House of Cards
The dirty game behind the game –
confessions of a FIFA referee
Jonas Eriksson, Anders Cedhamre

Aniara

Copyright © Jonas Eriksson & Anders Cedhamre

Aniara, 2025

www.aniara.one

info@aniara.one

Original title: *Korthuset : en domares berättelse om kickarna och spelet bakom världsfotbollen* (Forum, 2021)

Translation by Aniara

Cover Photos: Getty Images (Jonas Eriksson), Unsplash (Arena and Smoke)

Cover Design: Ingrediensen AB

ISBN print: 978-91-89954-33-5

ISBN e-book: 978-91-89954-31-1

All rights reserved.

No portion of this book may be reproduced in any form without written permission from the publisher or author, except as permitted by EU. copyright law.

Contents

1. Kickoff — 1
2. A Referee's Upbringing — 3
3. Out into the World — 36
4. The Season from Hell — 57
5. The Journey to the Top — 82
6. The Championship Debut — 113
7. In FIFA's Beautiful World — 149
8. The World Cup Dream in Brazil — 191
9. The Promise in Berlin — 255
10. European Championship in France — 298
11. The Last Chance — 319
12. The Way Out — 366
13. Overtime — 399

Kickoff

It's precisely that sound I miss the most.

That cold, echoing, hard sound when the studs of the boots rhythmically strike the mute cement floor, creating an echo that says the kickoff is imminent.

Ideally, it should be screw-in studs against the stone floor. New studs that you fasten before each match. Fewer in number, slightly harder material, but louder sound.

That's probably what I miss the most. Standing there in the tunnel and hearing that sound.

From a distance, it sounds like a short click, then another, and then several more. Eventually, it grows with increasing strength as all the steps come closer and closer.

It approaches a crescendo when twenty-two people and twice as many feet and shoes arrive at my position, where I've been standing perfectly still for a few minutes, waiting for today's main actors, the players.

The sound fades as slowly as it began.

The first player to arrive comes to a halt. Then a string of eleven players lines up on each side. Finally, nearly three hundred studs have found their way, and the cold, echoing sound ceases. I smell the scents of sweat, liniment, sometimes perfume, always adrenaline. When the echo of the studs has silenced, it's replaced by voices and shouts. Encouraging, threatening, and testosterone-fuelled dark tones in various languages try to instil courage in their teams -- and simultaneously dominate their opponents.

I stand silently, savouring the moment. I smile.

I know I earn the least of everyone on the pitch, but at the same time, I'm the one who risks facing both hatred and threats every time I go to work. Yet despite this, I absolutely wouldn't want to change jobs or trade places with anyone in the world.

In a few minutes, it will be time for kickoff, but in just a few seconds, I'll take the lead and walk onto the green turf. It reaches me first, the deafening cheer from the crowd in the sold-out arena.

As I walk in, the twenty-two players obediently follow me, eighty thousand spectators scream out their joy, and several hundred million viewers settle in front of their TV sets worldwide.

Ahead of me lie ninety minutes where I'll be forced to make several hundred important decisions. All lightning-fast, with no opportunity to call a meeting, talk to a friend, or sleep on it.

I have no idea how the match will unfold, what decisions I'll need to make, or what difficult situations I'll have to resolve.

What I am certain of, however, is one thing -- what has driven me here and what has made me continue with my job for thirty-one years. I love refereeing football.

A Referee's Upbringing

It's the 23rd of April 2002. I'm twenty-eight years old and have been a FIFA referee since the turn of the year. I've just received my license to officiate international football matches, but I've barely refereed any competitive matches abroad and only officiated thirteen matches at the highest level back home in Sweden. This spring, however, I've been the fourth official in Anders Frisk's team and found myself at the centre of world football - the Champions League playoffs. First at the Stadio Olimpico in Rome, then at Anfield in Liverpool, and now at Camp Nou in Barcelona.

Anders is about to blow the whistle to start the Champions League semi-final, and it's not just any semi-final, but El Clásico, Barcelona versus Real Madrid. I have to pinch myself. Even though I'm a newcomer, I already know that unexpected things can happen. After the round of 16 match between AS Roma and Galatasaray in March, absolute chaos erupted when the players were leaving the pitch after the match. Leaders and players from both teams clashed, and we in the referee team tried to intervene as stars like Francesco Totti, Gabriel Batistuta, and Fabio Capello came to blows. I was never scared, even though I was hit by an elbow to the back of the head in the midst of the melee. That time, we had to leave Rome escorted by police all the way to the gate at the airport.

As the fourth official, one of my tasks is to perform the customary equipment check on the players before the match. As I try to find my way around the enormously large dressing rooms at Camp Nou, my sense of uncertainty grows. There are world stars everywhere. In the home team, Frank de Boer, Luis Enrique, and Patrick Kluivert. In the team from the capital, Roberto Carlos, Zinedine Zidane, and the ever-sympathetic team captain Raúl. I'm more nervous than I've ever been before, almost panic-stricken with respect for the task ahead of me.

When Anders and the rest of the team go out to warm up, I follow. Down the long staircase that leads the players, on either side of a wire fence, towards the pitch. Past the chapel on the right side where players and leaders are given the opportunity to pray before and after matches, and then the steps up towards the large pitch, the steep stands, and the perfect grass. As I stand watching the warm-up, the Slovakian referee observer approaches. He kindly asks if I'm prepared to take over if Anders, for some reason, is forced to abandon the match. Although deep down I'm aware that I don't have the experience, despite every fibre of my body screaming at me that I'm definitely not ready, I calmly reply, "Of course, that's why I'm here!"

My journey towards the big arenas began in the summer of 1987 at Örnäset IP in Luleå. I was thirteen years old and lived barely three kilometres from what was IFK Luleå's main arena for youth football, in a completely ordinary two-storey house, in a completely ordinary residential area, in the shadow of the steel mill that in many ways characterised the entire city.

The family consisted of my two-year-older sister Jenny, my mother Ann-Britt who was a nurse at the hospital, and my father Hans who worked as a sales manager and was voluntarily involved in IFK Luleå. When my club called for a referee training course for young people in the spring of 1987, I had been the first to sign up. A career choice that surely surprised many of my friends, teammates, and referees who had officiated me as a player in IFK Luleå's boys' team, where I was a hot-tempered, mean, and dirty-playing centre-back or midfielder. Far too often, I was angry at the referees who came to officiate us. Not infrequently, they arrived five minutes before kick-off, were uninterested, often stood in the centre circle, and when you asked a question, you sometimes got a nonchalant snort or a scolding for asking. My match - even if I was a young lad and it was just a match in the local boys' league - was clearly the most important thing for me that week. And it never worked if the referee didn't take it seriously.

There were often conflicts, not infrequently fights, and often I had a guilty conscience for my behaviour when I went to bed in the evenings after the matches. In retrospect, I know that many of the referees disliked me. Most referees I encountered in Luleå have probably given me a yellow card. If it wasn't for a late and tough tackle, it was instead for my unpleasant attitude and my annoying chatter. How could someone who was such a pain as a player become one of the world's best referees? I think that maybe it's precisely because of this that I became so good. I knew exactly how to handle all the arrogant, unpleasant, and demanding players because I had been just such a player on the pitch myself. I was at times a difficult bastard on the pitch, and moreover, I was a poor loser. As a child, it was impossible for me to listen to such nonsense about how it was supposed to be most important just to participate - not to win. If I couldn't win, I usually didn't participate at all. My parents and my patient sister Jenny can still testify today that they always let me win the first three times in a game, and then play "normally" the fourth time. Because if they played seriously the first times and I didn't win, then there would simply be no more games in the family.

If I didn't win, those around me would know it. Loudly and for a long time.

At home in the house, paper and banknotes in Monopoly were torn apart, game boxes and dice were thrown against the wall, my mood changed when I was heading towards a loss. I cried, screamed, threatened, and threw things around me. My childhood friends in Luleå claim that they always gave me a few games when we played tennis to keep the mood up. Moreover, it was good to spare my racket a few more hits on the hard asphalt we played on. Individual sports were therefore not for me. Team sports were everything: hockey, basketball, and football. Fighting together and feeling the shared joy when we won was wonderful, but above all, I had someone to share the disappointment and frustration with when we lost. It was easier to share a stinging defeat with eleven lads in a football team than to handle a defeat on my own.

I officiated my first match on a summer evening in 1987 at Örnäset IP.

I don't remember how I was selected for the match or what compensation I received - but I remember that I cycled there, arrived in good time, made an attempt to warm up so that everyone would see it. I proudly wore my newly purchased black referee shirt of the Sportjohan brand, and had with me a black Acme Thunderer whistle that I had just bought with my own money... and I remember that I was nervous.

The lads I refereed were four years younger. It was my club, IFK Luleå, against the arch-rival Luleå SK. The match went well, I think. Or maybe that's just how I want to remember my first fifty minutes as a referee.

I remember that players and leaders thanked me after the match, that none of the parents around the pitch commented on my decisions, shouted or called angrily after my rulings, regardless of whether I had judged right or wrong. I'm grateful for that. With other players, leaders, and parents around the pitch, my refereeing career could have ended the same evening it began. But I was lucky. When I went to bed in my boys' room that evening, I realised that I had found what really was my dream job: I had gotten to move around, see and be part of a football match, and even got paid for it. This is what I wanted to do again.

Already the following year, I got to travel outside Luleå to referee. Someone at the Norrbotten Football Association must have seen me referee some match, sensed a little talent, and selected me for my first real tournament, Storsjöcupen in Östersund.

Just over six hundred kilometres one way in a minibus was followed by several matches per day, overnight stay in a cabin together with some colleagues, late nights, fun gatherings, and enormous fatigue when I went home after a week.

I realised that there were many more referees than the few I had met in Luleå - many were incredibly skilled, driven, friendly, and had completely new ways of handling players than what I was used to. It was an eye-opener, an incredible inspiration, and I got a taste for more. Even though the best referees in the tournament were already officiating in divisions 5 and 6, I didn't make a fool of myself in any way. The more I refereed, the more matches I was involved in, the better I became at developing my theories, my leadership, and my way of refereeing. For me, refereeing became more and more about understanding the players and their motives. I thought already from my first match, in the summer of 1987, that I would put myself in the head of the players I was refereeing, switch places with them for a second. Referee Jonas would for a second during the match switch places with player Jonas. My thought with this mental place switch was to understand how the latter felt, what the player was thinking, and how they would want to be addressed and with what words - so that referee Jonas could handle the player in the best way.

As a player, I had also encountered good referees who were friendly and happy, who showed commitment and, when needed, explained their decisions in a pedagogical way. Referees who met me as a fellow human being, with respect, even though I was both much younger than them and moreover a whiny figure. They were usually good people who I might not always agree with in substance, but who I could still respect because they could explain what I had done wrong, who let me react but were still clear about where the boundaries were. I always appreciated a referee who could acknowledge their own uncertainty or even an incorrect decision.

If I as a referee had always been reactive, that is, had run after the ball was played, I would always have been hopelessly behind. It was like looking into the future for me as a football referee. To always be prepared before it happened, to be in the right place at the right time and, if possible, prevent potential problems. I tried to kindly tell players when they made a small mistake, a little admonition that could prevent them from making a bigger one later in the match. It also happened that I talked to another player and told him that his teammate was causing problems and that I needed help to stop him, so that I wouldn't be forced to unnecessary free kicks, penalties, or yellow cards. There were referees in my youth who loved to punish, who never told a player in advance but rather waited for a mistake - just to blow the whistle and maybe give that yellow card. Throughout my career, I was exactly the opposite. I would rather prevent, tell what could happen if a player continued with an error and at least try to minimise my punishments - but at the same time not be cowardly and yielding the times when a player directly crossed a clear line. And I laid the foundation for that style already during my first years as a youth referee in Norrbotten.

The summer of 1989 in Luleå was special for a fifteen-year-old, football-loving lad with refereeing dreams. Not just because for the second summer in a row I got to travel to a tournament, this time to Hudik Cup in Hudiksvall. But above all: the newly crowned champions of the English league, Arsenal, had set up their training camp in Luleå. For me, it was like living in a dream. To wake up in the morning, cycle down to Örnäset IP and see world stars like Michael Thomas, Alan Smith, Paul Merson, and Tony Adams warm up, do exercises, play internal matches, and practice finishing. That Arsenal chose to set up their training camp for the season in Luleå may seem almost unreasonable, but it was because the club IFK Luleå had for several years arranged tours and matches with English teams. Each year, bigger and bigger clubs came to the capital of Norrbotten. Here, the English league teams could be in peace, the grass pitches were good in the summer, and there were opportunities for the players to go out and try the local nightlife without the English tabloids writing loads of articles.

One evening during Arsenal's visit to Luleå, I came home from having refereed a tournament in Piteå. For once, I heard a group of voices talking loudly in our living room. When I closed the door, it went quiet for a second, then I heard my dad speaking English.

I didn't understand anything. Who was sitting in our living room? I went in, curious, dressed in my referee tracksuit, and dad introduced me.

One of the unknown persons stood up, well-dressed and with a firm handshake he shook my hand and introduced himself. Although it wasn't really necessary.

Arsenal's manager, George Graham, I of course recognised. He was one of the world's leading coaches at the time, and had just led Arsenal to a title in the English league. Now he was sitting in our living room drinking whisky together with other important people from Arsenal, and parts of IFK Luleå's management.

When Graham, as a conclusion a few hours later, looked into my boys' room, he saw that it was teeming with posters of football players and teams that I liked. Maybe Graham was a bit disappointed that it wasn't Arsenal and their stars that were wallpapered on the walls but Nottingham Forest - my favourite team. The Scot with the difficult dialect saw that football was my life. "Focus first on becoming a player," he said. "If you don't become as good as you want, then focus on becoming a referee. The game needs referees who understand the game, and you do that best when you've played." I said I promised to think about it.

In parallel with my budding refereeing career, I continued to play football for IFK Luleå. As a supporter, I also followed our A-team who played in the second-highest division at the time. I watched all the matches, hung around at the training sessions, and quickly got to know the English players who played for the club for several seasons. One of them was Paul Proudlock. He was a professional at Middlesbrough FC but at times on loan to IFK. When he returned to England in the autumn of 1988, we kept in touch. It ended with me the following year, fourteen years old, travelling all alone from Luleå to Hartlepool to visit Paul and his wife and do my work experience. For a week, I got to stand on the sidelines and watch a team in the English league's highest division train, hear how the manager shouted, watch matches from the VIP stand, hang out with the players in the Players Lounge after the derby against Newcastle. And I got to train with Hartlepool's junior team myself, practice diving headers and sliding tackles like I'd never done before. It was an absolutely fantastic week that gave me a taste for football at the highest level, for travelling, for being in new and unfamiliar international environments. The visit to northern England gave me a thirst to discover the big football world that existed outside little Luleå, which at the time actually had a team that was at the top of Division 1 North and knocking on the door to the Allsvenskan.

My next big football trip I made in the spring of 1990. UEFA's Cup Winners' Cup final was to be played at Nya Ullevi in Gothenburg, and somehow my friends Lars and Henrik and I managed to buy match tickets, and in an even more miraculous way convinced our parents that it was a good idea for us, three sixteen-year-olds, to see the match in person. We got, or took, time off from school and flew down from Luleå to see the match between Sampdoria and Anderlecht on site. It was like living in a dream for three days. We marvelled together at the atmosphere on site, the screaming supporters, the crazy hooligans, and the enormous performances during the match by stars like Roberto Mancini, Gianluca Vialli, and Arnór Guðjohnsen. The Cup Winners' Cup final was a transformative experience, could football be so amazing?

A month later, my international football journey continued when my dad and I travelled to Italy to see Sweden play in the World Cup. For ten days, we travelled around northern Italy. In Turin, we saw Tomas Brolin score against Brazil, but Sweden lose

1-2, and in Genoa, the result was the same when Scotland beat Sweden, and I remember shouting from the stands at the, in my opinion, cowardly Paraguayan referee. The last 1-2 loss, the one against Costa Rica, we watched on TV back home in Luleå. The trip to the football World Cup in Italy was a great experience. I had never before been at such a big event, and I loved everything I got to experience. Back home from Italy, I decided to put my savings towards an expensive present for myself: FIFA's official World Cup watch for referees during the 1990 championship in Italy. It was fantastically stylish with a green ring around the watch itself, a white dial with a black and white football in the centre, and had functions such as time display, countdown and count-up, as well as regular timekeeping. I was guaranteed to be the only referee in Norrbotten who had such a watch. I bought my Seiko Chronograph in Luleå for the dizzying sum of 1,995 kronor. But that watch would be well used, and stayed with me all the way until 2011 when I replaced it with the heart rate monitor that then became a requirement for all referees.

With my new World Cup watch on my arm, my refereeing career progressed forward and upward at a rapid pace. Starting to referee adults when I was 17 years old myself was tough - but at the same time fun and challenging. I hoped that I would be judged for my competence, what I did - rather than my age. And usually I managed to get the players on my side thanks to being serious, running a lot, and having my very own way of solving problems that arose.

My older colleagues in Luleå were fantastic. They were kind, generous, supportive, and I felt that they always wanted me to succeed. There was never any jealousy or begrudging over my rapid advancement through the divisions. The secret behind my climb from Division 5 to Division 1 in seven years was actually simple. I always, regardless of division, stuck to my philosophy of fundamentally always trying to be friendly, communicate with players and leaders, be clear, and try to have fun. I let the players react and give their views on the decisions as long as they did it in a friendly way. At the same time, I never compromised on what was right and wrong.

During my journey up through the league system, I gained the somewhat painful insight that I was actually a better referee than player, or at least that I could reach much further as a referee than as a player.

Sure, I was okay as a player, but honestly, I wasn't a great talent - even if I had a good understanding of the game, the physique, and a decent touch on the ball. If I had bet everything, I might have made it to Division 1 at best, and then it would have required enormous amounts of training and above all, I would have been forced to give up everything else for a few years.

I realised that my qualities were better suited for pursuing a career as a referee, that there I could make use of my ability to communicate, to convince people of my decisions, and not least my understanding of the game.

Moreover, it didn't appeal to me to reach the middle ranks as a player.

Just as it didn't appeal to me to play something I couldn't win at. Then I'd rather not participate at all.

As a player, I could never be the best, so I quit.

As a referee, I understood that I could be the best, so I continued.

Moreover, as a referee, I could pursue a parallel career with something else I liked, which made the choice much easier.

When I was five years old, I was sick with a stomach bug for a few days and spent a lot of time in the bathroom. With me in the bathroom, I had a publication that perhaps isn't the most common reading material for children of that age: an almanac with all name days. A few days later, I wanted, as always on Friday evenings, to perform for my parents and my sister. I played "Hylands hörna" and demonstrated my newly acquired knowledge for them. I had memorised all the name days of the year.

If any of our daughters at the same age had shown the same knowledge, I would probably have become worried and started googling strange diagnoses. My wise mum and dad, on the other hand, they laughed, showed that they were proud, and encouraged me to continue learning even more things in the future.

My sharp memory has helped me several times in my refereeing career. I remember almost all the names of players I've refereed, which clubs they've played for, who I've cautioned, why, and in which minute of the match. My good memory wasn't the only thing that stood out during my childhood. I already had a strong drive early on to do fun and exciting things. I also very much wanted to be seen and be in the centre of attention.

At five years old, I learned to read, count, and write. And therefore, it was, at least for me, obvious to write and send in my own letter to Ulf Elfving's classic radio program "Upp till tretton" (Up to Thirteen). The popular program involved children participating in radio, talking with Ulf, answering a question, and winning an LP record. A week later, Ulf Elfving called, and on December 13, 1979, I sat and talked with the radio legend.

It was anything but a quiet, shy, and cautious little boy from Norrbotten who spoke on national radio for almost eight minutes. I talked a lot, quickly, and with a clear northern dialect. I ended the conversation by telling that I dreamed of becoming a bus driver and wished for the song "Tommy som knarkade" (Tommy Who Did Drugs) by Janne Önnerud, a song that was actually called "Tommy" and was a dark ballad about a guy in Gothenburg who overdosed in a bathroom. Not a common song choice for a five-year-old.

Two more times I would be on "Upp till tretton". In the last program I was in, when I was nine and probably broke some kind of record, I had changed my dream job to sports journalist. The dream job contained everything I loved as a child: sports, being seen, and writing. Everyone who worked on TV was a great role model and idol for me: Lennart Hyland, Arne Hegerfors, Fredrik Belfrage, and Ingvar Oldsberg. To get to watch sports during working hours, to be at the big arenas, meet the stars, be on TV and commentate matches for the entire Swedish people, those were all things I dreamed about.

In Luleå in the early 1980s, there wasn't exactly an abundance of sports stars to interview, and the opportunities for a nine-year-old boy to try working as a journalist were, to put it mildly, very limited. But I was lucky. Peter Lundgren, sports editor at the local newspaper Norrländska Socialdemokraten (NSD), had a father who happened to listen to my third program with Ulf Elfving. Immediately afterwards, the father called Peter and told him that there was indeed a nine-year-old boy from Luleå on the radio who seemed forward and whose main dream was to become a sports journalist.

A few days later, the phone rang. Peter called and wondered if I wanted to try working as a sports journalist at a hockey match with my idols in Luleå Hockey. Did I want to?!? Of course! Shortly after, I had my first article published in NSD. It was an enormous pride to see a picture of me in the newspaper, an article where my name was at the bottom, my own text published. I got an enormous kick, a boost forward, and the feeling that this is what I wanted to do again.

During the years that followed, I got to hang around at the editorial office, follow along to league matches in hockey and football, but also to championships like the Swedish Ski Championships in Luleå in 1984. I often got to help with small things. When Peter, stressed by a deadline, tried to put together texts from matches and lacked quotes, he sent me down from the stands to the locker room. I took a few quotes from a player and ran back up to the stands, gave the quotes, and the article was complete.

More assignments followed, and I became unofficially the newspaper's junior reporter. With that experience under my belt, it was obvious for me to apply for a job as a junior reporter on Sveriges Television's successful program "Barnjournalen" (The Children's Journal) a few years later. Full of self-confidence, I thought it was entirely possible to become one of the six selected reporters, despite there being over ten thousand applicants.

To my great joy, I was called for an interview at the City Hotel in Luleå. I remember dressing up nicely in white jeans and a turquoise polo shirt with a matching belt. At the interview, I talked at length with the fantastic Lasse and Birgitta Hjelm from SVT in Malmö. When asked who I would most like to interview in the whole world, I embellished the truth and didn't answer any of the idols Diego Maradona or Johnny Ekström in IFK Gothenburg. Instead, I chose the more serious answer Nelson Mandela.

Afterwards, I was satisfied with the interview, so confident and sure that I would be one of the six junior reporters that I may even have told some people that I would get the job - before I officially got it. Fortunately, the message that I had got the job came with a letter a few weeks later.

The year at "Barnjournalen" was fantastic and extremely educational. I got to interview Jan Guillou about the Palme murder, sports leaders who collected money for cancer research, and also the dream gig: a full-day interview with Johnny Ekström before his move to professional life in Italian Empoli. I was living my dream. I appeared on TV, got to work as a journalist, got to travel alone by plane to Malmö, Gothenburg, and Stockholm several times, I got 90 kronor a week in compensation, and I got to know friendly, kind, and coaching journalists who had come a bit in their careers. One of them was Pelle Thörnberg. He really took me under his wing and became a fantastic mentor for me and my journalistic dreams.

All the steps I managed to take at a young age taught me early on that everything was possible, that there were no limitations, and that much of it was about daring to ask and keeping yourself in the forefront. My parents supported me all the time, drove me where I wanted to go, gave wise advice but were neither pushing nor bursting any balloons that contained my dreams.

I remember that they really told me that everything was possible. They did this by taking me seriously; never did they smile, laugh, sigh, or in any way diminish the dreams I presented to them. There's a difference between saying that you support and believe in a person - and really supporting and believing for real. My parents knew the difference.

My schedule as a teenager was to say the least packed. I played in IFK Luleå's junior team, trained four times a week plus a match, refereed a couple of football matches, attended the social science program at high school, worked extra at a nearby petrol station, was chairman of the School Sports Association at the school, and was also involved centrally in the Swedish School Sports Federation. I was forced to become good at planning and was careful to write everything down in my nice Filofax in brown leather that contained all the information I needed. The days were long and I always slept too little - but I was forced to acquire discipline, realise that I had to prioritise, and not least: I became an inveterate time optimist. I still am today.

The dream of becoming a journalist was always there - parallel to everything else I did. When I was sixteen years old, I switched newspapers in Luleå, from NSD to Norrbottens-Kuriren. There I worked extra as a reporter and got a press card, which meant free entry to all sports events. I wrote about everything that happened in the world of local sports and was given great trust by my bosses. I worked all the time, never said no to a request - only my own match as a player or referee stopped me. But not always. There were occasions when I was both player and reporter - or referee and reporter - in the same match. Of course, questionable from a neutrality point of view, but no one put a stop to it or came with any comments.

I had now started my first own company. And as a freelance reporter, I discovered that there was another part that I liked even better than just writing reports of what had happened. I started to think of several different angles of a competition that could generate more income than if I just wrote a single good article. The best thing I knew was an orienteering competition with many classes and participants from all over Sweden - it provided an enormous number of possible combinations of winners in different classes, and thus many potential buyers of articles. However, it would take a few years before I realised that I liked business more than good articles, that it was the deal that gave me a bigger kick than the publication itself.

When it was time to do military service a few years later, I had a clear goal: to be accepted as a journalist at Värnpliktsnytt (Conscript News). I understood that it was difficult, even harder than getting into journalism school. But I put everything into making it happen.

I flew down to Stockholm, took the subway to Gärdet and walked to Sandelsgatan where the editorial office was located. The editor-in-chief explained to me that the positions as reporter were fully booked more than a year ahead, but that there might be an opening as an editor, with some reporting assignments, if I could use the QuarkXPress computer program. Of course I could, I lied tactically, and got the assignment.

In reality, I had no experience at all with QuarkXPress and editing in general. I thought to myself that it couldn't be that hard.

When I started at Värnpliktsnytt at 19 years old right after high school, I thought I knew everything, that I wrote the best texts, came up with the best angles, and knew best.

After an hour at the newspaper, I understood why it was so difficult to get into the newspaper. Most were extremely sharp, smart, quick, skilled, driven, and I felt like a beginner for the first time. But the environment fostered me, I was forced to get better at everything I did as a journalist. I realised that it was the environment that made me better, that the surroundings inspired me, that it was beneficial that everyone around me was faster, smarter, and more efficient. I was forced to improve myself to keep up, and already then I realised for the first time how much you can learn from having skilled people around you.

When a few months remained of my military service, I got calls from the personnel managers at Aftonbladet and Expressen. Both offered me a job directly after discharge, without me really having to apply. To be picked up directly by an evening newspaper without having to apply for the job was perhaps the best grade one could get in my world. The choice was not obvious, but Aftonbladet was at that time the underdog, number two, the newspaper that punched above its weight. It felt like they therefore fought a little harder for me to start working there. The personnel manager called a little more often, offered me longer temporary positions and even a slightly higher monthly salary.

If the pace had been high at Värnpliktsnytt, it was nothing compared to my time at Aftonbladet. After a couple of years, I had managed to be a reporter, editor, and night chief in the sports department, work during the Olympics, World Cup in football, hockey, handball, athletics, and a European Championship in football. I belonged to the sports department but also worked for news, entertainment, magazine, and economy.

I watched all football on Aftonbladet with a special eye for the referees. When the 1994 World Cup final referee, Sándor Puhl, was announced, I set the headline "Kul, Puhl -- du får döma VM-finalen" (Cool, Puhl -- you get to referee the World Cup final). During the summer of 1996, I watched all the European Championship matches from the editorial office at Aftonbladet and rejoiced in the successes of the Swedish referees Leif Sundell and Anders Frisk. I tried to highlight their good performances in my texts, and defended the mistakes that especially Sundell was criticised for after his quarter-final between Germany and Croatia.

At Aftonbladet, I took every chance to work, to fill in, learn more and get better. I enjoyed it tremendously, despite the shifts being both many and long, but felt after two and a half years that it was time to move on and try something new. Maybe journalism wasn't my dream job after all.

The years 1993-1997, during military service and my first years in Stockholm, I kept a low profile with my refereeing career. For three years I only refereed twenty-five matches. I didn't feel like starting to referee in Stockholm but instead only took matches when I was up in Norrbotten now and then. Stockholm was a large football district where I knew neither any colleagues nor any players. I also didn't have a car to get to the matches that were often played on hard and dusty gravel pitches. So I prioritised my job, but also having fun with friends - what you perhaps should have when you're around twenty, living in central Stockholm, earning relatively good money, and have many people around you in the same situation. But I never had any thoughts of quitting refereeing. I just lowered my ambition level to have time for work and also have fun.

Sometimes I tried to bring my friends along to matches around Sweden. If I, for example, had a match in Division 2, Selånger versus Edsbyn, often a group of friends would come along, sit in town and drink beer while I refereed the match and then we'd do Sundsvall together. At times it was a struggle to manage everything, and my friends probably wondered why I travelled around the country to referee at such a relatively low level. Still, during these years I had a fairly steady development curve, where I almost advanced one division per year.

The last weekend during the Olympics in Atlanta 1996, I had worked all night at Aftonbladet whereupon I took a taxi home, packed a bag while the taxi waited outside, went on to Arlanda, slept on the flight to Luleå, was picked up by my parents at the airport, slept on the way to Boden, had a coffee and went out to referee a top-division team for the first time in my life: Umeå FC was visiting Boden for a match in the Swedish Cup. My preparation left a lot to be desired, but there was no alternative since as an employee at a sports editorial office, you obviously couldn't take time off in the middle of the Olympics.

My referee colleagues in Luleå had heard a rumour a week or so earlier - there was talk that Bo Karlsson, the new chairman of the Swedish Football Association's referee committee (later referee commission), for some inexplicable reason was visiting Norrbotten and that he would see me referee the match. Bo Karlsson from Målilla was a tall and lanky man, almost two meters in his stocking feet. He was always clean-shaven and smelled of a distinct aftershave. With his charisma and personality, he always owned a room when he stepped in. Bosse, as everyone called him, was a self-evident leader, a natural authority.

Karlsson was one of seven Swedish referees who had refereed in the World Cup through the years. It became one championship, the summer of 1994, and just one match.

The year before the World Cup, he had been injured and had surgery on his Achilles tendon, and for the championship, he hadn't found his way back to the form he had had when he was selected. In the match Argentina-Nigeria, he managed to give a correct warning - but to the wrong player - and in the same second his tournament was over.

Returning home from the World Cup, Bosse became chairman of the Swedish Football Association's referee committee - and was generally and a bit carelessly referred to as the referee boss.

During warm-up, I looked for the tall man from Småland, but didn't see him. A little later, when I was standing in the tunnel waiting for the players, he came walking down the corridor. He shook hands as if we already knew each other and wished me good luck before the match.

I don't remember anything from the match itself, but I remember that Bosse was satisfied afterwards. He said a few kind words, that I was an unpolished diamond and had a fine future, before I had to leave the referee room to go back to Stockholm and the next night shift at Aftonbladet that started at eight the same evening.

It was my first meeting with Bosse, who over time became an extra dad in the referee world, a sounding board, my biggest supporter and the one who became happiest when I succeeded and saddest when things went badly.

Later that same year, I left Aftonbladet to start at the production company OTW. There I would be a media consultant with the task of developing newspapers. It was new and challenging, and the job meant that I got to travel around Eastern Europe. However, I wanted to learn more about TV production, which was OTW's other business area. So when I wasn't travelling on the continent or refereeing Division 2 matches around Sweden, I hung around unpaid at TV4 to learn how to produce TV, what it takes, and what happens behind the scenes.

At TV4, I got to know a nice guy from Växjö named Peter Jihde. He was already then a skilled presenter and was, like me, relatively new in Stockholm. He was also single and liked the nightlife in the capital. We found each other immediately.

In the winter of 1998, he tipped me off about a new job. He had been offered it himself and knew the owners, but thought it seemed more like something for me. In April 1998, I started as a salesperson of TV broadcasting rights at the company IEC in Sports. I was the first employee in the company and after a year I was offered partnership and also became sales manager responsible for salespeople and customer contacts worldwide.

In addition to the new job, I was also selected during the winter of 1998 to attend the last formal education to be allowed to referee elite football in Sweden, step 5. This meant more travel, a pressure to referee more matches, prepare better and prioritise football a bit more than before.

My boss, the CEO and founder of the company, was named Jonas Persson and was an incredibly football-interested person. From the very first day, I was honest and said that my ambition was to become a really good football referee, and that I needed to have the possibility to be able to go to matches, tournaments and assignments. He was understanding and kind, and quick to say that it was no problem, but probably didn't quite realise then what he was approving.

Parallel to my professional career, my refereeing career began to approach the very highest level. In the autumn of 1998, I made my debut in Division 1, did a few more test matches in 1999 before I became a regular elite referee in 2000. It was special, and extra difficult, to move up that year because the two Division 1 series were merged into a completely new series called Superettan. The second highest division would instead of two series with twenty-eight teams become one series with only sixteen teams. Of course, this also affected the number of referees. Instead of thirty-two referees, we were only twenty referees selected to referee the two highest divisions.

I was really the last one in of all the twenty who became elite referees. I had passed the small eye of the needle last of all, by grace, perhaps not primarily on competence but thanks to my young age. I had to skip the first round in Superettan, a clear signal that I belonged to the worst referees in the group. During the spring, I would get seven matches in the series, all at smaller arenas like in Åtvidaberg, Ljungskile, Umeå and Gunnilse. I had a way to go before getting to referee the big teams like Malmö and Djurgården on their home grounds. But step by step I learned to handle the stress and pressure, how to prepare, what worked and what didn't work at the higher level I was now at.

In the summer of 2000, I also got to make a "semi-international" debut in front of one hundred and fifty spectators at the idyllic

Vinåvallen in Vinberg outside Falkenberg. Sweden's U17 national team played against the Czech Republic in an annual training tournament.

It didn't really feel like an international match. I would never have been allowed to referee a competitive match between the teams since one of the teams was the Swedish boys' national team, but it was still a wonderful feeling to line up with the teams before the match and listen to the national anthems. It was also completely new for me to be forced to referee without having language as my main asset. I was forced to reinforce body language, be even clearer about what I was blowing for, why I had made a decision and really convince the Czech players that they could trust me - especially considering that one team was just a Swedish boys' national team, and I too was Swedish.

I also had my boss, Bosse Karlsson, in the stands. He had driven the 170 kilometres from Jönköping to Vinberg and after the match he came into the dressing room and said: "Damn, Eriksson, you've got something good going. I think you refereed better today than in Superettan where you have to run around and talk to everyone all the time. You were clearer and more determined when one team didn't speak Swedish."

Maybe he was right, I pondered. I had always talked a lot with the players, maybe too much. If I toned down my chat, avoided my constant explanations of decisions, maybe it could benefit my career. At the same time, I didn't want to lose myself and my way of refereeing.

However, I understood that I should listen to Bosse. He only wanted what was best for me, and he had after all been there himself and knew what it took to get to referee internationally and reach a World Cup.

After the international match in Vinberg, the dream of getting to referee internationally felt within reach. My goal at the beginning of the millennium was to conquer the FIFA badge, get to stick it on my chest and thereby get a license to start refereeing internationally regularly. But to do that, you had to have refereed two seasons in the top league.

In the spring of 2000, I felt like a newcomer in Superettan because I was always refereeing the smaller teams at the bottom of the table. After the summer, something happened. When autumn came, the teams were changed and also where in the table I refereed. I realised that I had taken a big step, without anyone telling me. Suddenly I was refereeing big teams like Mjällby AIF, Västerås SK, Landskrona BoIS and not least: Malmö FF with a not entirely easy-to-referee Zlatan Ibrahimović on the pitch.

The first time we met was on August 14, 2000. It was a top match against Västerås SK and I refereed my first match at Malmö Stadion. Already after ten minutes, Zlatan stamped in a cross in a duel with his future friend and national team colleague Daniel Majstorović. The goal was followed by wild protests from the VSK players, who wanted a free kick for a high kick. I remember that I was as surprised as everyone else and thought: Can you really score a goal like that? Are you really allowed to score a goal like that? VSK fought their way back and had 2-2 with two minutes left, but then Zlatan decided the match. After a perfect ball in depth and a well-timed run, he waited out the VSK goalkeeper and placed the ball ice-cold in the right corner. Zlatan celebrated the goal by taking off his shirt, swinging it over his head and of course getting a yellow card from me, which he completely ignored.

Already when I refereed him for the first time, I saw that Zlatan had qualities that almost no other player had - a charisma, a certainty, control of ball and body and an instinct that breathed: it won't be possible to stop me.

The match in Malmö gave me proof that I could handle refereeing top teams like Malmö FF - but also that I could handle difficult players like Zlatan. The fact that I got better and better matches made me realise that my performances had been good and that I had climbed from being one of the lowest ranked referees in the series in the spring to being one of the highest ranked in the autumn.

At the turn of the millennium, I was travelling more than ever before. In my job, I flew between world metropolises like Los Angeles, Bangkok, Dubai and Madrid. Then I went home and refereed football matches in Åtvidaberg, Umeå and Västerås. It was tough to manage everything and keep both parties satisfied - IEC and the Swedish Football Association. There was always some party that was a little dissatisfied, but I myself had tremendously fun all the time and couldn't imagine giving up either of the jobs.

At the end of October 2000, I had an extremely important work week ahead of me with a packed trip to Asia where I would manage eight customer visits with TV channels in Hong Kong, Taiwan and Thailand in four days. Then I would go straight home to be back at Arlanda on Friday morning - all to be able to referee in Superettan's last round on the weekend.

When I'm packing my bag, it's Sunday night. Earlier that same day, I refereed Västerås SK-Umeå. In the second half, I got terribly painful in my back, but gritted my teeth and accepted the pain. On Monday morning, I can't get out of bed. I have to cancel my trip to Asia. It's out of the question to sit on a plane for sixteen hours when I can barely get up. Just then the phone rings, it's Bosse Karlsson. I answer, but don't say anything about my sore back. "Hi Jonas," he says cheerfully. "What do you say about making your Allsvenskan debut on Saturday? Trelleborg-Västra Frölunda." I'm both overjoyed and completely cold, because right now I can't even get out of bed.

During the week, I get help from a naprapath, eat insane amounts of painkillers and muscle relaxants, and the following Saturday I blow the whistle to start my life's first Allsvenskan match at Vångavallen.

I'm proud and nervous, but the match goes well. So well that I get new chances right at the beginning of the next season.

My unexpected debut in Allsvenskan also meant that I had qualified to be selected and referee internationally, albeit only for boys' international matches. And in February 2001, I was selected to referee in an international tournament in Portugal for boys who were fifteen years old. The players were making their first international matches and I was perhaps not selected because I was good, more because I was Swedish and the Swedish national team was expected to bring a referee on the trip.

But still. I was going to make my international debut. For real.

Torneio Internacional de Juniores B was the name of the tournament played at Estádio Municipal de Torres Novas, just over an hour's bus ride from Lisbon. I was to referee the home nation Portugal against South Africa, and despite having refereed hundreds of matches before in my career, I was very nervous.

None of the players spoke Swedish, I hardly knew if and at best how well English the players could understand, I had new assistant referees that I had no idea what level they were at and above all: it was a real international match.

When the national anthems were played on a scratchy speaker, I felt proud and happy in my gray and black, far too large referee shirt.

I could already see during the national anthems that the players were also nervous. It was also their first real international match and in the stands were a number of scouts from large, international clubs. A good match could mean that eyes would stick to just them.

One of the players stood out particularly during the eighty minutes the match lasted. He had number 17 on his back and was elegant, nonchalant and moved a little more smoothly and faster than his teammates and opponents. He had a perfect posture, a hairstyle that didn't have a single hair out of place and celebrated as if he had decided a Champions League final when he celebrated his match-deciding 2-0 goal. On Saturday, February 24, 2001, it wasn't just me making my international debut - Cristiano Ronaldo also made his first international match that day, and his first international goal.

With me, he was calm. He didn't say a word, just concentrated on playing, thanked kindly and smiled when I said "obrigado", thank you in Portuguese, in the center circle after the match.

Immediately after the match, I didn't give him much thought.

During all the boys' and junior international matches I have refereed over the years, I have seen so many talents, young stars and promising players who then haven't become anything. But Cristiano Ronaldo managed, and still manages to surpass himself and set new records.

When the 2001 season started, I was a regular referee in Allsvenskan.

I, who the year before had barely refereed in Superettan, now got to referee Sweden's finest football league regularly. I was crazy proud and honored, but knew that I had to perform to stay at this level.

I didn't get to choose who I would have in my team as assistant referees, who were previously called linesmen or line judges. But it didn't matter much, because almost all assistant referees were nice, friendly, generous, supportive and helpful. Stefan Wittberg became a favorite. He was so calm, cool and always fun to have in the team. But he usually refereed with the established FIFA referees in Allsvenskan, like Anders Frisk, Martin Ingvarsson and Leif Sundell, and therefore I rarely got the chance to referee with him.

My fifth Allsvenskan match I refereed at Olympia in Helsingborg.

I still remember today the feeling when I walked out on the perfect grass pitch, where a few months earlier Champions League had been played and big teams like Bayern Munich and Paris Saint-Germain had visited.

I almost had to pinch myself in the arm and realize that it was actually ME who was going to referee the match, that I was in Allsvenskan, that I got to fulfill a dream almost once a week.

The highest level meant a much greater media interest in my decisions on the pitch. When the sending off of Pelgander ended up on a list in Aftonbladet of the worst decisions during the spring season, I didn't let it affect me. As an established Allsvenskan referee, I was now close to getting my long-awaited FIFA badge, the license required to referee internationally. To get the license, you had to be ranked as one of the seven best referees by the national referee committee, you had to be older than twenty-five years, speak at least one language other than Swedish and be presumed to pass the physical tests that FIFA had. Concretely, it was about getting a large, white, embroidered fabric badge with the magical large letters clearly prominent, FIFA, and then which year it applied to. For it was not a lifetime gift - every year FIFA approved or rejected the applications that the national associations sent in.

Sometimes, however, you could go along on international assignments as a fourth official without having received the FIFA badge - but then the intention was always that the license should be imminent for the current referee. Anders Frisk was the brightest shining Swedish referee star during my first time as a referee at the elite level. He was always tanned, slightly unshaven and wore his referee shirt unbuttoned at the neck. Anders was easy-going and fun, a happy devil who was curious, smiled a lot and loved meeting new people. We became close, and I learned enormously much from him - as a referee, but also as a person. He appreciated me and my company and somewhere I think he saw that I had potential as a referee.

Anders Frisk was the one who introduced me to the big football world when he took me along as a fourth official in his team in the autumn of 2001. My first trip with Anders Frisk's team went to Turin, where Juventus would meet Porto in the Champions League. TV4 reporter Patrick Ekwall was along on the trip and made a report about what it was like on the job for one of Europe's best referees. I kept in the background. Quiet and low-key, I soaked up everything that happened, learned from Anders' way of dealing with other people and preparing for the match.

A few months later, when the Champions League playoffs began in the spring of 2002, I had received my long-awaited license myself. When I traveled as a fourth official to the semi-final in Barcelona that spring, a large, white badge with four capital letters sat on my chest: FIFA.

Out into the World

From 98,260 fanatical supporters in the stands of Camp Nou to 250 quiet spectators in Slagelse in the Danish countryside. During my first year as an international referee, the contrast between my assignments was incredibly stark. After the Champions League semi-final in Barcelona in 2002, I travelled to Denmark to officiate the U17 European Championship for nearly a month. Becoming a FIFA referee marked a significant step in my refereeing career, but the leap to officiating the most prestigious matches was still considerable. All referees started with international matches for boys, then juniors, under-21 players, the initial rounds of international cups, and then progressed to officiating the best matches between major nations and club teams. Although in the spring of 2002 I was involved in the Champions League knockout stages as a fourth official in Anders Frisk's team, I still needed to follow the long path to become a referee at the very highest level.

The U17 European Championship in Denmark was indeed a youth tournament, but it was teeming with stars making their debut in a major championship: Cristiano Ronaldo played for Portugal, Wayne Rooney for England, David Silva for Spain.

I was assigned to referee a semi-final, England versus Switzerland, and in that match, I received the highest rating of my life: 9.5. As close to a perfect score as one could possibly get. My own international career had got off to an excellent start.

The referees' grading system was an unnecessarily complicated construction.

The grading scale ranged from 6.0 to 10.0. The score one was expected to have and which was considered equivalent to a pass in a match of normal difficulty was 8.4.

If, in the observer's eyes, you had missed a caution, you'd get an 8.3; if you missed two cautions, an 8.2, and so on. If, as a referee, you made a significant, clear, and crucial mistake such as missing a penalty (or awarding an incorrect one), missing a sending-off (or dismissing a player incorrectly), disallowing a clear goal (or allowing an incorrect goal to stand), you'd receive a reduction of 0.5. This would result in a score of 7.9, and if the observer deemed you had made two major mistakes, you'd get a score of 7.4.

If the match was more challenging than what the observer considered normal, that is, quite demanding and requiring one or more important correct decisions, then the standard score would be 8.5.

At all elite-level matches in Sweden and at the international level, an observer was present. Without exception, they were men, and invariably individuals who had previously been referees at the highest level. The observers graded the referees' performances and wrote a detailed report.

When I began my career at the elite level, observers had considerable influence. Their judgments were final - if a referee had performed well, it was described as such in the report submitted to the Swedish Football Association for Allsvenskan matches or UEFA for all matches in Europe.

For international matches, observers came from neutral countries. They were independent and did not rely on TV footage but formed their own opinion of the referee they saw officiating the match. I liked the system with observers. You were assessed by a neutral person on-site, who wasn't hunting for mistakes, which easily became the consequence when one could use aids like TV replays endlessly. And above all, I liked that they were independent, that no one could or wanted to interfere with the observer's job and influence the score he would give. Even in the 2002/2003 Champions League season, I was entrusted as the fourth official in Anders Frisk's team. Now the aim was set on getting the final, after having officiated a semi-final the year before. In April 2003, we were in the Spanish capital to referee Real Madrid against Manchester United, one of the quarter-finals in the tournament.

Before the match, I was chatting with our local referee liaison.

"There aren't two referees more different than Frisk and Collina," he said.

I had never met Pierluigi Collina at that point, but I heard stories from several people about what he was like as a person: meticulous, nitpicky, and quite stern. It was said that he even decided what food everyone in the team should eat to ensure the best possible preparation. But regardless of this, he was undoubtedly the world's best referee of all time - among other accolades, he was named the world's best referee six years in a row. Moreover, he was an extremely recognisable figure with his bald head and large ice-blue eyes. With his stern gaze, he could command respect from any player he chose to stare down.

Anders was the complete opposite in manner. His unwritten motto was freedom with responsibility. He wanted to have fun, meet as many people as possible, and draw energy from his surroundings.

Match day was as usual. We had a security meeting at the stadium at ten o'clock, then we returned to the hotel. Off with the UEFA suit, on with casual clothes, a walk in the sunshine, a coffee in Plaza Mayor, and lunch with the team at the hotel.

I had expected and what he truly deserved.

A year or so later, I heard through the grapevine that our observer had submitted a report stating that I, Anders, and one of the assistant referees had behaved inappropriately by drinking wine on match day, and that this was why Anders hadn't received more assignments.

The Italian observer who reported us to UEFA was named Pierluigi Pairetto. At the time of the quarter-final in Madrid, he was the head of all referees in Serie A but also the vice-chairman of UEFA's Referees Committee. He could influence which referees would officiate which matches and had full insight into all appointments. A few years later, he was a central figure in the major Serie A scandal, Calciopoli. As the tangle of crimes and other irregularities was unravelled, it was established that Pairetto had been in contact with Juventus CEO, Luciano Moggi, regarding which referees should be appointed for Juventus matches in both the Champions League and Serie A.

The fact that clubs could influence which referees would officiate their matches was extremely sensitive. There must be watertight barriers between referee committees that appoint referees and clubs. The Calciopoli scandal shook Italian football, Juventus was forced to leave Serie A, and Pierluigi Pairetto was suspended for several years.

The scandal surrounding Pairetto was not known in 2003. But everyone who followed international football knew that it was sensitive for Anders Frisk to referee Italian teams. On several occasions, the Swedish super-referee had come into focus when the Italian national team or an Italian club team played crucial matches.

The loss in the Euro 2000 final against France was perhaps what stung the most, where the Italians felt that Frisk had ruled against them.

The French striker Sylvain Wiltord had equalised in several minutes of added time, at least one minute too many, all Italians thought. But there were also a series of other controversial Champions League matches, for example, the chaotic match between Roma and Galatasaray, but also a number of sendings-off that affected Italian teams in other matches. The combination of Anders Frisk as referee and Italian teams was, in other words, anything but optimal. In the semi-finals of the 2003 Champions

League, three out of four teams were Italian. What actually happened, we may never know. Perhaps Pairetto's report was a deliberate attempt to prevent Anders from reaching a final that three Italian teams were striving to reach, a punishment for Anders having had controversial matches over several years where an Italian team stood on one side.

The 2002/2003 Champions League final became an all-Italian affair and was played between Juventus and AC Milan, officiated by German Markus Merk. And perhaps it was just his turn to get the final. Maybe he really deserved it after many good performances at the highest level. But perhaps it also played a certain role that the chairman of the referee committee was German at the time.

Less than two years after the scandal match in Rome, we surprisingly got a new match in the Italian capital: AS Roma versus Dynamo Kiev in the Champions League group stage. If the match against Galatasaray had been utter chaos, the match against Dynamo Kiev would be even more hellish. Usually, a referee's match ends at the final whistle. But sometimes it continues afterwards when you're forced to write a report on a sending-off. In exceptional cases, there's an exchange of letters where the player, coach, or team you've reported contests what you as a referee have written - and in that case, you have to respond to the reply received.

After our previous match in Rome, between Roma and Galatasaray in 2002, everything had been taken to the next level. It would be the only incident during my over two hundred international matches that became subject to the highest appellate body: the UEFA Appeals Body. Several of the players and coaches who had received punishments from UEFA's disciplinary unit had appealed their sentences. Therefore, I, Anders, and one of the assistant referees had been called to a trial where we were interrogated by lawyers from UEFA and the clubs - so that the players, including world star Francesco Totti, could potentially have their punishments reduced. The verdict was announced a few days later and meant that the players who had appealed their sentences had their suspensions reduced, while Roma, on the other hand, had to pay higher fines. With that aftermath, it was least expected that we would already be back at the Olimpico. This September evening, Roma were under pressure. They were trailing 0-1 just before half-time and were being booed. Home hero Francesco Totti was frustrated and was cautioned. And his teammate, French star Philippe Mexès, kicked down away player Māris Verpakovskis. Anders blew his whistle and immediately showed the red card. The crowd in the stands went wild. They screamed and whistled loudly at Anders and the rest of the refereeing team, but also at the home team who were playing terribly.

From my previous match as fourth official at the Olimpico just over two years earlier, I had learned that the stadium, built in 1928, probably had Europe's longest player tunnel. It went from a staircase at the halfway line and then along the entire long side before turning back towards the centre of the pitch again.

It was dark and extremely long, very difficult to overview, and there were great opportunities for players to confront each other without us referees being able to see what was happening. That's exactly what had happened in the match against Galatasaray, but we would avoid that this time. Therefore, we had talked about me going down into the tunnel in advance so that we in the team could spread out and monitor a larger area than last time.

When Anders blows for half-time shortly after the red card, the crowd is at its most frenzied. I immediately leave my area between the benches, go down the stairs and escort the first players through the long, dark tunnel and make sure no confrontations occur. We have decided that I will receive the first wave of players coming down the stairs, then one of the assistant referees will take the next wave, and finally Anders and the assistant referee furthest from the stairs will look after the last players. I'm standing outside our referee room when the stream of players suddenly subsides. After a while, two Roma players come. They look at me, and one of them points to his head and says to me in poor English: "Blood from his head. Frisk injured." I quickly run through the long, dark tunnel towards the pitch.

I nearly collide with several players on the way. When I reach the area where players and referees gather before going up the stairs and out onto the pitch, Anders is lying down, seemingly unconscious with blood on his face and on the yellow shirt.

In the replays afterwards, you can see that an object hits Anders in the forehead, that he reaches for his head and a second later the blood starts gushing. With the help of one of the assistant referees, he gets help down the stairs and then collapses and loses consciousness for a brief moment.

We first move Anders to a protected place where he can't be hit by more objects. The doctors are there, trying to stop the bleeding and checking how Anders is doing. UEFA personnel rush over - everything is in utter chaos. I catch myself for a few seconds thinking about the match, about the second half, maybe I'll now be forced to make my Champions League debut.

Anders is moved to our dressing room with the help of medical staff. He's actually feeling quite okay, but has a headache. He's got a proper gash on his head and now has a large bandage over his forehead. We in the referee team call our respective families back home to reassure them, in case they've seen what happened.

Despite what happened, UEFA wants the match to continue. For them, a referee is a thing, a product, a unit that can be replaced when needed. No one really cares about the person, about the injury, about our working environment. The show must go on. Always.

This was demonstrated not least by what happened after Christian Eriksen's cardiac arrest during Euro 2021, but also when my Swedish colleague Mohammed Al-Hakim and his team with Peter Allheim and Fredrik Klyver in the summer of 2018 officiated the match between Sturm Graz and Larnaca in the Europa League qualifiers. They were forced to complete the match despite Klyver being hit in the head by a glass bottle with twelve minutes remaining and the fourth official having to step in as assistant referee. Mohammed didn't have the status that was probably required to get the management to stop the match. But Anders has it at the Olimpico in Rome in 2004. He decides that the match should be abandoned, that there will be no second half at the Olimpico. At the same time, the Italian police are worried about our safety if we stay at the stadium for too long. We pack up our things, shaken, walk out to the bus and in the same second that we, escorted by three police cars with blue lights, leave the stadium, the announcer informs that the match has been cancelled. My colleagues and I are safe, and feel secure.

Anders is taken to the hospital for examination, they do a skull X-ray and find a one-and-a-half centimetre long gash in his forehead, at the hairline. Additionally, Anders shows signs of a mild concussion, with headache and nausea. When the reports have been written, we go to the flight with full police protection, and just like after the match against Galatasaray, we have a police escort until we board the plane.

UEFA's verdict after the match was harsh and clear. Dynamo Kiev was awarded the victory with a 3-0 score. Roma was forced to play their next two home matches behind closed doors. Despite the turbulence in Rome, I personally received positive feedback from UEFA. The referee observer on site, a very strange Croatian that many Swedish referees had had problems with over the years, for some incredibly odd reason gave me the highest score in the team for how I had acted after the match. I received praise and the highest score for obvious things like taking care of my friend and colleague who was injured and needed help. At the same time, one of the assistant referees received harsh criticism because his shorts were far too short to be worn during a Champions League match.

Sometimes I really wondered what criteria UEFA actually had for those they appointed as observers.

For Anders, it took a while before everyday life returned. The news hunt from Swedish and international journalists was intense. Everyone wanted a comment, a picture, an opinion from the Swedish referee who had abandoned a match in the Champions League. It went so far that a group of Italian journalists staked out Anders' house in Mölndal, they were on the property and crept up to look through the windows when they thought no one was home.

Less than six months later, Anders Frisk chose to quit refereeing - despite still lacking the Champions League final he had dreamed of and the 2006 World Cup lying just around the corner. Anders said that threats, hate, and harassment were the reason.

After the Champions League knockout match in February 2005 between Barcelona and Chelsea, coach José Mourinho accused Anders Frisk of having had a private meeting at half-time with Barcelona's coach Frank Rijkaard. Anders denied the allegations but confirmed that they had briefly greeted each other - without talking about the match.

In the aftermath, Anders and his family received several death threats from Chelsea supporters and were forced to have police protection for a time.

A few weeks later, he chose to end his career for good.

What happened to Anders and his family made me feel sorry for him on a personal level, that his dream and ambitions were not fulfilled. It was terrible that hate and threats from supporters forced him to quit.

But I never connected what happened to me as a person, that similar things could actually happen to me in the future if I continued with a career at the highest level. That even my family could be affected by my choice to become a referee at the highest level. At this time, I had met and fallen in love with a fantastic girl. We got together, moved in to an apartment on Nackagatan in Södermalm, Stockholm. A year later we were expecting a child and a couple of months before our first daughter's birth, we bought a house in idyllic Sigtuna. The fact that it was fifteen minutes from Arlanda was no coincidence, it facilitated my constant travelling. Moreover, there was an additional advantage to the new residence: I could now referee teams from Stockholm in the Allsvenskan since Sigtuna was considered part of Uppland. In August 2005, we got a fantastic new addition, a little daughter whom we named Melisa. At the same time, these years were my toughest in life. I was a new parent and homeowner, an Allsvenskan referee, officiating my own international matches, and had the role of sales manager at a rapidly growing global company with forty employees and five offices around the world. I slept too little, trained poorly, ate carelessly, and had to struggle to make my life puzzle fit together. I was heavier than before, the scale even showed three digits at times. But I chose to ignore it, and instead cheerfully focused on the fact that I had always passed my fitness tests without problems. When I was at my heaviest and least trained, the injuries started coming. My Achilles tendon was constantly inflamed, and I officiated my matches with painkillers. Throughout my refereeing career, I had maintained a parallel professional career, and I'm convinced that I would never have become such a stress-resistant, successful entrepreneur with high work capacity if I hadn't been a referee at the same time. And in the same way, I would never have become a successful referee if I hadn't got to practice my leadership in other environments.

During the IT bubble shortly after the turn of the millennium, we who owned IEC in Sports had sold our shares to an English company. The idea was that the company would grow through acquisitions, an increasing share price, and new opportunities to buy TV rights.

I received a small amount of money paid out in connection with the sale, a small bonus for the hard work I had put in during the first years. Above all, however, I was paid in shares in the buying company. When the market crashed hard, the compensation in shares turned out to be completely worthless. With that, all the prerequisites for building the company in the way we had intended disappeared. We owners grew tired of the situation. In the spring of 2003, when everything looked at its darkest, with recessions in our most important markets and an ongoing acute SARS epidemic in Asia, we did the brave thing: we bought back the company that we had sold barely two years earlier.

Shortly after, two things happened that would come to affect the company's future in the right direction. First, IEC signed a contract to be responsible for all sales of TV rights for Real Madrid's pre-season tour in Asia. Then David Beckham, the world's most famous football player, signed for the club and the value of the rights quintupled overnight without it costing us a single penny extra.

The timing when we bought back IEC was, in other words, fantastically good. SARS became just a local epidemic in Asia, not a global pandemic, and the world economy turned upward from having hit rock bottom. After the summer of 2003, the company grew rapidly again. But having two parallel careers took time and energy, and I knew that at some point I had to focus on refereeing if I wanted to reach where I dreamed: the World Cup, the Euros, and the Champions League. Because even though my work was stimulating and I was successful at IEC, it was the career as a football referee that drove and attracted me more than anything else.

With each international assignment, I got more and more of a taste for refereeing. The Allsvenskan was good, but internationally it was better.

The matches abroad were inspiring with new stadiums, larger crowds, better atmosphere, more skilled players, and more unpredictable matches.

I constantly got to visit new countries and experience new things.

When the Allsvenskan season ended in the autumn of 2005, I got a U21 match that made a strong impression. Usually, a U21 international was a rather tired affair, played far from the capital, in a smaller arena, often with players who only cared about their own performances and less about the team's result.

But this match was different. It was England against France in a direct decisive playoff match at White Hart Lane. On that fantastic, tight, noisy arena, the attendance record for U21 football in England was broken that night - 34,491 spectators. It was there I understood that this was what I wanted to do. I wanted to follow in the footsteps of players like Franck Ribéry, Gaël Clichy, and James Milner and make the career in football that I understood they would make. I grew as a referee when I stepped into the big arenas with better players, more people in the stands, and matches that were broadcast on TV. The kicks became greater the more was at stake, my dose of adrenaline increased after each match - at the same time as I almost always had a new assignment to look forward to immediately after the match. It felt more and more like I had found my home, in a profession and mission that actually seemed to suit me and my qualities in the best way. I liked the wonderful unpredictability of sports. The only things I knew were that the match started at a certain time, that the score was goalless then, that the match time was two times forty-five minutes, and how the rulebook was written. After that, there was nothing more I could know or have control over. The rest was advanced improvisation and adaptation. I had to solve things as they arose or even better: ensure that no problems occurred. The feeling of going out to difficult assignments with good players, lots of people in the stands, and three hundred difficult decisions in front of me during ninety minutes was like no other. It brought out my competitive instinct, triggered me to perform better, and I loved the challenge and the intellectual stimulation it gave. On my birthday in March 2007, I was to referee a match between Bulgaria and Albania in the Euro qualifiers. The legend Hristo Stoichkov was the national coach for the home team, and in the tunnel, he was shocked when he first saw me and then my fourth official Markus Strömbergsson. Markus looked much younger than the thirty-two years he was at the time, and Stoichkov exclaimed: "My God, you look like a little boy. Are you going to referee this match?" Markus shook hands, answered Stoichkov that he was the fourth official and that it was me who would referee the match, but that I was actually only a year older than him. Stoichkov looked at me with a scrutinizing gaze, sighed a little and then said: "I guess I'm the one who's starting to get old, when the referees are so young." The match was by no means a big match in European football, but all the more important for me. My observer was the chairman of the referee committee, Volker Roth, and I knew that a good word from the German would give my career a push in the right direction. Roth was pleasant and correct but the review after the match was extremely short. It was done in a passport queue at the airport in Munich when the German turned to me and said: "Good match, you have a future. Be ready. Your score is 8.4." As usual, I had worked the hours before the match. The workload meant that I could never take completely off for three days to just focus on football, I always brought work with me wherever I went. During the days in Sofia, the starting shot was fired for a race that ended a few months later. Together in the ownership group, we had decided that it was time to sell IEC and had found a hot buyer, the French media group Lagardère Group. Ten minutes before it was time to go to the arena, I stressfully wrote the last lines of an introduction to the company and pressed the send button. Three months later, the deal was done. We had sold our company for crazy many millions. My namesake Persson, the company's CEO, had finalized negotiations in Paris all night and day, and in the afternoon he sent the email that contained no text, just a headline: "Congratulations, you're aprik!" I was thirty-three years old and suddenly what you loosely call financially independent. I, who was a hyperactive workaholic and performance junkie, actually never needed to work again from that day. The joy was great, but not overwhelming. The path to the millions had actually been more fun than the moment when I realized that I never needed to worry about money again.

The money didn't really change me in any significant way. I had worked far too long and hard for it when it finally came. But the money gave me a calmness and security - capital and space to tell people to go to hell if needed. I could now focus only on what I wanted, what I believed in, and what gave energy or a kick.

I chose to continue working at IEC because it made me feel good, to have a context, a stimulating task, and to be in demand. At the sale, I signed a contract valid until 2010. Everyone who knew me understood why. I couldn't sit still, but always wanted to move forward. And that's still the case today. I'd rather sit at the computer and write than in front of the TV watching a series. I'd rather have an exciting meeting than be alone at home. I'd rather start a project than have a few weeks off.

Money was never my biggest driving force, either as an entrepreneur or as a referee. My primary goal was different: the desire to create something, to get somewhere, to accomplish the impossible and reach a set goal. In my best years as a referee, I had an annual salary just under a million Swedish kronor from all my assignments in Sweden and abroad. A match in Allsvenskan gave eighty-nine thousand kronor, a group stage match in the Champions League close to fifty thousand, while a match that could decide which country went to the World Cup gave a significantly lower compensation: just over ten thousand. Compared to many others in society, the salary and compensation were of course good, even really good. But if you thought about the fact that I was one of Sweden's best in my profession and that everyone around me was extremely well-paid, the salary was low. Especially if you compared with players internationally, the greatest star of all in sports, Portuguese Cristiano Ronaldo, earned an insane 2.2 million Swedish kronor per day during 2016. My annual salary didn't even reach half of what Ronaldo earned in a day. Yet I was supposed to be his boss on the pitch. Even though I had fun at my job and was passionate about it even after the sale, I knew deep down that I couldn't forever continue to have two parallel, demanding careers. I didn't have time to train as I wanted, wasn't as available as either FIFA, UEFA or the Swedish Football Association required, and barely had time to see my family. The journey towards the best international matches continued after the assignment in Bulgaria in March 2007. I started coming back to arenas, teams, and cities. In February 2008, I was back at White

Hart Lane to now referee Tottenham Hotspur against Slavia Prague, and in the autumn of the same year, I was back in Bulgaria - but now to referee a decisive Champions League qualifier between Levski Sofia and FC BATE Borisov.

Slowly I learned the game, became wiser, more strategic, and minimized the risks. The grades also became better and better - and the big debut was just around the corner. I now began to form a team around me for the international assignments. Mathias Klasenius from Örebro was already at that time a more or less permanent second assistant referee in my team. He was always meticulous, serious, willing to put in the time to be the best, and above all: he dared to challenge me on my decisions. He always said what he thought and thus always helped me to become better. We were also the same age, and I knew that if I managed to reach the top, I could have Mathias in my team for almost my entire career.

As the first assistant referee, I had Peter Ekström. He was considerably older and more experienced. He had been in Anders Frisk's team before, but had to start over after Anders quit.

With his routine and experience, Peter contributed perfectly to our team's collaboration.

Markus Strömbergsson was always a given as the fourth official. He was calm, sympathetic, extremely good at putting refereeing into words, helping me to make the right decisions and analyses afterwards. Having the right people with you in the team was important throughout my career. And it became even more important after 2007 when UEFA's top referees were equipped with communication equipment and the collaboration developed into something completely different than it had been before. From the communication between referees having been limited to eye contact, gestures, discreet signs, and feedback during the break, you now got feedback in real-time - input from everyone in the team on the performance, on decisions to be made, that had been made, and tips on what to focus on during the match. Some referees couldn't handle the transition to the new technology and became stressed by all the voices shouting in their ears. Others, including myself, loved it and became experts at having a lot of information in our ears, being able to evaluate it carefully in a few tenths of a second - but then always making decisions that felt right. On December 10, 2008, I reached my first goal, a debut match in the Champions League: Real Madrid versus Zenit Saint Petersburg. I arrive in Madrid together with my then Dream Team - Peter, Mathias, and Markus.

    I, who usually always sleep before the match, can't find peace just this afternoon. I'm too nervous, too jittery, and feel too much tension. The fact that I have been entrusted to referee in the Champions League feels unreal. In the car on the way to the match, I can't help but ask our referee liaison if there will be a lot of people tonight.

    I walk as if in a bubble when I escort the twenty-two players to their positions, turn around and then stand facing the benches, the VIP stand, all the TV cameras, and get to hear the wonderful anthem that introduces all matches in the Champions League.

    It doesn't matter that it's a chilly evening, I'm not cold. It's unimportant if I'm nervous, right then I don't feel anything. It doesn't matter if I possibly doubt myself, right there and then I believe I can handle anything.

It's in that moment on that day in Madrid that I realize that this beats everything else. I don't care about the job at IEC, all the money I have, and my successes as an entrepreneur and businessman. I want to referee football and I love it.

The Season from Hell

While in 2008 I had to wait until December for the year's finest present, my first match in the Champions League, 2009's best gift came as early as January 23rd.

In the midst of the annual Swedish referee course in Jönköping, our second daughter Milla was born at Karolinska Hospital in Solna. Fortunately, the delivery was planned, which meant I could be there to support my wife, take a few days off, and be in that wonderful bubble one experiences as a new parent.

A couple of weeks later, I packed my bag to head off to the year's first match, a friendly international in Marseille between France and the South American superpower Argentina.

Friendly internationals were special. It was the only time when the respective national associations could choose who would referee their national team. Many associations therefore saw it as a relationship-building and very important opportunity to invite a referee, butter him up a little extra, and let him become familiar with the national team under friendly circumstances - all in preparation for upcoming competitive matches. The fact that the world-class nation France invited me was an honour in itself, but it was even more special considering Argentina was the opposition and the World Cup was just over a year away. For me, it was a test, an important match. Absolutely not a friendly international where no one cared about the result. It was two top nations teeming with world-class players: Thierry Henry, Franck Ribéry, Carlos Tevez and, above all, the then 21-year-old wonder boy Lionel Messi. And even more special - it was Diego Armando Maradona's second match as manager of the Argentine national team. I didn't have many idols in football, neither as a referee nor as a player in my youth. Apart from a few local stars in IFK Luleå during my upbringing, there were really only two players. The first was IFK Göteborg's Torbjörn Nilsson, who in the early eighties was at the centre of Blåvitt's enormous success in the UEFA Cup.

His way of moving, shooting, celebrating, and he always looked so kind.

Moreover, he seemed to be a bit different. He didn't want to turn professional, and he even declined to play for the national team... things that a young boy in Luleå found hard to understand.

The other was the great hero from the 1986 World Cup in Mexico - Diego Armando Maradona. It was the first World Cup tournament I followed seriously. I always stayed up late at night, too often fell asleep during the late night matches and had to quickly cycle down to the kiosk in the morning to buy Aftonbladet to understand what I'd missed when I fell asleep.

It was in the summer of 1986 that I became spellbound by the sport that would become a big part of my life. But there in front of the TV, it wasn't yet my plan to become a referee. I wanted to be a player, I wanted to be Diego Maradona. It was like him I wanted to dribble, shoot, and pass.

As an adult, as a referee in various contexts, I got to meet both Torbjörn Nilsson and Diego Maradona. But even though both Torbjörn and Diego had sat as idol portraits on the wall in my childhood room back in Luleå, it never occurred to me to treat them differently from the other players and leaders. For me, it was as simple as it was fundamental: the day you as a referee treated players and leaders differently depending on who they were, what they had done previously, and what relationship you had with them - then you were no longer suitable for the task. The little Maradona seeks me out in the tunnel before the match. He shakes hands and holds on for a second. With wide eyes, he talks quickly and gesticulates. The interpreter explains that Maradona has asked me to protect his players, especially Lionel Messi. Messi doesn't need to worry during the match. I do my part to protect him, but unexpectedly, I have the best help from one of his opponents - the French defender Éric Abidal. Abidal was Messi's club teammate at Barcelona. How would it look if he as a teammate tackled Messi in a friendly match? Not all the players see it as a friendly international, though. For two of them, Frenchman Thierry Henry and Argentine Gabriel Heinze, a personal war unfolds on the pitch. Just before a corner is about to be taken, I blow the whistle when I see them engaged in a duel that looks more like a wrestling match. Henry is upset and claims that Heinze always plays dirty against him, while Heinze in turn claims that Henry is exaggerating and always complains about him.

I keep an extra eye on Heinze and Henry for the rest of the match. There are a series of tough duels and there's an enormous amount of emotion between the players. Sometimes they're close to the line, but my colleagues and I make sure the players don't cross it.

Afterwards, I understand why it's so tense. They have a long history of playing for rival top clubs in both England and Spain, and have met many times before in decisive and prestigious matches.

Most of the players are satisfied afterwards. Carlos Tevez gives me a thumbs up for the advantage I played when Messi scores to make it 2-0 in the final minutes, and the crowd's booing afterwards is not directed at me but at the unpopular French manager Raymond Domenech.

In the dressing room afterwards, I can breathe a sigh of relief. I've shown everyone that I can indeed handle internationals of this calibre.

Then suddenly there's a knock on the door and in comes Diego Maradona along with his interpreter and a person from the Argentine management team. My childhood idol shakes hands again and looks me in the eyes.

He thanks me for the match and says he's very pleased with my performance. I also receive an Argentine national team shirt as a memento from the match.

I thank him shyly for the shirt and for the praise, and before Maradona can leave the dressing room, I speak up again and ask for something I've never done or will do again during my refereeing career: I wonder if we can take a picture of us in the team with Maradona.

If the door to the dressing room hadn't been closed, I would never have taken the picture. For me, it was important that no one outside saw what we were doing, and if Maradona hadn't sought us out in the dressing room, there wouldn't have been a picture either.

It has to be an exception to confirm my own rule: to always treat everyone equally.

The spring season of 2009 continued with fine matches, better assignments than before and greater trust from UEFA. Reaching the knockout stages of the UEFA Cup was a milestone in my career - refereeing AC Milan and a football icon like David Beckham was another. But the encounter with Beckham made me believe, for a minute, that my refereeing career could be over.

It's a late and cold Thursday night in Milan. The temperature barely rises above zero, and the cold bites hard at the twenty-five thousand spectators who have braved the chill and come to the classic San Siro to see a star-studded AC Milan play in the round of 32 in the UEFA Cup against Werder Bremen.

Milan are big favourites to win not just tonight's match but the entire UEFA Cup. The team consists of world stars like Paolo Maldini, Andrea Pirlo, Ronaldinho and David Beckham. The English star is at that time and place the world's most famous football player. Perhaps not just for what he does and has done on the pitch - but also for his glamorous life off it.

The start of the match is tough and the atmosphere between the skilful Italians and tough Germans is on the verge of getting out of hand immediately.

Out on the left wing, at the corner of the penalty area, he steps back, looks up and shoots towards goal, whereupon the ball is stopped by a German defender with his arm.

Beckham goes crazy, gesticulates and shows the whole world that the free kick hit the hand. But it's not because of Beckham's protests that I blow for a penalty - I've seen it, and I also get it confirmed by my fourth official.

At half-time, Werder Bremen's leaders are angry. They remain in the long corridor, shouting angrily in German and gesturing that we in the refereeing team would be corrupt, bought and influenced by the home team paying us bribes. I choose to look away, not to see or hear, not to confront, report or send off.

I understand that in hindsight it may seem cowardly, submissive and perhaps disloyal to my colleagues. Or maybe it was wise. Reporting a bunch of leaders and preventing them from being on the bench during the second half would probably have created more chaos, an even bigger scene and even bigger problems.
The most important thing I knew myself: I am absolutely not influenced by bribes or pressure from the home team. Milan lead the match 2-0 and seem to be through to the next round, but in the second half the home team suffers a collapse.

First, the away team reduces it to 2-1. Then Beckham tackles the away team's Claudio Pizarro in the penalty area.

I'm well positioned and wave dismissively. The ball goes out for a corner. Beckham turns around, gives me a thumbs up, as a confirmation that I've made the right call and that it's not a penalty. The away team, who will go through if they score one more goal, are furious and shout and gesticulate.

A minute later, Werder Bremen make it 2-2, which becomes the final result.

The star-studded home team is eliminated. The crowd at San Siro boos and shouts out their displeasure after the match. The players flee the pitch quickly, all except one. David Beckham.

He runs up to the home supporters and throws up his shirt, but the booing continues. When Beckham, as the last player, has left the pitch, I and my two colleagues - Mathias Klasenius and Peter Ekström - also step off the green turf and go down the long tunnel under San Siro.

David Beckham is walking a few steps ahead of us, he shakes his head in frustration and disappointment, but when he hears us, he turns around and extends his hand. He apologizes for being rude to me when he wanted a free kick in the first half. I assure him it's no problem.

The morning after, I fly home to Arlanda, and I get home to my family in Sigtuna after three intense days in Milan. I'm tired, as always after too little and poor sleep in connection with international matches. My body aches.

After reading a bedtime story to our oldest daughter Melisa, I fall asleep early myself. After about an hour, she comes into our bedroom feeling unwell. She lies down between me and my wife and twists and turns anxiously.

Suddenly she vomits. Then she vomits again. The winter vomiting bug has been going around at the preschool, and of course it's her turn to be affected.

I lift her up, carry her gently towards the shower, look straight into her crying face and try to comfort her. I have time to think that right now it doesn't matter if I get sick, I've already refereed my most important match.

Then she vomits again. Right in my face. Her vomit runs down my face and the smell makes me feel like I'm about to throw up myself.

On the way into the shower, I quickly glance at the clock, 22:30. It's exactly twenty-four hours since I was running on the same football pitch as David Beckham. It's to the minute a day since I was in charge of a bunch of world stars in front of twenty-five thousand spectators and got them to do exactly as I wanted. Regardless of what profession you have, it's a given that you sometimes make mistakes. The only way to get better and avoid making the same mistake again is to accept and realize that you've just made a mistake. As a referee, when you make over three hundred decisions in ninety minutes, you always have to be extremely convinced that you're doing the right thing yourself to be able to convince the players, the audience in the stadium and everyone at home in their TV sofas. That's why it's sometimes difficult to realize immediately after a match that you've actually made a mistake. You have to force yourself into a decision bubble where you really only have one mantra in your head: "I'm going to make all decisions correctly today, no matter how difficult it is and what happens." I have on several occasions come in after a match and met a person (maybe an observer, journalist, colleague or player) who's told me that I've missed a clear penalty, but when we've looked at the TV pictures together, we've seen completely different things. When I've let go of my protection, my guard, after a day or two and can look at the situation more soberly and without the match's post-psychological walls with new eyes, I've often been able to admit that I've made a mistake.

Immediately after a match, it was usually impossible. Not because I didn't want to, but just because it was so insanely difficult to go from "I know everything and make no mistakes" during the match to "sure, I made a mistake and decided the match" minutes after a final whistle.

But sometimes, when the mistake has been all too obvious, it has been important to be able to capitulate immediately, even if it was painful at the time. The Allsvenskan premiere in 2009 between Helsingborgs IF and IFK Göteborg was such an example.

The stands are full, there's a fantastic atmosphere, and I'm pumped full of confidence after a pre-season where I've refereed world stars like Messi, Beckham and Ronaldinho.

Just before half-time, I see a defender in IFK Göteborg handling the ball, and I blow for a penalty. Helsingborg make it 1-0 from the penalty and that also becomes the final result.

After the match, several players from IFK Göteborg come up. They are disappointed. The player who caused the penalty, Ragnar Sigurðsson, is understandably the most frustrated.

In the dressing room, my colleagues and I celebrate a successful premiere, we are convinced that all major decisions are correct and I am completely comfortable with the evening's performance.

There's a knock on the door and in comes our referee observer. He looks a bit stressed and has an important message to give. The observer has received feedback from others who've seen the match on TV and believes that my decision to blow for a penalty is completely wrong. That if the ball even hits, it's unintentional handball.

I sink down. Canal Plus has asked me for an interview that I've already agreed to. For a moment I consider not going out to them, to delay it so long that the broadcast is over when I finally come out.

But I change my mind. I realize that I've actually made a mistake and therefore must own up to it. My steps out from my "I do everything right" bubble in the dressing room to the interview are heavy.

In the interview, I immediately admit and acknowledge that I've made a mistake.

As I remember it, I more or less escaped follow-up questions. A referee agreeing to an interview was not common, and for him to then admit a mistake was even rarer.

I agree to another interview with SVT's Staffan Lindeborg, with the same type of questions and I give the same answers. When the camera is off, I get praise for daring to admit that it went wrong. When I return to the dressing room, Ragnar Sigurðsson is there and wants to talk to me. He's angry, upset and disappointed about the incorrect decision against him. I immediately admit that I was wrong and apologize. When Sigurðsson then goes out to the press gathering waiting outside our dressing room, ready to snap up juicy quotes on what was said behind the closed doors, he says: "I think the referee makes a big mistake, but everyone can make mistakes so there's nothing to say about it." One of the biggest and most public mistakes of my career somehow turned into a success. I probably never received so much praise from players, leaders, colleagues and media, despite having actually made a match-deciding mistake.

All international appointments of referees were governed by which category you belonged to in UEFA. Belonging to the top group, ELITE, was therefore the most important when UEFA sorted referees into groups twice a year.

The selection for the groups was based on a series of official and unofficial criteria such as merits, ratings from matches, physical ability, experience, potential, language skills and so on. The best referees in each group were moved up, and the worst were moved down. Just like for teams in an annual league play. The year you turned forty-five, you were removed due to age reasons, so there was always a need to fill up from below. June 26, 2009 was a big day in my refereeing career. After a good spring season with big teams and good ratings, UEFA's referee committee decided to move me up to the highest category, along with eight other referees. Among

UEFA's top referees, there was a major generational shift going on, and great investment was promised for all new referees in the autumn Champions League. All nine referees who were moved up actually also became championship referees at Euro 2012 or 2016. In other words, UEFA had scouted well and already in 2009 picked out the top referees of the future. For my part, however, the autumn began in the worst way, and I was slowly drawn into a downward spiral that made me start to doubt myself. Was I up to this level? Was I really as bad as some seemed to think? The start was a friendly international between England and Slovenia at Wembley in early September. Once again, it was a match with world stars in a row and before the match, Beckham came up to me. He recognized me from Milan a few months earlier and greeted me cheerfully. I grew a few centimeters. The fact that one of the football world's biggest players recognized me and came up to greet me made me proud and happy.

But during the actual match, I was poor. I don't know why, but the flow and confidence I had felt all spring was suddenly gone. I awarded a dubious penalty in Wayne Rooney's favor. For me, there and then, it was a super clear penalty that couldn't be discussed, but I got enormous protests.

What was worse, the player I thought had pulled Rooney's arm, the Slovenian captain Boštjan Cesar, got injured in his foot in the same sequence and was forced to leave. I had to show a yellow card when Cesar was lying on the ground outside the pitch receiving treatment.

The fourth official in the match at Wembley was Mark Clattenburg, who over time became one of my closest friends in the refereeing world. We had dinner and toasted to the future after the match. In the hotel room afterwards, I noted that I was dissatisfied with my performance, but tried instead to look forward to the Champions League that was waiting during the autumn. But if my first match in the Champions League in December 2008 was a dream, my second match would become a complete nightmare. A few weeks after my weak performance at Wembley, I land again on the British Isles. In Glasgow, I'm met by persistent rain, terrible humidity, and a cold that eats through all clothes. The pitch is spongy, slippery, and barely playable. But of course, the match will still be played.

Glasgow Rangers are hosting Sevilla at Ibrox in front of forty-five thousand extremely loud Scots who do everything to lift their team. Maybe Rangers have the loudest supporters I've refereed - or maybe their deafening volume is due to what happens just before half-time. One of the forwards in the home team, Steven Naismith, is fouled in the penalty area, but I'm stressed, tired, feel that I'm in the wrong place, read the situation completely wrong and let the play continue. The replays, however, showed their clear language. I was wrong. Terribly wrong. It should have been a penalty and a sending-off for the Sevilla player, Frenchman Abdoulay Konko. What happened after that, I barely remember. I just want the match to end, to get away from there, blow the final whistle and disappear. As if to add to that feeling further, it's Konko who gives Sevilla the lead five minutes later and the away team eventually wins comfortably 4-1. At the dinner afterwards, I barely eat, don't drink the beer that has been set out but wait for the review from our Dutch observer. It's a scathing critique without end. It continues in the subsequent written report. The grade that lands a few days later is record low: 7.6. The consequence of the grade and report is clear: I will be suspended for one match from the Champions League. Afterwards, I received harsh criticism in the media. The comments in the newspapers the day after were painful to read. The Scottish football legend Gordon Strachan didn't hold back when commenting on my performance: "Eriksson should never referee football again, he was worthless ..." On the flight home, I looked out the window and saw the sun setting. Was this the end of my refereeing career? My hesitation and worry were exacerbated by all the calls and messages that pounded into my phone after the match. I happened to answer the first call and accidentally read a message. Then I stopped.

I was hunted by journalists who wanted a comment, supporters who wanted to shout out their hatred and other people who threatened my life if I ever set foot in the arena again.

I was never afraid. I knew the threats were empty, and that I wouldn't return to Ibrox again in my career anyway - that UEFA would remember my match and therefore never let me referee Glasgow Rangers again. But I was unsure if I would even have the strength to continue at all. I logged out, didn't read my texts and didn't tell anyone in my surroundings about what was happening. I felt like shit for a few days. It's life-threatening for a referee to start doubting himself and his decisions. As soon as you even think you might make a mistake… you do just that. Throughout the autumn of 2009, I increasingly wondered about my capacity, my decisions, whether I could handle refereeing at the highest level I was at. And as soon as I started to wonder, the decisions more often became wrong. I did some okay matches, but the questions about my own competence constantly gnawed in my head.

I was now indeed suspended by UEFA from the Champions League, but I got a match from FIFA in the last round of World Cup qualifiers: Poland versus Slovakia.

A bit depressed and dejected by the autumn's performances, I could follow the group's other results in the days before our match and conclude that my match would be directly decisive for whether Slovakia would go to their first ever football World Cup. With a victory, the ticket to the World Cup in South Africa would be secured. I realized that FIFA hadn't thought the match would matter so much when they appointed me to it. It made me shaky. And my nervousness didn't exactly decrease when a few hours before kick-off, I pulled back the curtains to my hotel window in Katowice and saw absolute snow chaos. We were incredibly unsure if there would really be a match, and when we arrived at the stadium, it was completely white on the pitch. At Stadion Śląski, built in 1956 and barely renovated since then, the last match was now to be played before a total reconstruction would take place. We were forced to realize that the match would be played with a red ball on a white snow bed with the lines brushed out now and then.

It would be a complete parody of football.

The Italian FIFA delegate took me aside and told me that the match must be played, that the group must be concluded tonight no matter how bad the weather was. Cancelling was out of the question - even if it would have been the fairest. I joked that I was used to snow on the pitch from Luleå. Jokes aside, I was also comfortable in the cold and slippery conditions, and understood better than most what would happen under the extreme circumstances.

When I blew the final whistle after ninety-four minutes and saw the Slovakian players celebrating their World Cup place, I felt no joy myself, just a great relief at not having ended up in focus once again.

On home turf, I refereed with a completely different confidence during the autumn. As the gold match at Ullevi between IFK Göteborg and AIK approached, there was speculation that I would get it after a good season.

In AIK's penultimate match, at home against Örebro, I was the fourth official and afterwards AIK's coach Mikael Stahre came into the referee room as usual to thank for the match and asked in confidence if I would referee the final. I said I thought it would be Martin Hansson.

It was indeed he who got the classic gold match. He was the best referee at that time and deserved the assignment. I had to see myself as a good second, as Sweden's second-best referee.

During the latter part of the 2000s, Martin Hansson, born in 1971, had emerged as the most promising Swedish referee in many years. He was mentally strong, fearless, had a physique that an elite athlete would be jealous of, was good at communicating and just crazy enough to handle the pressure that existed in the big matches. Martin narrowly missed out on selection for Euro 2008, but fought on towards the 2010 World Cup. He was ranked number one in Sweden and refereed Champions League, and was selected for the pre-World Cup in South Africa, the FIFA Confederations Cup, in the summer of 2009. He got to referee the final of the tournament, where he excelled and was praised for his performances. That he would be selected for the 2010 World Cup was as obvious as a kick-off always being taken from the centre spot of the pitch. His future would, however, unexpectedly be crushed one evening in Paris. On November 18, 2009, a decisive playoff match between France and Ireland was to be played. A place in the 2010 World Cup in South Africa was at stake. The big favorite France had, as expected, won the first of two meetings 1-0. But in the return match, Ireland, the lowest ranked team in the playoff qualifiers, puts in a heroic effort. Ireland leads 1-0 after full time. When both teams have scored the same number of goals at home and away, it goes to extra time. It's a nightmare situation for a referee. During extra time, the players get more and more tired, make simpler mistakes, the quality drops, more and more lose their temper and strange situations arise. During the match, Martin referees incredibly well, almost flawlessly. But during extra time, something happens that radically changes Martin Hansson's refereeing life. France has got a free kick in the centre circle. Midfielder Florent Malouda plays the ball towards the French captain Thierry Henry who is in the penalty area. Henry is surprised, and as a reflex, he takes the ball with his hand before passing it on to his teammate William Gallas who scores from close range.

Martin doesn't see the situation and approves the goal. There's great French jubilation and wild Irish protests. France wins the match and is through to the World Cup. Martin becomes the villain, the scoundrel. He is hung out to dry and criticized in media worldwide. In the aftermath, it's only he who is criticized, who is pointed out as guilty, and he receives death threats from supporters. The headlines will very little be about Henry, the person who cheated in the situation and who, in my opinion, should actually be hung out to dry.

I suffered with Martin when it happened, I knew it could just as easily have been me, and I understood what hell he and his team were going through. Martin was strong in the midst of the storm, he stood tall.

He said that he had always in his career been fair and judged according to what he had seen, but that this time he had not seen anything and therefore could not make a different decision.

Despite the scandal in Paris, Martin was still selected for the 2010 World Cup.

But once there, there was no match for Martin and his team.

Even though they were told they were selected for a match, the selection was stopped by political forces higher up in FIFA who did not want the Swedish team to referee in the tournament. Martin and the team had to return home extremely disappointed. After the World Cup, Martin's time in football's fine room was over. In the autumn of 2010, Martin was gradually frozen out by the new leaders within UEFA. Empty words about better matches would prove to be worth nothing. Somehow I managed during the winter of 2010, after an okay round of 16 match in the Europa League between Wolfsburg and Rubin Kazan, to gain UEFA's trust to referee a top match. Or was it a last chance to show that I was at that level? A test that would decide my future as a referee? The fact that UEFA had introduced a change in the number of referees in the matches also contributes to my feeling of uncertainty before the upcoming quarter-final. When the Europa League replaced the UEFA Cup in the 2009/2010 season, President Michel Platini and UEFA had decided to test a system with five referees instead of three. My quarter-final in the Europa League would be the second match I refereed with the five-referee system.

The system had been tested at lower levels for a couple of years and was the UEFA president's solution to the increasingly loud demands to introduce goal-line technology and technological aids in refereeing. Platini and UEFA wanted to keep human decision-making on the pitch and the solution became to place two extra assistant referees, equipped with headsets each, behind each goal to help with important decisions in the penalty area. FIFA didn't believe in the idea of five referees and would never come to implement it. I had benefited from the expanded communication possibilities that had been introduced earlier and looked positively at the five-referee system. Our former fourth official Markus Strömbergsson now became one of two penalty area referees in my team and Stefan Johannesson often filled the other role. While my assistant referees were completely specialized in refereeing from the line, my new penalty area referees were usually main referees. Having several people in the team who could both help and challenge me was positive, but at the same time I would need to stand even more firmly and be able to trust that what perhaps only I saw on the pitch was correct and should be judged for.

Our newly formed five-man team would now referee an English team, and I myself thought back to the hell autumn when I had failed with both England and Glasgow Rangers. I hoped and prayed that it would go better to referee Liverpool in the Europa League quarter-final away against Benfica in Lisbon.

It's Maundy Thursday, and at 20:05 I blow to start the match.

I want a calm match, no big, difficult decisions or situations that put me in focus. It becomes exactly the opposite. Early in the match, I send off Ryan Babel of Liverpool for pushing a hand into the face of home player Luisão. I see from close range what happens and don't hesitate, but become uncertain when my colleague Mathias shouts loudly in the microphone after the red card is shown. He's stressed and hasn't seen the same thing as me. I myself am confident with my decision, but of course am affected by his opinion. It creates an uncertainty that remains during the match, and then escalates.

Liverpool score a goal, but because a player was clearly offside much earlier in the attack, I disallow the goal. Certainly, it's completely correct, but I've blown late after neither hearing nor seeing my assistant referee on the line. I'm forced to take a humiliating walk with the ball that has just been in the net, back to the point where the offside occurred and where the free kick should be taken.

In the second half, I award two penalties. Both against Liverpool.

The first happens after 58 minutes when Emiliano Insúa fouls Benfica's quick Argentine midfielder Pablo Aimar. I see what happens, think it's a clear penalty, but the last few months' less good performances mean that I'm no longer the absolutely certain and clear referee I once was.

I hesitate for a short second. Before I blow, I want to hear what my colleagues have to say. When I need help the most, it's echoing silence in my earpiece. Not a sound is heard. Since it broke in the first half, maybe it has broken again, I have time to think.

I follow my instinct, trust what I've seen and blow for a penalty. I point to the penalty spot and walk slowly there. Sixty-two thousand spectators cheer loudly, while eleven Liverpool players are crazy, gesticulating and shouting at me.

Then suddenly my communication equipment works again, and I hear both my colleagues synchronously shouting: "No, no, no!" When I needed it the most, I heard nothing - now when the decision is made, I hear that none of my colleagues think it's a penalty. It's spinning in my head. Should I change my mind? I think, ponder, talk simultaneously with the Liverpool players, argue why I'm blowing for a penalty, try to show convincing body language and at the same time negotiate with my inner voice and then bottom out that I still have to trust myself. When Óscar

Cardozo equalizes to 1-1 and I walk up towards the centre circle, I'm dejected. It's quiet again in the communication equipment. But not because it's not working. Usually, our communication is filled with praise, pep, encouragement and happy words. Now it's completely quiet. Everyone has heard what happened. Two in the team have clearly said no - but I've still awarded a penalty.

The second penalty I don't see myself, Stefan Johannesson helps me blow it - a clear handball on Jamie Carragher.

A good half hour later we're back in the referee room. We've navigated past a bunch of furious players and leaders from Liverpool and can lock ourselves in our room. Mobile phones are turned on, and despite my feeling that everything has gone to hell, we get a series of messages that are positive: The sending-off is correct according to UEFA's new guidelines. Both penalties are correct. The five warnings are correct.

We breathe out a little cautiously, but what friends in Sweden write doesn't really matter. It's UEFA's words that weigh the heaviest. And our Northern Irish referee observer is delayed. After fifteen minutes, Alan Snoddy comes in, takes my hand and says we'll talk after dinner.

I have an uneasy feeling, because I know deep down that I haven't been good enough today. If I've got all decisions right despite my poor performance, it's not about skill. Then it's just luck.

It feels like dinner takes forever, and afterwards at the hotel Snoddy begins the review. He can, reluctantly, support the sending-off and the two penalties - but not much else is positive.

The observer thinks I've been too shaky in my judgment, that I've at times lost control of the match. In the report that was sent a few weeks later, I was thoroughly criticized. The grade was 8.0 - the absolute worst grade you could get after getting right on a sending-off and two penalties. It should rather have been 8.8 if I had done an acceptable job.

The journey home to Sigtuna was heavy. After four hours of direct flight, I landed at Arlanda and again I was peppered with calls and messages, especially from England. This time, my email address had also leaked out, and supporters from the away team were spamming my inbox. I didn't take any calls, deleted all texts that came from unknown numbers and refused to read a single one of the threats directed at me. I felt worse than I ever had in my refereeing career and I thought to myself that now I'm giving up, this is not for me. At the same time, I was going through a tough time off the pitch. As the only top referee in Sweden with a civilian job, as sales manager at IEC in Sports, it felt like I constantly needed to clone myself. When my Swedish refereeing colleagues came home from an assignment, they could be off, recover and be with family.

I could of course have quit my job and got the same position as the other referees - but I was in the last six months of the contract we had agreed on when we sold the company in 2007. I had promised my colleagues to stay at least until autumn 2010.

I gritted my teeth and knew that everything would soon change. I too would soon be able to referee full-time, and then fully focus on becoming not only Sweden's best referee - but also one of the world's best. If I now had the strength to continue.

On May 12, 2010, UEFA's annual meeting and revision of the categories that the referees belonged to awaited. A year earlier I had been promoted to the highest level. Now, after twelve months, it was time to evaluate us referees again, and I honestly knew that I had at times been terrible during the past year. My performances had been uneven, the big mistakes too many and I had not shown that I could handle the new level.

If I was demoted, I had decided that I would quit as a referee with immediate effect. If I invested in something, I wanted to be the best. If I didn't belong to the best, I might as well quit.

For me, it had always been like that.

Every time the phone rang in early summer 2010, my heart pounded a little extra. If it was my boss, the Swedish referee chief Bosse Karlsson who was also on UEFA's referee committee, the call could mean that it was over with the community and joy that football had given me since I turned thirteen and refereed my first match.

Finally he called. We first talked a bit generally about UEFA's new referee organization. Bosse told me that in the future it would be run by three people with Pierluigi Collina at the helm, and that the previous chief Yvan Cornu would disappear. I thought it sounded good, as I had never felt that I had Cornu's real trust. I didn't know Collina. Bosse dragged it out but finally told me that UEFA, even though they weren't at all satisfied with my last season, had decided to give me one last chance. I felt relief and joy.

Of course I couldn't celebrate and tell the whole world that I had gotten a second chance, that I had been so close to taking a step back in my career, but I decided in the same second as I hung up the phone that I would stop working and focus on my refereeing career full-time.

I decided to make more changes in my refereeing. I didn't know exactly how and what I would do, but by autumn I would show myself to the new leadership, referee differently, better and without big mistakes. In the middle of the break, during the World Cup in South Africa, I got an email from Bosse Karlsson that made me think about the future. He pointed out that it would be good if I could lose a few kilos before the UEFA course in September: "I'm not saying you're 'fat' but you have a heavy bone structure..."

The Journey to the Top

I have just eaten a typical breakfast for a match day with my colleagues. A plate of yogurt, muesli, coffee, two sandwiches, some fruit, and a fried egg. Afterwards, I go out to Strøget on my own, and at a café I meet two people I haven't seen in a while: my father Hans and uncle Stig-Åke. Dad has flown down from Luleå to Copenhagen, and my uncle who lives in Lund has taken the train across the Öresund.

We hug each other, have a cup of coffee and talk for just under an hour. Then I walk back to my hotel in the chilly and damp February cold. I then spend just under an hour at the computer before going down to the restaurant to meet my colleagues and have lunch.

It's a salad for starters, a main course with pasta and meat sauce, and as always, when available, tiramisu for dessert. After drinking my usual cup of tea after the meal, I go up to the hotel room and lie down to sleep deeply for just over an hour. The preparation for tonight's friendly international between Denmark and England has been just as usual, according to my routines, and everything feels really good. I'm happy and proud that my dad and uncle will be sitting in the stands at Parken with tickets that

I personally have bought from the Danish Football Association. Sure, I could probably have got free tickets, but that wasn't an option. Accepting tickets as a gift could lead to my neutrality being questioned. I absolutely don't want to expose myself to that. Moreover, a referee should never accept gifts from a club worth more than two hundred euros. There were extremely few occasions when I had the opportunity to bring family or friends to the matches I refereed. It was actually forbidden, but there were exceptions when it was actually possible. It was allowed at big finals, matches during championships - and at friendly internationals.

I have lost almost four kilos in the last six months. I'm lighter, faster, have more endurance and have had to go down a size in my referee clothes. They fit tighter and I like it when I run out onto Parken with my team this February evening.

When the match is over, almost all players have thanked for the match and I walk off the pitch, I can discreetly raise my hand in the air as a greeting in secret to my two relatives and supporters in the stands. It was my first match of 2011, and the new year had gotten just the start I wanted. I was in top form, physically and mentally, felt a balance and harmony in life, was in love and happy, had children who were growing and doing well - and since the turn of the year, I was a full-time referee. On the flight home, I get further confirmation that I'm on the right track. In an email to all Swedish referees at the elite level, coaches and instructors, the referee boss Bosse Karlsson writes a number of praising words about me. He describes how I've really shown my willingness to change and improve with my weight loss and my increasingly better performances on the pitch. He ends with the words: "Thank you Jonas for listening during 2010 regarding your physique." The praise warms of course, but I didn't really need it to understand that I had done something right. I knew myself that I was on the right track and that I had moved on in my career from the hell season of 2009/2010 when most things went wrong. It had been almost eight months since Bosse Karlsson in June 2010 urged me to focus on losing weight. I was never offended by Bosse's tip. In fact, it was the opposite. I got inspiration and understood the seriousness. I knew that Bosse meant well, that his words were for my best - that he wanted me to come back in the autumn of 2010 in front of UEFA's new leadership and show that I was indeed prepared to make a clear change to take a step further in my refereeing career. In my notes on my mobile phone, I can see exactly what I weighed on June 22, 2010, the same day Bosse emailed me and urged me to think about a change. I went down to the basement, dusted off the scale I had avoided for several years and stood still looking down at the display: 99.2 kilos. Over the next eight years, I lost nearly ten kilos. I went from being a referee who was heavy and untrained - to being light and well-trained. It was a work that took time, that didn't happen in a week, a month or a year. It was a long-term work, filled with patience, tough decisions and priorities. But it was also the beginning of a change that gradually meant stress, pressure and discomfort around the tests that UEFA's top management had introduced. You didn't just need to be a good referee and make the right decisions, it was also about prioritizing diet, looking like a top-level referee, that weight and fat percentage were right, otherwise you risked being scolded, getting fewer matches and ending up in the cold. When UEFA replaced its referee organization during the summer of 2010, Pierluigi Collina introduced a number of changes. It was the same things he had previously introduced in Italy during his years as head of the Italian elite referees. During Collina's first year, there was an extreme focus on the referees' physique, measurements of weight and body fat, and mandatory vision tests. Vision tests for referees might sound like a given, but it wasn't before. At the courses, visual tests were introduced that not only examined basic things like being able to read small text at a certain distance, but also other, more specific tests that were completely adapted for professional football referees at the highest level. The result was that some referees were found to be color blind. Another referee turned out to be blind in one eye and was forced to quit when the result of the test became known. At least that's what the rumors said, but no one knew for sure - because regarding the results of the vision test, nothing was revealed in larger groups. For me, the vision test was a reassurance, it was obviously good to have a check of the most important sense you have for refereeing football. It signaled professionalism, thoroughness and a desire to get better.

When it came to tests of weight and fat percentage, however, I mostly felt just disgust, anger and humiliation. It wasn't the tests themselves that were the problem, but the way UEFA chose to conduct them.

The first time I was forced to endure the humiliating procedure was in the autumn of 2010 at our annual course with UEFA. This time we were in Ljubljana, Slovenia.

On the first morning, the referees were divided into three groups of about fifteen people each. When my group had entered the large, cold conference room where we were to gather, the management urged us to undress down to our underwear. We looked at each other, but no one reacted or dared to say anything. Instead, we slowly took off our clothes, garment by garment.

The evening before, we had received clear instructions not to eat or drink anything in the morning, but to be as empty as we could when we were to undergo the test. Of course, it was about weighing as little as possible, and having as low a fat percentage as possible.

And to look like a referee should according to UEFA's model.

There we stood in a conference room, fifteen guys in a long row. In just our underwear. We were Europe's absolute best referees, elite athletes, role models, adults, parents, strong personalities with great integrity... but no one said anything. We barely looked at each other, our gazes flickered a bit nervously while we were called forward two by two. There stood the new chief Pierluigi Collina and observed us from top to bottom with an ice-cold gaze. Silent and observant. We stepped onto the scale one by one. I sucked in my stomach, straightened my back and held my breath as if it would make any difference to the weight. One of the instructors looked down at the result and loudly announced: "Eriksson, Sweden, 96.2 kilos." I felt how Collina paused, looked at me and scanned my nearly naked body. I turned off all emotions, went into my bubble and thought to myself that this is damn not worthy. I'm an adult and forced to stand here and be examined and judged.

I stepped off the scale, it felt like I was standing in a fog.

The same instructor who had just read off the scale and loudly called out my weight came forward with a kind of pliers, a polygraph-like tool that he began to pinch me with on different parts of the body. The caliper, as the instrument was called, was cold and I flinched a little every time it touched a new point on my body.

The instructor squeezed, pulled, pressed, measured, measured again, mumbled something inaudible, pressed again and pinched my skin and body fat. After each measurement area, he called out my value, that is, the number of millimeters he could measure with the caliper.

I had no idea what the numbers stood for, if it was good or bad. It took a total of maybe just over a minute, while I stood there half-naked and was measured and judged. The person who was secretary and assistant efficiently entered the numbers into a document, and when all four values were established, the document quickly calculated my total fat percentage. My value was announced without discretion, for all to hear: "Eriksson, 18.7%." I turned off all emotions, slowly wandered away, got dressed and could see how the other referees underwent the same procedure that I had just been forced to endure.

When I had dressed, I could from the side follow how Collina himself scrutinized the half-naked referees, his ice-cold gaze. At times he could almost snort a little, shook his head and seemed to get irritated when the fat percentage was too high to fit his guidelines.

What he had said and done when my weight and fat percentage had been called out, I don't know. I just turned off all emotions. I neither heard, saw nor felt anything.

Why didn't I, or anyone else, say anything? Why didn't we stand up and say what everyone really thought: that it was degrading. But I didn't say anything. If I had raised my voice, talked about how I experienced it, I would have simultaneously signed my career's death sentence. If I had questioned or challenged the methods that Collina had introduced - then I wouldn't have gotten any matches, I'm convinced of that. Of course, I also wanted to become more fit, weigh less, reach my goals and become a world-class referee. It was quite obvious that you shouldn't be overweight as a referee, equally obvious that you should be fit - and sure, maybe the entire referee corps needed a professionalization to take another step. But it was wrong to try to get there through a humiliating weigh-in and an agenda where the most important thing was to lose weight and minimize your fat percentage.

Our two annual courses with UEFA thereafter followed the same pattern.

Weigh-in, measurement of fat percentage, running tests, rule tests, reviews of interpretations, group work and then at the end of the course everything would be summarized, including the physical tests. On a document, we all got personal facts about our own physical profile - a summary of how the weight was, how our fat percentage was classified, arrows pointing if we were going in the right direction (down) or wrong direction (up).

In front of the entire group of referees, referees' fat percentages were summarized and categorized into five different groups. An approved result was if you belonged to excellent or very good. After that, there was a red, clear line that extremely distinctly told that the groups below that limit were not acceptable. At the course in Slovenia's capital, it was communicated that over seventy percent of all referees had a clearly failed result and had to improve.

So did I, who in the autumn of 2010 was in the poor category.

At UEFA's referee course the following year, Pierluigi Collina took the floor to talk about diet, the importance of preparation and bad examples of referees who did not prepare professionally. Collina fixed his gaze on us, and everyone looked down. Like scared schoolboys in front of an angry, strict and grim principal who had just caught the students doing something stupid.

After that day, my colleagues and I secretly laughed at Collina's story about the oyster and carbonara-eating referee. How incredibly unhinged and crazy it was that our highest chief had people who checked what we put in our mouths before our assignments.

At the same time as it became a standing joke about what one could eat, there was a slightly uneasy feeling of being monitored, even when you eat. And wherever we went in Europe from that day on, we thought about what we should order. It definitely wasn't oysters and definitely no pasta carbonara. All possible sweets disappeared from the courses. No desserts were served - just fruit. And if at any time, often by mistake, there was any cake or sweet left, hardly any referee dared to approach it. Alcohol during courses and tournaments was phased out completely over time. Between certain colleagues, a weight hysteria was created. There were competitions about who had the lowest fat percentage and who had decreased the most in weight since the last measurement. Of course, it was neither beneficial nor healthy. In connection with our courses, positive examples were highlighted of referees who had lost weight and reduced their fat percentage - instead of being praised for their decisions on the pitch or performances in difficult matches. I was never mentioned. Despite knowing that my weight journey was exactly the same as many others. Somehow it drove me further - towards becoming lighter and reducing my fat percentage. Of course, I also wanted to get attention and praise for my weight, for my hard work and for my ever-improving fat percentage.

Under Collina's leadership, it became more important to look good than to be a good referee. I know of at least one occasion during the 2010s when a referee should actually have refereed one of the biggest finals, based on performances, merits and achievements. Everyone on site, tournament management, referees and all others involved, were in complete agreement that it was precisely that referee who should referee the final.

But UEFA's leadership and Collina, who had the last word, said no and another referee was assigned the match. The reason was clear.

The referee everyone thought would get to referee didn't look fit enough. It didn't matter that that referee was actually the best and most suitable for the assignment.

The year that had just begun with the international match between Denmark and England was exciting. I looked forward to a series of fun matches and I knew that everything would culminate on December 20 when the referees for Euro 2012 would be selected. It felt like a long shot, but I had allowed myself to dream and at least aim for it. Because even though my career was now heading in the right direction, it was just over six months ago that I had barely managed to stay in UEFA's highest category.

I more often had time to train, especially during the daytime, which meant more time with the family. With my secured finances, I could also spend money on hiring my own personal trainer who helped me push my physical limits. I could also, without thinking about the cost, choose to go to a naprapath preventively, get massages regularly and even visit a podiatrist to make sure my feet stayed in the same shape as the rest of my body. I also spent more time recovering after matches and preparing for assignments. The results were clear: I gradually became a much better referee in every way. My recipe was actually quite simple. Since I no longer had a job that required over a hundred travel days per year, I could now more easily avoid business dinners, late nights, alcohol and junk food. Instead, I could eat better and above all train more often. Despite the muscles getting bigger, the weight decreased and my fat percentage likewise. But I lived a normal life in parallel with it. Drank alcohol occasionally, but in much smaller doses. Ate cinnamon buns and candy - but maybe not every day, just on Saturdays. And the last few weeks before each weigh-in, I reduced my intake of everything - to set records on the measurements. Of course I felt pressure from UEFA. Being weighed and inspected twice a year was tough - and I really didn't want to stand there in front of Collina and feel his glances and hear his sighs over my weight and body shape again. But my hunt to lose kilos and do what UEFA wanted and expected of me probably also made me a better referee.

The year 2011 had started in the best way with a great international match, a praising email from my Swedish boss, Bosse Karlsson, and a self-confidence that was stronger than ever. A few weeks earlier, I had learned that I had crossed a new barrier - that for the first time I would get to referee the knockout stages of the Champions League.

It was an incredibly important message. To belong to the sixteen best referees in Europe was a milestone, to get to referee a return match (which is considered more difficult and more decisive) was yet another sign that my work and my performances during the last six months had yielded results with UEFA. The autumn's Champions League matches had gone exactly as well as I could have dreamed of. I felt light, strong, unshakable and full of the self-confidence that was missing a year earlier when I had been in a completely different place in my career with other thoughts about my capacity. Now I had been entrusted to referee the round of 16 match between FC Schalke 04 and Valencia CF. I had had plenty of time to prepare in the best way. I watched the teams play in the Bundesliga and La Liga, I learned their tactics, studied names, trained strength, ran intervals, went cross-country skiing, got massages, went to yoga and looked forward to the match of my life on Tuesday, March 9, 2011. My observer in Gelsenkirchen, where the home team Schalke played their matches, was Englishman Mike Riley - in his day job the head of referees in the Premier League. We had met at several courses over the years and always got along well. Moreover, he had had the Swedish referee boss, Bosse Karlsson, as his mentor earlier. It felt reassuring. I knew that he was basically positive towards us, that he liked me and the team, and that he usually judged what he saw on the pitch without thought of politics or expectations. When we gathered at the hotel two hours before kick-off, I joked with Mike and said jokingly that I thought he looked nervous. It turned out that he actually was nervous, because he had been told that none other than Pierluigi Collina himself would be the TV observer during the match.

Now I also became very nervous.

It was a completely different build-up to the match than what I had expected, but I realized at the same time that it was just to roll up my sleeves and go out and do as good a job as possible.

When I put the whistle to my mouth shortly after half past ten in the evening and blew the final whistle, over fifty thousand spectators had seen the home team advance with a 3-1 win, and we in the refereeing team had nailed the match. We were careful not to look too happy as it could be misinterpreted as being satisfied with the final result. Actually, I wanted to smile, laugh, shout loudly and hug everyone who came near me... but that had to wait.

No one could say a bad word about our performance, we hadn't ended up in focus and our observer should be super satisfied. And probably Collina in front of the TV too, I thought. Inside the dressing room, with the door closed, it was allowed to show emotions. We could cheer, hug, celebrate and breathe out.

Mike Riley came in and joined us. He praised us as expected but also came with a disappointing message: Collina had canceled at the last minute. After all, it wasn't he who had been the TV observer for the evening. In the midst of the joy over a perfect match, I suddenly felt disappointment that Collina hadn't seen the match. I so wanted to show myself to the highest chief, who I knew it had become increasingly important to be seen by.

Pierluigi Collina's appointment as responsible for UEFA's referees in 2010 had been part of larger changes in how refereeing was led. UEFA President Michel Platini and General Secretary Gianni Infantino had chosen to employ three Refereeing Officers to take care of the daily operations regarding everything concerning UEFA's referees and lead the referee committee. By appointing Pierluigi Collina, Hugh Dallas and Marc Batta in turn, they took the first clear step away from a more democratic process governed by elected representatives from all over Europe towards a more person-controlled process where a few paid individuals decided everything, without much insight. The troika led by Collina was assigned a main responsibility for management and selection of referees for matches and tournaments, establishing strategy and technical development. The work that had previously been shared between a larger number of elected representatives in the committee now ended up more and more with the three individuals.

The system with TV observers was one of the novelties introduced by the new referee management. The change meant that the independence of the independent observers decreased. Now all observers who were on site at the arena knew that there was another assessor following the TV broadcast, another observer who could study replays and be influenced by others' opinions about the matches.

After my successful debut in the Champions League knockout stages, a spring followed where success bred success, and my self-confidence constantly gave me new challenges and matches. After also a round of 16 match in the Europa League, I was up for a quarter-final in the same tournament between Portuguese Braga and Dynamo Kiev.

It was an extremely tough match. I was saved by my goal-line official Daniel Stålhammar when the home player Paulo César during the first half, without warning, brutally kicked down a Kiev player behind my back.

Our Spanish observer was very pleased after the match and gave me a grade of 8.6. I now had eight straight international matches with a grade of 8.4 or higher. My average grade was as high as 8.5, even a little better than UEFA's already high expectations.

I informally learned from high-ranking people within UEFA that my grades for the past season were impressive. That I stood out in comparison to other referees.

After eight straight matches with good grades, it was time for a fail again. I barely remember the situation that lowered my grade - but from the match itself, a Euro qualifier between Romania and Bosnia-Herzegovina, there are two events that have etched themselves into my memory. Our fourth official had during the equipment check an hour before the match met a player in the Bosnian team who spoke Swedish. The player had introduced himself as Zlatan. We understood that it wasn't a certain Ibrahimović, but we still became interested and googled to find out that it was Zlatan Muslimović. He was born in 1981 in Banja Luka and had both Bosnian and Swedish citizenship after coming to Sweden from Bosnia-Herzegovina in 1993, when the civil war in former Yugoslavia was ongoing.

Muslimović came to Habo and then played for Husqvarna FF, IFK Göteborg - before he made a longer professional career in Italy and in 2011 Zlatan played for the Greek top club PAOK. I had never encountered him as a referee, as far as I remembered, but I knew well who he was and that he had had a long and relatively successful career abroad. When we went out to warm up, all the Romanian supporters had already gathered in the stands.

Just below the Romanian supporters, the Bosnian team was doing their warm-up. When Zlatan Muslimović saw us in the team, he left his teammates and ran happily towards us - as you do when you meet Swedish acquaintances somewhere in the world. We managed to exchange a few words and a high-five before we were interrupted by a hurricane of boos, thrown objects and screaming home supporters who were crazier than any other audience I had encountered before.

It took me a few seconds to understand what I had done that had made them so angry and upset. It was my innocent and friendly greeting and conversation with Zlatan that had started it all. It was seen as almost a declaration of war against their own team and country.

I reacted instinctively and called to my assistant referee, the experienced Stefan Wittberg. He read the situation just like I did and I asked him to join me on a round to some of the Romanian players and greet them with a high-five each. I chose a player at random who looked quite surprised, but happily accepted my greeting.

Stefan went a step further. He ran up to the goalkeeper of the home team, opened his arms for a hug and said something inaudible, but had a big smile on his lips, and then they united in a long and heartfelt hug.

The crowd fell silent.

A long hug with an extremely surprised home goalkeeper and a high-five with an equally astonished home player had saved us.

We had shown that we in the refereeing team certainly had friends in the home team as well, and our act had at least made it possible for us to start the match without having too much hate and opposition from the stands.

But that wasn't the end of the trouble. Just before kick-off, absolute chaos broke out in the small section where the five hundred traveling supporters from Bosnia-Herzegovina had gathered. Chairs were broken and thrown in, the noise level was high, supporters were screaming and the players suddenly left the pitch before I had even managed to start the game. I went over to the Bosnian bench to hear what had happened and what had created the reaction. The Bosnian leader pointed agitatedly towards the stands in response to my question. I turned around and saw a banner that read: "Free Mladić". It was the home supporters who had put up the banner about the convicted Serbian war criminal Ratko Mladić. The purpose was clear: to provoke, taunt and anger the away team and all their supporters who were present.

It's hard as a Swede to understand and feel the pain that name creates for all Bosnians. Most of the players in the Bosnian national team that played against Romania on Friday, June 3, 2011 were around ten years old when Ratko Mladić was the Bosnian Serb commander and got the hideous nickname "The Butcher of Bosnia".

Mladić had been arrested the same year and would be convicted at the war crimes tribunal in The Hague in 2017 on ten of eleven counts, including genocide and crimes against humanity. Among these were the Srebrenica genocide in 1995 and four years of terror bombing of civilian targets during the siege of Sarajevo where up to twelve thousand people are estimated to have been killed.

Football has seventeen rules, but the eighteenth is perhaps the most important. Common sense, when you go outside the rulebook, outside the protocol. You have to do that sometimes.

Instead of arguing, discussing or forcing the Bosnians out to start the match on time, I calmly replied that I certainly wasn't going to start the match until the banner was gone. The team leader's anger subsided. He felt that I was on his side, that I had shown myself to be both understanding and empathetic. The banner eventually disappeared. And after a five-minute delay, we could start the match.

The first half was calm. Romania was much stronger, and led clearly 2-0 after forty-five minutes of play. But a few minutes into the second half, the Bosnian section of the stands exploded again, kicked-apart chairs were thrown onto the pitch and flares were lit.

I immediately understood what had happened, blew the whistle to stop the game - and pointed at the banner that had come up again. I bent down, picked up the ball and calmly put it under my arm - as if to send out a message that I had all the time in the world. There would be no further play until the banner was gone.

This time the away team was calm, still and anything but upset. I had won their trust.

After the match, the team leader came up to us in the center circle. His team had lost 3-0, we had disallowed one of Bosnia's goals for offside and also incorrectly given Romania a penalty. But he was still satisfied. That I had shown respect for them and their history was more important than all other decisions I had made during the actual match, it turned out.

The Italian observer also praised my actions after the match. That I got a failing grade that evening didn't matter, I felt that I had made the right decision about what was really important. It trumped any shortcomings in the judgment.

I knew that I would be tested even more during the autumn of 2011. The match between Austrian Sturm Graz and Belarusian BATE Borisov in August might not sound like a prestigious top match in any way - but it was perhaps the year's most important match for the clubs involved. It was namely the directly decisive match that would determine which team would advance to the group stage of the Champions League. In the extremely warm evening in Graz in August, both teams were extremely interested in the nearly eighty million kronor that the winners would receive. Despite the fact that it involved big money and I hadn't refereed that many matches of the same magnitude, I was neither extra nervous nor felt extra pressure. When a lot was at stake and it was most important, I usually became calmer, more focused and often performed at my best. Somehow it was easier to enter a bubble of concentration and believe in myself the more the matches mattered. And the annually recurring playoff matches to the Champions League were the most fateful I refereed during my entire career. They were the most charged matches where there was the most to lose for the team that was eliminated.

Football-wise, however, they were rarely top matches. More fight than beautiful play, and that's exactly how it was in Graz. The away team BATE Borisov advanced after an utterly mediocre affair. For me, the money in the eighty-million match in Austria's second largest city was completely unimportant. I was chasing something else - a number, a grade that would take me further towards the Euros the coming year. Since my observer in Graz was one of UEFA's three most powerful people in refereeing, Frenchman Marc Batta, the oral review after the match was more important than usual. He said that my cooperation with colleagues was brilliant and that I acted professionally and with confidence. Then he leaned forward, looked me in the eyes and said: "Jonas, continue as you do today. We are starting to look at which referees we want to have for the Euros next summer and you are one of those on the list." The grade came after a few days. 8.4, maximum grade for the match's difficulty level.

Despite the influential Batta's words and grade, I was still a bit surprised when I got the best match I could be appointed to as my next assignment: Manchester City versus SSC Napoli.

I felt like a real top referee when I began the slow march, took the ball under my arm and stepped out onto the pitch.

During the short walk, I had a big smile on my lips.

I hate referees who are stone-faced, who never show their emotions. During the ninety minutes that followed, I found myself in a bubble where nothing could go wrong. When the match was over, I had handed out five, clear-cut, yellow cards, seen Cavani give Napoli the lead and Aleksandar Kolarov then equalize with a fantastic free kick. The match ended 1-1, but of everyone on the pitch, it wasn't a player who had shone the most of all. I received praise from basically all journalists on the sports channels, including the legendary Ray Wilkins who thought I had been best on the pitch. Swedish media joined in the positive tone and Expressen wrote that I had been "the giant of the match".

Sure, I was satisfied after the match, but not as overwhelmingly positive as the journalists were. Sure, the match had gone exactly according to my plan, but I knew I had that capacity in me - that I could referee so well, if I just got the chance.

I enjoyed it. This is where I had strived, this is where all the training and all the priorities along the way had led me. I understood that I wouldn't have come here if I hadn't put in all the work over the past year. And now I knew that I probably had two more matches in the Champions League before the referees for Euro 2012 would be selected in December.

On Friday, my boss, referee chief Bosse Karlsson called. He praised me for my performance in Manchester before telling me that another referee had made a blunder in an important Euro qualifier match, which now according to UEFA's regulations led to the referee being suspended for the next round. This referee was supposed to have refereed Olympique Marseille versus Borussia Dortmund, but now I would instead get that match.

I understood that someone high up in UEFA had seen our match in Manchester, and then immediately afterwards chosen me to fill the vacancy in the Champions League. A few years later, Pierluigi Collina himself told me that it was he who had seen the match.

Our extra Champions League match was won by Marseille with a clear 3-0, and it was a loss that not even the away team's charismatic and outgoing coach, Jürgen Klopp, could blame on us in the refereeing team. Even though I blew for a penalty against his team, Klopp came out to the center circle after the match and thanked us.

When the Swiss observer had his review, he was satisfied with my performance, but was not at all as sure as I was that the penalty I had awarded was correct.

My angle was perfect for making such a decisive decision. It was a penalty, without doubt and discussion. I could celebrate my second top performance in the Champions League in two weeks.

At this time, I significantly changed my preparations for the important international matches. Previously, I had been a bit careless, accepted planning that I actually might not like and let others in my surroundings have too many opinions on how we should prepare. In the autumn of 2011, I put my foot down and dared for the first time to be a bit uncomfortable. I became a selfish team player. I put pressure on my team, on UEFA, on the travel agencies that booked our flights and on local referee hosts. After all, it wasn't people around me who were going to referee the matches. Nor was it they who received criticism when the decisions were wrong. It was me and my team, and therefore I thought it was important that the preparations suited me and us in the best way. In October, I was to referee a match that was directly decisive for whether Russia would go to the Euros, away against Slovakia. The match was played on a Friday evening, and UEFA's travel agency suggested that we should travel Thursday morning via Vienna, then take a nearly three-hour car journey to Žilina, where the match would be played. Previously, I would probably have accepted the travel plan without reflections or comments. Mostly, I had been grateful that I had got the match - and been a bit afraid to be uncomfortable and perceived as "difficult". But now I insisted that it must be possible to solve it in a better way. It ended with us instead flying via Prague from where on certain days there were direct flights to the small airport in Žilina. Now we arrived already on Wednesday and had plenty of time to prepare on site.

After a 1-0 victory, Russia was clear for Euro 2012. No focus fell on us in the refereeing team, we collected another top grade. Now there were only two matches in the Champions League left before the selection for the Euros, and even though the autumn had been a success, I knew that a single clear mistake or a bad report could change everything, and I understood that neither I nor any of my colleagues had room to fail so close to the finish line.

The penultimate step on my long and tough road towards a Euro ticket was to travel to the Spanish east coast and referee Valencia versus Bayer Leverkusen in a Champions League match. The away team's world star, Michael Ballack, was the obvious key player but the question was whether he would be able to play the match. A few days earlier, in a league match against Freiburg, he had broken his nose. And if he came to play, it would be with a specially made face mask. At the traditional match meeting in the morning, representatives from Bayer Leverkusen came and wanted to show me the mask, and convince me that it was okay, but I said that I wouldn't approve it now, but that I wanted the player to come with the mask to our dressing room seventy-five minutes before kick-off. I wanted to take the chance to build up and strengthen the relationship with one of the players. I had learned and understood that a few words, eye contact, a little chat, a laugh before the match always gave a better relationship with a player. Then it was a little harder for the player to get angry with you if you made a decision that they didn't agree with.

It was for this reason that Michael Ballack, surely not overjoyed at being forced to go to the referee's room, later knocked on the door. I was lying on the massage table in an adjacent room for a short treatment when I heard the door open and Ballack along with their team doctor stepped into the referee's room. I got up, put on my pants but then waited ten seconds... a little power play to show that it was I who decided, set the time and agenda, both before and during the match. Then I stepped out and greeted them cheerfully in my clumsy school German. It immediately lowered any potential barriers and put them in a good mood. We laughed heartily together while I apologized that I wasn't very sharp in German, but that I understood the language quite well. Then I approved the face mask with a quick shrug before Ballack left the dressing room.

My little theater and my attempt to build a relationship with Ballack succeeded. He, who could otherwise be both brusque, shouty and energy-demanding during the match, kept calm. Not even when he was cautioned for diving in the first half did he get really angry, but instead just stated that he got a yellow card instead of a penalty.

He started arguing with my goal-line official, Tobias Mattsson, but I immediately shouted loudly and looked at Ballack with slightly feigned angry eyes. It worked, Ballack looked down, then barely said a word for the rest of the match - despite Leverkusen losing 3-1. It was becoming a positive habit that I had satisfied observers after every match. The match in Valencia was my fifth straight full score in terms of grades, and our Russian observer whom I had met several times during my career was really lyrical. Since it was matchday four in the Champions League, and the referees for matchdays five and six would be appointed the day after, the observer was in a hurry to send in the grade. He did this both via text message and by entering it into UEFA's internal system FAME, Football Administration and Management Environment. It was an extremely expensive system that administered everything around a football match such as delegates, security, protocol, registration of players and leaders. For us referees, all appointments, matches, grades, travel plans and documentation about matches were available in the portal.

The system had a number of advanced functions - but the security was poor and there were several loopholes, which I and several of my European colleagues had discovered. For example, you could easily through certain keystrokes read the secret grade that the observer had entered. You could see in real time how it was written, how line by line was added as the observer saved the document. Moreover, you could see secret information about which matches you were selected for and which dates UEFA planned for you to referee.

The morning after the match, during the stopover in Madrid, I logged in, performed the secret keystrokes and two seconds later I could see the grade and read the entire report. I happily noted that we had received a phenomenal 8.6 and informed my colleagues. Great cheers broke out. It was a fantastic grade and yet another big and important step towards the goal: Euro 2012.

But we neither could nor were allowed to tell anyone that we had received that grade, because through UEFA's lack of data security we had been able to read it before it became official. A few days after returning home, referee boss Bosse Karlsson called. As a member of UEFA's referee committee, he often got to see our grades before they officially reached us. Previously, I had received his calls with great excitement, curiosity, but also a great deal of uncertainty: what grade had the observer given? Since the summer of 2011, a completely new row had also been added to the otherwise so standardized report: UEFA Referees Committee Intervention. Most often this box was left completely empty, meaning that the three people who were at the top of the hierarchy - Pierluigi Collina, Hugh Dallas and Marc Batta - agreed with the observer in his opinions, thoughts and evaluation of the referee. But it happened occasionally that the highest leadership did not have the same picture and view as the observer on site, and then UEFA's three highest chiefs could personally go in and change. It was, I understood in retrospect, here that a tool was created to be able to centralize, control and strengthen the three persons' power over the referees and their grades. It officially came to be called quality assurance, but in reality it was about limiting the neutral observers' influence and ensuring that the last word ended up with the referee chiefs.

In short, it meant that an observer could give a more than approved grade, but that three people could choose to lower it to a fail. It was enough that they in front of the TV had a different view than an observer who had traveled halfway across Europe to assess the referee's performance. Sure, it could also be in the referee's favor, that a failed performance was changed to an approved one, but this happened very rarely. Collina's changes created in the future increasingly cowardly observers who didn't dare to set the grade they actually wanted. They often sought support from other people, didn't trust what they themselves thought or what they had experienced on site. Relatively often, I know from personal experience, messages were sent to the highest leadership where observers asked for their views before they sent in the report. After all, no one wanted to have their report changed afterwards, be corrected and forced to rewrite the report and adjust the grade. It was probably the worst criticism you could get as an observer. From the summer of 2011, observers increasingly set the grade they thought the three governing persons wanted to read. This meant, I understood in retrospect, that referees from the countries that Collina, Dallas and Batta represented - Italy, Scotland and France - as well as other referees who were on the leadership's positive side generally received higher grades than referees from other countries and referees that the leadership disliked. And with higher grades, they of course also got more and better matches. The leadership could in this way in theory steer in the right referees from the right countries, and in the same way steer away referees who were not desirable. Of course, I occasionally had help from politics and support from the governing in my career. But when Bosse Karlsson called that morning in November, I had no thoughts about how UEFA's referee activities in general were developing. A few days had passed since the match in Valencia and I knew that the report now, officially, had gone for review and approval by the three. Bosse Karlsson and I made small talk for a while before he asked me to guess what the grade had become. I had seen the observer's report thanks to FAME's security loophole, which Bosse didn't know about, so I "guessed" happily: "8.6?" To my surprise, Bosse replied: "You weren't that damn good, you had to settle for 8.4." When Bosse emailed me the grade shortly after, I could read that UEFA's inner circle had got the Russian observer to lower his grade, because the match wasn't difficult enough to be able to give the grade 8.6.

Officially, it was constantly claimed that the text in the reports was more important than the actual numerical grade, that it was the text in the grades that would develop you and that was important for the leadership.

It was bullshit. All referees, including a performance-addicted person like me, looked directly at the number in the grade and then more or less ignored the actual text that described the referee's performance. Because everyone knew that UEFA only summed up the referee's grades and that it was that number that determined what your next match would be. A number that was 8.3 or higher meant a new match at the same or higher level - a lower number signaled a question mark to UEFA and eyebrows would be raised: Was one really ready for a new match? Had Eriksson really reached the top of his capacity? Could he continue to perform at this level? For a time, you were even suspended for the rest of the season if you had a grade that was 7.9, that is, if you had made a (in the observer's eyes) big, clear and obvious mistake. Fortunately, UEFA abandoned that stupidity and instead set the limit at 7.4, meaning suspension for two big mistakes. The stress of getting a grade around 8.3 was always there and was obvious to all referees. Not least for me. Despite the slightly annoying lowering of the grade for our performance in Valencia, there was now only one obstacle left for a possible selection for the Euro finals next summer. A match in the Champions League during matchday five or six was the last step for me before the referees would be selected during December. Part of me longed to know which match I would get to referee - it was yet another sign of how much trust UEFA actually had in me. But another part of me absolutely didn't want to have any match at all. That part almost hoped that I would get injured or sick and not be able to referee anything more during 2011, so that my grades were uninterruptedly good during the autumn. One more match meant the risk of failing, ending up in focus, getting a failing grade after five straight maximum grades.

It ended up being Olympique Lyonnais versus Ajax - a match where a place in the knockout stages was at stake for both teams. And for my part, a place in the Euros was likely at stake.

Everything felt good, I felt great, was healthy and injury-free and had an incredibly good team with me. Actually, there was only one question left that created uncertainty before the match: who was the observer who would assess the match? I hoped for a known name, someone who had seen me before and who maybe even had given me a good grade then.

On Sunday morning, two days before the match, the email from UEFA came that would give me all the information and satisfy my curiosity. I slowly scrolled through the email until I found the name of the observer: Alan Snoddy.

Damn, I thought. Snoddy had given me one of my career's worst grades in the Europa League quarter-final between Benfica and Liverpool a year and a half earlier. It felt like a punch right in the stomach. Didn't UEFA want me to succeed? Did they want to put a spanner in the works for my selection for the Euros? I was first really irritated by the choice but then gathered myself and told myself in my usual way that it was just to make the best of the situation. If Snoddy now thought I was terrible in the last match, there was room for improvement now.

In Lyon, we eat a fantastic dinner the night before the match, I sit as always next to the observer and have a nice discussion with Snoddy. I realize that despite his trashing of me in Lisbon, I like him very much. He's nice, funny, has a subtle and sarcastic humor that I appreciate.

During the warm-up the next day, I start up my body, everything feels good and the pulse increases as planned. I have a fantastic feeling in my body when I hear a familiar voice shouting loudly at me from the line of home players warming up together. It's Kim Källström, one of the nicest players I've met in my career. Wise from the experience of my greeting to Swedish Zlatan Muslimović in Bucharest half a year earlier, I tone down my body language so as not to anger the opposing team and its supporters.

The match ends 0-0. Not much happens until the second half when I twice - once for each team - wave dismissively at quite difficult penalty situations. After the match, Kim Källström comes up, shakes hands, thanks for the match and doesn't mention with a single word the denied penalty. It's a good sign, an indication that I made the right decision.

The feeling is good, but it means nothing until I have found out what the observer really thinks. We've barely made it into the dressing room before there's a knock on the door. It's Snoddy, he's rushed, intense and calls for me.

I have difficulty judging whether he's happy, angry, sad or disappointed. But then he smiles, takes the last step towards me, looks me in the eyes and gives me a hard and long hug and says:

"What a great game, Jonas." He's super pleased and says that we've done a completely perfect job. "I knew you had this capacity, it hurt not to see you succeed in Lisbon, but tonight you did everything right."

It's Tuesday evening and we're in the world's gastronomic capital. After the match, we can enjoy the world's best dinner at a restaurant signed by Paul Bocuse. I have just had the best season of my life and it's only a month until the Euro referees will be selected.

The Championship Debut

It's one of the darkest days of the year, the winter sun can barely be seen through the thick clouds. I'm sitting in the car on my way to Stockholm. I've dressed up a bit extra nicely, in a shirt and jacket. In the inner pocket lies a dark blue tie, which matches well with my blue jacket and white shirt. This particular day has been in my mind throughout the autumn, and not a day has gone by without me thinking about Tuesday, December 20, 2011, and what I want to happen then.

In my digital calendar, I've written down: "UEFA Referees Committee Meeting." The meeting is important, it will affect my life and the choices I have ahead of me. That I'm even being considered to referee a championship was unthinkable as recently as just over a year ago. But now I'm ranked number one in Sweden and have all the possibilities.

At Arlanda, I had picked up the person I had passed in the referee ranking. I had officially become Sweden's best referee in the summer of 2011 when UEFA's referee committee chose to downgrade Martin Hansson from the highest to the second-highest category. Martin's story is sad and shows how small the margins can be in a referee's career. It's millimeters that separate success and big matches from fiasco and the freezer. Despite the setbacks, Martin had maintained his good mood. That Martin throughout his career was so generous to me with praise and always kept his head high was impressive, and I admired him for it. We drive towards Solna and a meeting at the Swedish Football Association's office. We are both elected representatives in the Elite Referees Club in football, the referees' interest organization. What the meeting is about, I don't remember, probably about fees for the coming season, and when the meeting starts, I apologize that I will have my mobile on. I blame it on my daughter being sick and that I want to be able to be reached by the preschool if they should call.

I look sickly often at my mobile during the meeting, update the inbox and double-check that I have coverage. I let the phone lie face down, so that my display isn't visible and others can't see who's calling.

Just after 1:00 PM, my phone rings, I start, wake up, grab the phone and my pulse rises.

The display says Pierluigi Collina. UEFA's head of referees.

I excuse myself and leave the meeting room as I don't want to take this call with people around me. I answer with a calm voice, but also with a hard pounding pulse.

Exactly how the words came, what he told me, what I said, I don't know, but a few minutes later I'm standing alone in an empty room, so happy that I want to scream out loud, slide on my knees in the corridor, hug everyone I see and cheer loudly. But I have to keep calm. I'm in the middle of a meeting, and out of respect for Martin, I don't want to tell him or anyone else yet.

The phone rings again, it's Bosse Karlsson who wants to congratulate me. Apparently, the twelve referees were selected already the evening before during an informal meeting between the committee members, and then formally on Tuesday.

I then return to the meeting. I have to stay as neutral as possible... but inside I want to scream to the whole world: I'm going to referee the Euros! I long to get home and tell my family.

I've been selected for the Euros as the only referee from the Nordic countries. I am now officially not only the best in Sweden, but also in the Nordic countries. I am so proud, so happy, so grateful to everyone who has helped me on the way since I was thirteen years old and started refereeing football back on the gravel pitches in Luleå. I have received such help from my colleagues, from players, coaches and everyone else who has supported me. My family, my parents, my sister. In the afternoon and evening, I give a bunch of interviews, but the tie that had been in my pocket all day I never need to use. Then I celebrate with my family extremely cautiously with a glass of bubbly at home and a dinner at a restaurant in Sigtuna.

On Thursday, December 22, two days before Christmas Eve, the official email came from UEFA with the selection, the planning for the spring and information about the upcoming course in Turkey. I still felt great joy and pride over the selection, but when I read on in the email, I found something new that immediately created worry.

It was announced that at the course we would undergo a so-called yo-yo test, an extreme and challenging running test. If you didn't pass the test, you would not only miss the entire spring season in the Champions League, but also the Euro finals.

I had never run this particular test before, but knew by hearsay that it was incredibly tough and challenging, that it was about running until you simply couldn't go on anymore. And I had to pass it in five weeks. The lump in my stomach came immediately, I felt slightly nauseous at the thought that this could stop me from the Euros. I had been allowed to be unreservedly happy and joyful for two days. I was selected for the tournament of my life, but suddenly UEFA had chosen to introduce a new running test where the bar was set at a level that none of us referees had checked before, except for the Italians. Most of them managed after a longer period of tests and training to reach level 18:2, which was what UEFA required. I read up on what would occupy my thoughts around the clock for the next five weeks: Two cones are placed exactly 20 meters apart. There is an additional marking 5 meters behind one of the two cones.

You run the first 20 meters, turn 180 degrees at the line by putting your foot on the line and then sprint back the same distance. After finishing, you walk more calmly 10 meters (5 meters x 2) around the cone and then back for a new start.

The active rest was always ten seconds, but the time you had to run varied from fifteen seconds at the beginning to being down to eight, nine seconds at the end. An audio file coordinated the starts.

18:2, which was the requirement we had to meet, meant running for almost fifteen minutes with increasingly faster interval sprints.

If you were late at the finish, didn't round the cone or didn't put your foot on the line after twenty meters, you got, a bit amusingly, a yellow card and at the next error you got a red card and were thus disqualified.

I had never failed a running test in my career. After being overweight and in less good physical shape for a few years, I had since 2010 increased my training, lost weight, become stronger and generally improved my physique. But now I was faced with an extreme challenge and had five weeks to prepare. It was winter back home in Sweden and access to football pitches was not the best. In addition, I had planned to be on vacation in Thailand and Singapore for three nice weeks in January, the only month of the year when I could be off and travel with the family. But it was just to roll up the sleeves and give it everything. I set up a course and got started. I struggled, gave it all I could, missed some starts, deliberately turned too early... and after just over ten minutes I collapsed from exhaustion. Despite cheating so much that I was ashamed, I only reached level 16:4. I panicked. I was almost five minutes from passing the test, despite cheating in my solitude. And I was completely finished. I could see on my pulse watch that I had reached ninety-four percent of my maximum heart rate, and that there was thus not much more to give.

I walked around looking for excuses for why I had failed so badly. Was I using the wrong technique at start and turn? Had I played the audio file at too high a speed? Or had I measured the distance wrong? That's it, it must be. It was surely twenty-two meters. That explained everything.

But when I re-measured the distance, it turned out to be nineteen rather than twenty meters. I had even run too short. Hell.

I walked home, dejected and depressed. I had to train much harder to pass the test, otherwise there would be no Euros in the summer. I spent the following time an unhealthy number of hours at the computer, checking on YouTube how to turn, how to make the running more efficient. For a few nights I hardly slept at all. Everything revolved around the yo-yo test.

When we arrived at Koh Samui for vacation, it was mid-January. I had put together two weeks of really good training and in place in Thailand I found a tennis court. I paid the caretaker to take down the net so that I could run and I warmed up to do the test again.

The result was disappointing. It was certainly better than the previous 16:4, but it was still far from the 18:2 that was required. I was completely exhausted.

When the children had fallen asleep, my wife wanted to talk to me. She had noticed that my mood had gotten worse and worse, that my patience with the children had become shorter and that I had been more and more absent. She wondered if I wanted to cut the vacation short and go home to train for the test instead. I had always had fantastic support from my wife, which had been necessary for me to succeed with my dream. There and then, in a hotel room on a rainy Koh Samui, I understood that I had her to thank for everything. I was deeply grateful and happy for the fantastic support and during the night I considered going home.

But when I woke up the next day, I chose to stay.

Instead, I trained even harder and prepared like a professional.

Eventually, I thought I began to see a positive trend. My pulse didn't go up as quickly and when I had reached a high pulse, I could continue running at a high level for a longer period.

I got additional energy from texting with my referee colleagues around Europe. I realized that I wasn't alone. Everyone was having a tough time in the preparations. Most had failed not just once, but several times.

Ten days later, at the Hyatt Hotel in Hua Hin early one morning, I snuck out of the hotel room. I had bribed yet another caretaker to open the tennis court as early as half past six (to avoid the worst heat) and asked him to remove the net. At the starting line, I was as charged as before an important match.

As always, I had a high pulse from the first run, indicating nervousness. But I had now learned how my body reacted, that I had to hold back at the beginning, that it didn't matter if I didn't rush in the last meters, that I didn't need to walk so fast during the rest and that I should try to find an even pace.

14 minutes and 45 seconds later, I was lying on the ground. I was completely finished, breathing heavily, groaning loudly and screaming out my pain. But I didn't care. Because now I had passed the test for the first time. By the skin of my teeth, certainly, but I had run for almost fifteen minutes. I got up and shouted loudly: "Yes!" The caretaker who had been sitting and watching in wonder

as the tall Swede ran back and forth for a quarter of an hour shook his head and laughed.

It's one hundred and twenty-eight days until the Euro premiere when I wake up in Antalya, Turkey and prepare for the most important running test of my life.

In the breakfast hall where you usually hear a lot of laughter and cheerful shouts, it's completely quiet.

I'm starting in the second group of four. That's good, then I have time to wake up properly, eat breakfast, maybe take a walk and wake up the body before it's time to go to the arena.

The weather is, by Turkish standards, a disaster. It's raining, just above zero degrees and a wind bordering on storm. I think, in an attempt to cheer myself up, that this weather is made for a guy from Luleå. I always prefer to train in cool weather than in heat.

We arrive at the small arena where we're going to run, I go into the changing room, put on my football shoes to get a good grip and not slip. Then I go to the toilet. Inside, I close my eyes quietly and take a few deep breaths.

The pulse is higher than normal, I haven't felt such tension since I first refereed in the Champions League in 2008, when the pulse and impressions in the player tunnel almost made me faint.

Through the toilet window, I hear the pre-recorded, mechanical voice start the first group. Our entire group is curiously looking out towards the field from the changing room to see colleagues run the test under extremely difficult conditions with headwind the last twenty meters. Even if we don't see everything from the changing room window, we understand that it's extremely tough. Someone steps off, someone is removed after a red card, someone collapses, and when fifteen minutes have passed, basically the whole gang is lying down and gasping for air, completely exhausted.

I'm slightly shocked. I who had previously only run on a dry tennis court in Thailand and indoors in a sports hall with an even and dry surface understand that a wet, slippery and uneven football field with extreme winds is something completely different.

I see the leadership, UEFA's highest chiefs, members of the committee.

They are worried, the expressions are grim. Angriest and most concerned of them all is Pierluigi Collina - the one who decided that this is the running test that applies. He looks so angry that no one dares to approach him.

It feels like he thinks that the weak result in the first group is directed at him personally, that the referees are intentionally running so slowly and poorly to annoy him.

Those of us who are going to run in the next group start warming up and exchange a few quick words with the colleagues who have run the test before us.

One of them says that it's the worst thing he's ever experienced. After the warm-up, I drink a little, tie my shoes one more time and take a few deep breaths. I'm noticeably nervous, but I still tell myself that I will pass the running test.

When the start signal goes off, I look at my pulse watch (which registers every step and heartbeat). It shows fifty-five percent of my maximum heart rate. That's high, much higher than normal. On a normal day when I'm standing still, it barely shows thirty percent. I understand that it's the enormous tension and pressure that's raising the pulse.

When the test begins, I go into a bubble. I turn off emotions, sounds, the slippery surface - but the rapid breathing comes already after two minutes. I look at the clock. It shows eighty-three percent. Hell.

I keep going, turn after turn. Start counting backwards, thinking and conclude that I won't be able to maintain more than ninety-four percent of my maximum heart rate for more than the absolute last minutes.

I know that the pulse usually increases about one percent per minute, and when I reach ninety percent of my maximum heart rate after six minutes, I'm close to giving up. I'm several minutes ahead of my planned schedule, the breathing is heavy, I know there are nine minutes left and I only have negative thoughts in my head.

Then something happens. I notice that some of my colleagues start falling behind, missing the starts, being late in the turns, and that those near me are at least as tired as I am. It gives me energy.

We pass eight minutes, I have ninety-one percent of max heart rate.

Then ten minutes, the clock shows ninety-three percent. I'm over the limit now and shouldn't be able to go on any longer. The lactic acid is pumping out into my legs, I'm becoming more and more numb in them for each run, I'm breathing heavily, having difficulty perceiving what's happening around me - but I keep running. Count the number of laps left, think in minutes and am not even close to being able to read my pulse during the last five minutes.

I just run.

In retrospect, I can see that I'm actually running faster than I can handle in the last five minutes. The pulse reaches ninety-eight percent at the finish line and I try not to collapse. Instead of lying down, howling, panting and looking as tired as I am, I struggle to stand up, not put my arms on my knees and sink down.

I walk around and breathe heavily, but try to smile as best I can, try to look unaffected and above all show that I'm certainly not as tired as all the other colleagues who are lying knocked out on the ground around me. Some are disqualified.

Eight of the forty-eight referees at the course have failed. Among these, some experienced, more well-known referees - but above all, the failures are among the referees who were ranked in the category just below the top. Of them, the top referees of the future, many missed the test.

That whole group of referees went straight into the changing room.

I don't know if they were ordered there, or if they went voluntarily. But after the referees came the highest chief, Pierluigi Collina.

overweight to referee at the highest level.

To be scolded for your weight, your appearance is completely unacceptable to me. It never matters if the person criticizing is right in substance - you don't do that. And if as a leader you feel compelled to do it, it's definitely the wrong time to do it in a group in front of other people.

To scold the already slim referee in front of everyone crossed all boundaries and was beneath all dignity. Such incidents contributed to creating a culture of silence and weight fixation among us referees, driven by fear of Collina and his outbursts. There was always pressure to lose weight, to follow the ideal that UEFA under Collina's leadership had set up. That the smallest and thinnest referee of all was accused of being overweight was completely incomprehensible. No referee was lighter and smaller than the guy who got the scolding. I myself, for example, had much more to be afraid of. I knew that my kilos were too many, that I looked heavy. I had certainly begun a journey downwards in weight - but quite frankly, I risked becoming a target for Collina's wrath at any time. Another referee was scolded despite passing the running test. Collina's voice echoed through the door: "I gave you a match in the Champions League, and now you come here looking like this." The rest of us stood outside and listened, and were silent. But it wasn't because of my own overweight that I kept my mouth shut. We were all in an extreme position of dependence on the leadership and terrified of getting the same scolding, of also being hung out as fat and less good referees. It wasn't an option to stand up and say something. It would have been like signing your own death sentence as a referee. Collina's outburst of rage in Antalya was the first I seriously and up close got to experience, but absolutely not the last. They recurred regularly and not infrequently were about food, fat percentage, performances and referees who according to Collina did not act professionally. When I was selected for Euro 2012, the image of me changed. Suddenly I was a familiar name, a championship referee. "Experienced" could be written in the referee observers' reports, which had never been written before. I was seen through a new filter, as if I had received a stamp of approval from UEFA's referee committee. And then it took a lot for an isolated and lonely observer to go against what the referee committee already considered to be a referee of high quality. For it being the end of March, it's warm, really warm. Usually, the days are warm in Milan in March, but the evenings are cool and sometimes even chilly. But tonight summer has arrived. It's over twenty degrees outside and warm winds find their way down to the player corridor under San Siro where I stand with my colleagues. It's March 28, 2012, my birthday. Number thirty-eight in order. But it has been celebrated sparingly. The team and I hope to celebrate a little more later. Not just the birthday but that we're breaking a record - we've never refereed this far into the Champions League knockout stages as this quarter-final.

The meeting between AC Milan and Barcelona is also the most hyped quarter-final. Two big clubs against each other, a number of world stars who want to win at any cost, and a Zlatan who is pitted against the Barcelona he previously left under controversial circumstances.

Just like at the running test in Antalya eight weeks earlier, my pulse in the player tunnel is higher than it normally is. The players gather in the tunnel. Zlatan greets his former teammates, some more heartily and personally, some just briefly and matter-of-factly. We know about the strained relationship that Zlatan has with some of his former teammates in Barcelona, but none of that is visible in the tunnel. It's mostly high-fives, hugs and smiles.

After dealing with Barcelona, Zlatan comes up to us five Swedes and greets us.

"Welcome to Milan, guys. And good luck," he says and smiles broadly.

Zlatan walks around in the corridor like an obvious superstar. A leader in the group who with his one hundred and ninety-five centimeters takes over the corridor and owns his surroundings when the twenty-two players stand still in the tunnel and shout out their pep words before the march in.

He goes up to the match's other big star, Messi, who comes in a bit late in the tunnel and they shake hands a bit cautiously. It's not at all as relaxed as with the other players in Barcelona, but more formal, almost a bit reserved. I'm struck by the height difference between the two world stars - twenty-five centimeters separate them.

I myself am one hundred and ninety-three centimeters, and when Zlatan comes up and talks, I don't need to tilt my head back to look him in the eyes. It feels good, it's always an advantage to have the height with you when you're going to confront a player. The match is tight, difficult to referee, contains several penalty situations but we solve everything in a good way. Barcelona or Spanish media don't think so, but fortunately we in the team and above all our German observer think that we handled it in a good way. The grade becomes 8.3 in a match that is described as quite difficult.

What we in the team most of all took with us from this match, however, occurred an hour before kick-off. By chance, we came out for our warm-up just when the home team got to make their entrance. We got loads of energy from the crowd cheering for their home team. And at the same time, the intro to Guns N' Roses' "Sweet Child o' Mine" was playing. It was a powerful feeling.

We left Milan with two new lessons: to always, if possible, take the chance to go out with the home team and surf on the positive energy that their audience can give you.

And to always, as the last thing we did in the changing room, listen to the intro to "Sweet Child o' Mine".

We ended the club team season with a semi-final in the Europa League between Sporting Lisbon and Athletic Bilbao. My boss that evening was a Greek member of the referee committee. He was satisfied with the team and my performance. We got a maximum grade, but he thought something was missing. In the report he wrote that I could well lose two, three kilos in weight.

But as long as I avoided being examined in just my underwear or getting a scolding from Collina in front of others, I could accept comments and criticism about my weight in writing. After all, I and my team could sum up a fantastic spring. We had reached a semi-final and were now ready for our first major national team tournament.

On Monday, June 4, 2012, I and my team boarded the flight to Warsaw. Besides me, the team consisted of assistant referees Stefan

Wittberg and Mathias Klasenius as well as goal-line officials Stefan Johannesson and Markus Strömbergsson.

That it would be Stefan and Markus behind each goal was obvious. They were both skilled and promising referees with merits from the Champions League. In addition, they had been part of my team during much of the preparations in 2011. It was different among the assistant referees, i.e. the linesmen, where I had also had Fredrik Nilsson as an assistant in some matches over the past year.

Since I was new as a championship referee at the senior level, it was UEFA who had the final say on who would be included in my team.

That would change when I became more established, but before Euro 2012 we didn't know more than that the assistant referees would be selected during the spring.

The same day we were to referee AC Milan vs Barcelona, UEFA communicated their decision. It became Mathias and Stefan, who were also the assistants in Milan, who would go to the Euros. For me it was a good choice, those chosen had been in my team longer than Fredrik.

Since 2010, we had gotten used to being a larger team of referees at the matches. It created a different dynamic, it became more important to get everyone involved, make sure everyone felt the goal that had been agreed upon and constantly work towards it. However, it wasn't a problem for me, I almost always had the same guys helping me and my greatest asset was my team, my colleagues who dared to challenge me, who were always professional and above all - we had fun together.

When you referee a big championship, you really think all the time about which could be the next match. Already when the group draw took place in December, I had speculated, counted, analyzed and saw myself refereeing almost every match in the group stage - except in group D, where Sweden would play and I was thus disqualified.

Purely strategically, we didn't want to referee the opening match. It was always a powder keg and absolutely not the assignment you wanted to start with. Setting the tone for the entire tournament, being the one who shows exactly how the refereeing should be done is certainly honorable - but risky. We thought it was better to come into the tournament after a day or so, get the first match over with and then after that rest a bit and with new energy get into the next match. Preferably during the second round, before there were matches that were really decisive.

We had already been in Poland for a week in early May, on a preparatory course, so the actual gathering before the Euros was relatively short. We came to Warsaw just four days before the tournament started.

The Euro base was at the Hilton Hotel in Warsaw and we quickly created our routines there.

My team, who all lived on the same floor next to each other, always took a walk in the morning, ate breakfast together, had some time to ourselves in the room, changed clothes, went to the training facility which was fifteen minutes by bus from the hotel, went back, visited the hotel gym, took a shower, ate lunch and then had an afternoon with theory in a large group.

The weigh-in took place the day after arrival, and I was praised for having lost some kilos since last time. It felt good to be a bit lighter, and above all I knew that it sent good signals to Collina and the others in the leadership.

UEFA's increased focus on what the referees ate and drank, our appearance and weight, was clearly visible in the food in Warsaw. I don't know what the order looked like, but almost everything that was served was extremely dry, boring and tasteless. And when you eat three meals every day in the same restaurant, you quickly get tired of it.

In previous years and at courses, a small dessert could sometimes be served after dinner, maybe an ice cream scoop, a cake or something else nice.

You might think it would be okay for adult people, men who all train a few hours a day, who all have responsibility for their own body and weight and who need energy and above all maybe should be rewarded for the hard work they put in - but almost nothing like that occurred now. No one dared to say anything. It wasn't just the referees who had become quiet and didn't dare to question Collina's leadership style and manners - this also applied to members of the referee committee. The longer the tournament went on, the more tired all referees became of the food that was served. More and more teams completely avoided the dinners at the hotel - and instead went out into the city and paid for their food to be able to eat what they wanted. The atmosphere between the referee teams was a bit cautious at the beginning, everyone was a bit tense before their first matches and everyone was waiting for Friday, June 8 when the home nation would open the Euros by meeting Greece. The referees for that match would be announced on June 6, and we understood that it wasn't our match. Opening matches were to be refereed by a safe bet, a known referee, from a big country who had credibility and through his name would not be questioned.

When we ranked all the referee teams that were in the tournament, we realized that we were perhaps the lowest, or second lowest, ranked team in place.

We had come in at the last minute, and almost all referees were ahead of us in terms of routine and experience. Among the referees were four referees with merits from the 2010 World Cup, as well as one who had refereed the Champions League final a few weeks earlier. In addition, there were referees from large, important countries such as Spain, Italy, the Netherlands, Scotland and Turkey.

Here I was an underdog. I was actually just happy to be there, to have gotten the chance to be part of a big championship. My team and I were realistic, and realized in our constant speculations that our first match would be one with slightly less profiled teams. From a member of UEFA's referee committee, we learned that a preliminary selection had already been made for all matches in the group stage, but that we referees would not know anything until two days before each match.

He also mentioned that changes could occur in the planning if any referee made serious mistakes.

It's a puzzle to appoint referees. You can't just randomly distribute them according to a template or draw. A referee is not allowed to referee the same group as their own nation plays in, for example. A Scottish or English referee is not allowed to referee Ireland. A Slovenian referee is not allowed to referee any other country from the Balkans. If you as a referee have had problems with a team, such as Howard Webb had had with Poland in Euro 2008, when he disallowed a goal for them and afterwards received several death threats, you should not referee that particular national team. And so on. Besides this, UEFA wanted to arrange it so that the best referees got to referee the biggest nations and the most important matches, while those who lacked experience and were new got smaller nations and matches that meant less. The opening match was assigned to Carlos Velasco Carballo from Spain. It wasn't a big surprise. He was a safe choice, a referee from a big nation.

We were present during the match. For safety reasons, I and Stefan Johannesson, as the two highest ranked and most recognized in the team, had to put on the official suits, got VIP tickets with food and drinks included - while the rest of the team could go in civilian clothes and sit in the regular stands.

I and Stefan enjoyed the VIP section's buffet. Of course, we as adults drank a glass of red wine, but for the first time since I was underage, I hid my glass. When you were seventeen, it was about not showing your parents that you were drinking, now we were afraid that Collina would see us, despite the fact that we didn't have a match and that it could at the earliest occur seventy-two hours later.

It was dizzying to go out to the stands and see the teams come onto the field. Euro 2012 was about to begin and I was a part of it, one of twelve people who had been given the responsibility to referee.

It became an opening match that was special. Not for the result, it ended 1-1, but because the referee ended up in focus in the wrong way.

An extremely cheap second warning gave the Greeks a dubious sending-off already in the forty-fourth minute - and apart from that, Carlos' performance was not good at all. It lacked confidence, the decisions were shaky and it was anything but what UEFA had expected.

In tournaments, it's important that everyone succeeds. Referees are often lumped together collectively. No one remembers afterwards if it was the Swedish referee who was good, the Spanish or the Slovenian. We remember referees as a group, and if you stepped into a match and the referee in the match before hadn't been good, you started at a disadvantage. Moreover, it created a much better mood, atmosphere and harmony in the referee group if the results were good. Not to mention how it affected the leadership - UEFA's referee committee - who had been given the responsibility to select referees, coach them, make sure the referees didn't end up in focus and decided the matches. The match reviews during Euro 2012 were held in the "Executive lounge" on the twenty-sixth floor booked by UEFA with a fantastic view over Warsaw. The referee team came there the day after the match at an agreed time, got to give a brief account and then the appointed observer, who was a member of the referee committee, gave his view.

Then the committee's three Refereeing Officers (RO) took over: Collina, Marc Batta and Hugh Dallas. In several cases, an RO was also an observer, and then feedback came directly from the three who actually decided. What was said to other referees, we didn't know. There were sparse joint reviews throughout the championship. We got, via rumors, via someone who had been in the team or via some other person, to hear what the RO had for opinion about the performances. I was almost shocked. Not getting feedback on situations, assessments, interpretations and other things - not being able to calibrate your refereeing or adapt your refereeing was completely foreign to me. In total there were four groups of four teams - a total of twenty-four matches - to distribute among twelve referees, so we could expect two matches in the group stage per referee. We were impatient after the premiere, we wanted to get started and referee our first match and get into the tournament.

But we had to wait. When five match days, that is ten matches, had been selected, one referee had even already got his second match without us getting a single one.

In retrospect, I have understood that the plan for which matches all twelve referees would referee in the group stage was changed after Carlos Velasco Carballo's performance in the opening match.

His grade became poor, the committee felt that they didn't have confidence in him and were forced to make changes, which wasn't the easiest. There were major limitations on which referees could referee which matches, and to make as few changes as possible, I think the Spaniard was removed from the big meeting Holland-Germany.

That was probably how it happened when my first championship match became precisely that charged top meeting between the neighboring countries. I was incredibly happy, proud, honored - and at the same time completely terrified.

But of course I couldn't show that.

My international matches during 2011 and 2012 had all been less prestigious. Now I was going to referee the 2010 World Cup finalist Netherlands, known for their extremely physical play, against Germany - one of the world's most successful football national teams with four World Cup golds and three Euro golds.

Moreover, the Netherlands had very surprisingly lost to Denmark in the first round, while Germany had won against Portugal. The Netherlands had to win the match against Germany, otherwise they were sensationally eliminated from the tournament. The match was to be played in Kharkiv in northeastern Ukraine on Wednesday, June 13. The departure from our base camp in Warsaw took place the day before the match, and the return trip the day after. I understood that it would be a long travel day, probably with a change in Frankfurt or Vienna, but when I got the travel plan from UEFA it turned out that we would get to fly a specially chartered private jet to the match. This was a different level of arrangements than I was used to.

For the governing bodies in UEFA and FIFA, however, a private plane was everyday fare. It was a given, and the stories about how FIFA President Sepp Blatter traveled the world in his own plane are many and long. During Euro 2012, UEFA President Michel Platini, along with important people from the organization, also had their own plane ready to transport them from one destination to another. From Poland to Ukraine, but also within Poland. If you absolutely had to see a match in Warsaw with kick-off at 18:00 and another in Wrocław with kick-off at 20:45, a private jet was required.

We trained the evening before at the stadium in Kharkiv. It was extremely hot and humid. The thermometer showed 33 degrees a day before kick-off, and we understood that not only the match itself was a challenge - running for ninety minutes in the heat would require a lot from us.

Our observer was Frenchman Marc Batta, one of the three most powerful within UEFA's referee committee, and the one I had the greatest respect for. He had seen me live in Austria ten months earlier and I liked him as a person. He was always nice, curious and humble. He felt more like a colleague than a boss.

But he was nervous and worried, both I and my colleagues noticed that. Our impression that the top match we had in front of us wasn't really intended for our team, one of the least experienced in the entire tournament, was constantly reinforced.

But the closer to kick-off we got, the less I cared. We were in place, I felt confident. I understood that a lot was at stake but was at the same time convinced that I would handle it.

After a match where I've been really, really focused, there are hardly any memories left. Everything is in fragments, you remember certain sequences, situations, feelings and words that were said. The rest is a big haze. It's as if you force yourself to be so concentrated on the task of making the right decisions that the capacity to remember the actual match disappears.

I remember talking German with Germany's captain, Philipp Lahm, in the player tunnel before the match, saying that I've tried to improve my Swedish school German and I'll try to speak the same language as him.

I remember having to run properly, but that I never get tired.

That I'm determined and work with an extremely clear body language, that I have the players' full confidence, that no one questions my decisions. I constantly have that flow that you want to have as a referee.

And then I remember constantly longing for the final whistle.

In the dressing room we cheer together. No one talks about us referees afterwards, that's the best grade we can get. Markus reads what Swedish media has written. Not a negative line at all. Glenn Strömberg calls it a flawless performance on SVT.

We have shown that we can handle championships, big matches and enormous pressure. We have made a debut that leaves us wanting more.

A few hours later we have caught our breath, showered, eaten dinner, drunk a beer, a glass of wine and I'm all alone in my room at the Kharkiv Palace Hotel. It's a dizzying contrast to the packed arena a few hours earlier. I'm lying in bed, listening to music and answering all the texts I've received afterwards. All are positive. It's exclusively happy cheers, praise and encouragement. I respond personally to all messages, and at five in the morning I fall asleep. As usual, I sleep extremely poorly after a match, but already at breakfast our planning for the future, recovery and preparation begins. The speculation about which will be our next match is already underway. UEFA are satisfied, very satisfied. Batta, our French observer, is relaxed. On the way home to Warsaw in our private plane we are offered something to drink, maybe a glass of wine or beer? I look cautiously at Batta. He says we deserve a beer or two, but that we should be prepared for another match soon. Then everything goes extremely fast. Within an hour after we landed, we find out that we will referee again within forty-eight hours: Greece against Russia. And we find out that Pierluigi Collina himself will observe us. For the first time ever. I barely remember the review after the match, more than that we got enormously much praise for our performance in Kharkiv. One reason why I don't remember anything is that I was already focused on the next match. It would be played in Warsaw, so we could stay at the hotel and didn't need to pack our bags and travel away again.

It's a special feeling to blow the whistle for another match that is even more important three days after what you have experienced as the most important match of your life. The match between

Russia and Greece is directly decisive. It's a group final. One of the countries goes through - for Russia a draw or win is enough, for Greece only a win will do.

I'm incredibly happy about the new match, but become even happier that I - despite the tight time - manage to arrange for my wife and father to fly down to see the match. UEFA fixes tickets, I fix flights and hotel. And some time to get to see each other. A week before departure to the Euros, I and my wife have taken the plunge and got married at home in Sigtuna, almost ten years after we got together.

Getting support from my wife, the great love of my life, and my father in between two important matches makes me so happy and joyful. I get an extra energy boost, become secure and it feels like I - unlike all other referees in the tournament - get an opportunity to take part in the best from home, but still remain in the bubble. When I go out in front of the packed arena, I of course don't see my wife and father among the fifty-five thousand spectators, but I know that they see me, and it makes me calm and harmonious. The experience from Kharkiv three days earlier is with me and I'm in a zone filled with confidence. The first forty-five minutes of the match, almost nothing happens. We have full control of everything, there are no protests and there is an incredible flow in the match. In two minutes of overtime, Giorgos Karagounis gives Greece the lead after carelessness in Russia's backline. There's an enormous cheer among the Greeks and immediately after the goal I blow for half-time.

I understand that it will be much tougher in the second half, as Russia now has to attack and score - otherwise they are eliminated.

And in the second half, a lot indeed happens. It is described afterwards by the referee committee as the most difficult match of the Euros so far.

The goalscorer was the great Greek star at the time - Giorgos Karagounis. He had been with the national team since 1999, won Euro gold in 2004, played two World Cups and was now in his third Euro finals.

When he gave Greece the lead, he also gave his team and an entire country hope for a quarter-final.

After sixty-one minutes, Karagounis makes a breakthrough into the penalty area and challenges the slow Russian center-back Sergei Ignashevich. Everyone agrees that the ball is poked past Ignashevich's left side. Everyone also agrees that there is contact between Ignashevich's leg and Karagounis' foot. But about who creates the contact - there opinions differ.

Karagounis is absolutely certain it's a penalty when he falls.

I'm just as certain that it's Karagounis who creates the contact by seeking out the leg, and I blow for an indirect free kick for Russia and caution Karagounis for diving.

There are six cautions in the second half, but it's really only one situation that stands out. In the seventy-third minute, the Russian back Zhirkov runs into the penalty area and after a duel with the Greek Salpingidis he falls directly to the ground.

"Play on," I shout. I don't have a thought of cautioning for diving, but let the match continue. No one else calls for diving, not even the Greeks. When I blow the final whistle after ninety-four minutes, the Greeks cheer loudly. One of them, Kyriakos Papadopoulos, rushes across half the field. I think he's going to rush in and celebrate with all the other Greek players - but he runs towards me. For a second I think he's going to hit me, or push me. But when he reaches me he shouts: "Eriksson, I love you!!!" Then I get a Greek bear hug. I accept it a bit cautiously. It doesn't look particularly good for a referee to hug a player, but it wasn't on my initiative, and cautioning Papadopoulos for an unauthorized hug is not an option. In the dressing room we were all, especially me, exhausted and tired after two matches in four days. Now we were really just waiting for the verdict from our observer Pierluigi Collina: had I done right when I had cautioned Karagounis? The guys turned on their mobiles and started reading all the texts. It was basically only positive reports. After fifteen minutes Collina came down to the dressing room, gave me a high-five, smiled and praised us for a good performance. He said it had been a difficult match, but that we had solved it well. He even urged us to enjoy the dinner afterwards.

He added that we would talk about the situation with Karagounis the day after, but that I should be calm. I had his support.

Usually the observer always ate dinner with the referee team, but Collina excused himself and said he would eat dinner in his hotel room. When he left the dressing room, we laughed and cheered. Over the match, the praise and the information that Collina wouldn't join us for dinner. Apart from avoiding Collina at dinner, we also didn't need to eat at the hotel's boring restaurant and the tasteless food served there. Our Polish hosts had booked an entire restaurant, and when we arrived at Bacio di Angelo shortly after midnight, my wife and father joined. It became a fantastic evening and night, we could celebrate and enjoy two solid performances in four days. I knew it was at least five days until a possible match, and didn't need to worry about being tired the day after. When we came in for the review in the afternoon the day after, we were thus worn out, but still happy and satisfied with our performance. Collina was busy with his computer and asked a bit dutifully how the dinner had been at the Italian restaurant and what we had eaten. We answered that it had been very nice before Markus said: "For starters we ate oysters, and for the main course pasta carbonara." It was a standing joke among the referees in the group not to eat just oysters and carbonara in connection with assignments so as not to risk incurring Collina's displeasure, but now Markus dared to joke with Collina about the food we had eaten.

It became quiet in the room. Then Collina's colleagues in the committee started laughing. First cautiously, then louder. Finally, even the Italian himself understood Markus' spot-on joke, and laughed with us.

Although he maintained that oysters and pasta carbonara were things that a world referee should not eat in connection with a match.

The review was almost as positive as after our first match, despite this match being much more difficult. The situation with the diving caution was judged as a 50-50 situation, that is, five referees would give a penalty and five would give a caution. They meant that I had missed a caution for diving for Zhirkov, when he went down a bit too easily in the penalty area. But that was a detail in an otherwise very positive whole.

We didn't get a numerical grade for the performance on site in Warsaw, it came only after the tournament, but it didn't matter, we felt very satisfied. The days after were some of the best in my refereeing career.

I was basically walking on clouds after having completed my two group stage matches in a good way. Several members from the referee committee came up and said that I had really surprised, that I had taken a big step in my career and that I had now seriously become a top referee.

One of them hinted that there would be another match for me in the knockout stage.

The group stage ended on Tuesday, June 19 with matches in group D, where Sweden defeated France in a match insignificant for the group. At the same time, England played against Ukraine in a match that decided who would advance to the quarter-finals.

We in the team watched the matches in our hotel room in Warsaw. The mood was good up until the sixty-third minute of the match when the Ukrainian Marko Devic shot a shot that via goalkeeper Joe Hart slowly descended towards the goal line. There John Terry appeared and with a bicycle kick managed to save the ball from going into the goal.

Or did he? Did Terry really manage to save the ball before the goal line? The replays followed one after another and finally came the sequence that made us freeze and fall silent. On the last one, you could clearly see that the ball was over the goal line before Terry cleared it away.

On the goal line as the goal-line official stood the Hungarian István Vad. There and then he had only one task: to judge whether the ball was over the goal line or not. He had in a fraction of a second made a decision - an incorrect one. The home nation Ukraine lost the match and was eliminated, England went through. All focus fell on us referees, on the system with five referees, on UEFA's referee committee and not least on President Platini who had said that this was the future of football. It almost hurt to go down to breakfast the day after. The dining hall was dead silent, no one laughed or talked, everyone looked down and at the tables where there were discussions, it was mostly mumbling. When István Vad and the referee team led by Viktor Kassai later in the day returned from the match in Donetsk, it was with their tails between their legs. They snuck into the dining hall, sat down and basically didn't look up during the entire dinner. As a friend and colleague, I went up, patted Viktor and István gently and said I was sorry for their sake. Not much more could be said. That István Vad would end up in the freezer after the Euros, everyone understood, and so it was. But he came back, and it didn't become as one of the members of the referee committee said to me: "If President Platini had got to decide, he would never have refereed football again." Despite the chaos and the mood in the group, we Swedes were charged and looking forward to the next round of matches. We thought we would get another match. Still, we were nervous when it was announced later that same evening which referees would be sent home.

When the names of those sent home were read out, we understood that we would stay and that we were thus ranked top eight in the tournament.

Then the referees for the four quarter-finals were announced, and when I was already in the first quarter-final selected as fourth official, I realized that we wouldn't get our own quarter-final. UEFA bet on extremely safe cards in all four quarter-finals. While waiting for new assignments, we celebrated Midsummer at the hotel with brought-along herring, crispbread, Swedish schnapps, boiled potatoes and strawberries and cream. In my head there was always that one of the committee members had said that we would get more matches. From experience, I knew that we would never have received any information about an upcoming match if we weren't actually intended to get another assignment. Given what had been said to us, we thought we would get one of the two semi-finals, even though there were three other referees left who also hadn't had any knockout stage match: Cüneyt Çakır from Turkey, Stéphane Lannoy from France and Craig Thomson from Scotland.

On Monday after the Midsummer weekend, we trained in the morning. The body felt as good as ever, and I kept thinking about which of the semi-finals we could get: Portugal against Spain on Wednesday in Donetsk or Germany against Italy in Warsaw on

Thursday. When we got off the bus at the hotel after training, I immediately saw the chiefs Pierluigi Collina and Hugh Dallas. I met their gaze and greeted them cheerfully. The answer and look I got from Collina made me nervous: "Jonas, can you come with us so we can talk to you." I followed them and followed them up to a meeting room at the hotel. I understood from the silence on the way there that we had refereed our last match, that there would be no further match. Collina began by saying that they were very pleased with our performance, but ... Then everything became a haze. I zoned out.

I remember how clearly I felt my own pulse, how incredibly angry I became, while at the same time I was sad, disappointed and felt betrayed.

But I didn't show any emotions there and then.

I perceived both Dallas and Collina as a bit ashamed when they described my Euro 2012 as a great success, that I had the future ahead of me, but that they just this time couldn't give me more matches, even though I actually deserved it, and that I should see the tournament as a springboard for the future. But that I this time wouldn't even get to stay as fourth official. When I left the meeting room, I didn't know what to do. I ran out onto the street, took a walk around the block and looked at my mobile phone. I had several missed calls from Bosse Karlsson.

I called back and he began by asking if Collina and Dallas had had time to talk to me. I explained what had happened, that they had taken me aside, what had been said during the meeting and how sad and disappointed I was.

Bosse understood and explained that they hadn't planned to tell me in a personal meeting, but just to announce that we would be sent home, but that Bosse had forced them to take it with me.

I hung up. I had to tell my colleagues in the team what had happened. They were waiting up in the corridor by our rooms, and I heard them as soon as I stepped out of the elevator. "We saw that they took you aside," one of them shouted when I reached the team. "Tell us, which semi-final do we have? Will it be Donetsk or Warsaw?!" I was silent. I didn't dare look up because I was afraid I would start crying. I gathered myself and said tightly: "You can pack your bags now." The guys cheered, and I didn't understand anything.

"We're packing our bags, it's a semi-final in Donetsk: Spain against Portugal," they shouted. "No," I replied. "We're packing our bags because we're being sent home. We're going home. Tonight." "But you're joking, we have a semi-final, right?" "No, I'm not joking. We're going home." I went into my room and banged my fists against the wall. The emotions welled up when I was finally alone, and my eyes teared up. Then I called my wife and told her that I would be coming home already that same evening. She comforted me as best she could. Even though I longed for my family, I would have gladly stayed another week and gotten to experience one more match. A few hours later that same day, we were home at Arlanda. I felt completely empty and exhausted. I could barely watch TV when Çakır from Turkey refereed one of the semi-finals. Or when Lannoy from France - the influential big nation with both Batta and Platini in high positions within UEFA - refereed the other. It took several weeks before the spark and desire to referee football was back. The referee in the Euro 2012 final, which was played between Spain and Italy, was ultimately not selected by UEFA's referee committee, but rather by which teams had advanced. I myself hoped for a final between Portugal and Italy, because then my favorite, the skilled Englishman Howard Webb, would have gotten the final. He couldn't referee Spain after his World Cup final in South Africa 2010. If Spain had gone to the final against Germany, however, Nicola Rizzoli would have gotten the final. Now it became Spain against Italy, and then only the Portuguese Pedro Proença remained as an alternative to referee the final.

My big lesson in the summer of 2012 was that I learned that as a referee, it's about having luck in the draw and results or great skill and help within the political game that affects who gets to referee which matches. In the summer of 2012, I didn't have that when it really mattered.

In FIFA's Beautiful World

"Nice meeting you, Mr. Blatter. I am Jonas Eriksson from Sweden."

FIFA President Sepp Blatter looked at me and replied: "Where from?"

"Sweden," I said cheerfully. I naively thought that he might have forgotten all the harsh words and quarrel with my countryman Lennart Johansson, and that he instead had something positive to say, that he might bring up Swedish refereeing which for many years had been prominent and among the world's best.

But it was exactly the opposite.

"Thank you," Blatter replied quickly and looked away.

It was generally known that President Blatter generally didn't like Swedes. The reason was probably that Lennart Johansson had challenged Blatter for the position of FIFA President in 1998. Blatter won that election with the score 111-80, but afterwards it has been proven that the vote was decided by a bribery scandal where, among others, the then FIFA President João Havelange was proven to have paid six million dollars from FIFA to secure votes for Blatter's presidential campaign. And after the vote, Johansson had harshly criticized Blatter. The road to refereeing in the World

Cup was long, maybe too long, if Blatter didn't even spend five seconds on me, I thought as I moved on and made room for the next of the fifty-two referees who like me had been selected for the preliminary squad for the 2014 World Cup and who at the first referee meeting got to shake hands and take a picture with the FIFA President.

Howard Webb, who had refereed the World Cup final just over two years earlier, had stood before me in the queue to Blatter. He had met the president on several occasions and they had hugged as a greeting. Their chat had been long and cordial, and Blatter seemed genuinely interested in Webb's stories and they laughed happily together.

The FIFA course in Zurich at the end of September 2012 was my very first under their auspices. Although I had just been to a European Championship and surely more than ten courses with UEFA, it was a completely new experience in many ways. We had been accommodated in a five-star hotel and not least the food was more normal than what UEFA served. Here there were sauces, spices, french fries and desserts of various kinds, and it was possible to have a glass of wine with dinner if you wanted. The atmosphere was also better at first, more relaxed and less stressed with a schedule where there was plenty of time to recover and rest.

The theory sessions, however, were extremely long and almost never included questions, dialogues or discussions - they were rather unstructured, far too long and unfocused lectures by the highest referee chief within FIFA, Massimo Busacca.

Massimo Busacca was, at forty-two years old, a sensationally young chief in the refereeing world. In 2011, he had been appointed by Sepp Blatter to lead FIFA's refereeing department into the future, to many people's great surprise. Busacca reported directly to Jérôme Valcke, FIFA's General Secretary, and his title was Head of Refereeing.

Busacca was slim and wiry, had thick and tousled black hair with grey streaks and intense eyes that could switch from being kind and friendly to becoming filled with irritation and rage a second later.

Busacca's body language was expansive and could easily be interpreted as arrogant. At the same time, he was a great language talent and switched quickly and easily between English, German, Spanish and of course Italian. He always had answers to all questions, never showed any uncertainty, and if he was contradicted or got a question that he maybe didn't have an answer to, he not infrequently chose to go on the offensive and question the person who had asked the question. Some of the referees he became boss over from 2011 were older than him, had more routine and had been better referees who had refereed My brief and stiff meeting with Sepp Blatter took place on a sunny day in Zurich in September 2012, outside the House of Football, FIFA's pompous main building.

more high-profile matches than Busacca. Sometimes it felt like Busacca was a person who had to assert himself and show who was in charge. He was anything but a natural authority.

Despite his age, however, Busacca had managed a fantastic career on the pitch with a series of finals and fine matches. But there were also other events that stood out in Busacca's career.

On September 12, 2009, Busacca was the referee in the Qatar Stars League between Al-Gharafa and Al Khor. While all players were waiting for a corner to be taken, the Swiss referee took the opportunity to urinate on the pitch, in the penalty area. According to media reports, he then apologized to the Qatari hosts, referring to "health problems".

A week later, on September 19, 2009, Busacca was the referee in a match in the Swiss Cup between FC Baden and BSC Young Boys. After FC Baden supporters had verbally attacked him, the Swiss top referee got tired and gave the finger to the supporters.

At first, Busacca completely denied that he had shown the finger. When photographic evidence then emerged, he was forced to apologize. The Swiss Football Association suspended Busacca for three matches for the finger.

That he still got to referee the World Cup in South Africa nine months later was astonishing, but probably also testified that he had very loyal contacts who supported him, swept things under the rug and helped in the political game. In South Africa, it became only one match for Busacca and not even strong support within FIFA could save him from being sent home. Busacca refereed South Africa against Uruguay in the second match. In it, he gave Uruguay a penalty when Luis Suárez fell after contact with goalkeeper Itumeleng Khune, who was also sent off in the same situation. Suárez fell, as so often, very easily, as soon as he felt the slightest contact. Maybe the Uruguayan was already on his way down when the contact came, maybe he hadn't even reached the ball, maybe it was also offside in the situation before. The home nation was more or less eliminated after the match, and the national team's Brazilian coach Carlos Alberto Parreira was furious: you don't mess with a home nation in a World Cup as a referee, and therefore Busacca got no more matches in the tournament. Busacca's style as chief for his fellow referees was also notoriously bad. During Euro 2008, UEFA produced a documentary - Kill the Referees - which followed the referees behind the scenes during the championship.

For the first time, viewers got to follow the referees' internal chat with each other and the players, as the communication equipment was recorded for the first time. During the match Sweden-Greece, which was refereed by Busacca, you could hear how the Swiss referee swore and scolded his co-worker.

Massimo Busacca had not left his temper on the pitch when he stopped refereeing. In the middle of a lecture, he could throw out an open question to everyone in the audience. As it was in our group of fifty-two referees, everyone hesitated, no one raised their hand but everyone looked down and hoped that they wouldn't get the question. Because the risk of answering incorrectly was overwhelming. You almost never knew what answer Busacca was looking for, and then it was better to avoid answering at all.

It made him flare up. After the question was repeated, some hands came up in the air.

Busacca gave the floor to someone who reluctantly held up their hand, and when the person had started to answer, he was usually quickly interrupted by the head of the refereeing department who scolded the person in question for answering incorrectly.

It was the same on the pitch when we conducted training. An incorrect decision, a hesitation or a misunderstanding of a poor instruction could make the moody Busacca lose it completely. During all the years I worked for FIFA and Busacca was at the helm, it happened numerous times that he had outbursts and scolded referees in front of everyone else.

Massimo Busacca's leadership style did not exactly stimulate discussion, dialogue and openness. Instead, the referees became closed and quiet. The fear of making mistakes was much greater than the will to do right or come up with the right answer.

We European referees always fared better. It was usually referees from other confederations who took the biggest hit. Towards the referees from UEFA, he was always a little kinder. Kicking downwards was Busacca's thing. Scolding the weak but not daring to communicate in the same way towards the stronger European referees was a clear part of his leadership. Something that was new to me at the FIFA course was the practical training. It was also extremely prioritized by FIFA. In short, it was a training where FIFA had called in players to play a match that was choreographed by the leadership. For example, the players were given instructions to dive a lot, to knock down a player behind the referee's back, to fall just on the edge of the penalty area, to start quick counter-attacks, to kick each other and to score goals with their hands. The practical training was a foundation in FIFA's education and development of referees. It was an important tool for selecting referees and seeing how they handled various match-like situations - without it being a real situation.

I hated it thoroughly. Every minute of practical training, every faked situation, every whistle I was forced to make was terrible. I didn't enjoy it at all. It was theater, a game without anchoring in reality and matches - far from refereeing in a real situation, which I really liked.

When the players were instructed to dive, they dived all the time. In all situations. And when the instructions were to create penalties, there were fouls and pushes every time a player approached the penalty area. A practical training of five minutes could involve between ten and fifteen penalty situations. And most became extremely obvious, as the players did everything to create penalties. In the end, you blew the whistle as soon as someone fell, without having any idea what had happened.

It wasn't realistic, it gave me nothing. But I obeyed orders. Tried to be concentrated and do my best, even though 95 percent were meaningless sequences and situations that we had to judge. The risk of injury during the practical training was also extremely high. Often we were forty referees who were to train at the same time, and since only one or at most two could be active, it meant an enormously long wait before you were then thrown into five minutes of maximum work where Massimo Busacca often stood and shouted angrily at you to sprint. Afraid of getting a scolding, I ran faster than I had ever done before. The trainings were also extremely long, often well over two hours. The first twenty minutes were warm-up and extremely much of the time thereafter was waiting when you had to try to keep warm. The physical coaches who were present thought the setup was completely crazy. Their mission was to keep everyone fit and injury-free but when they approached Busacca with feedback or criticism, they often got a scolding. Before we came to the World Cup in Brazil, two of the main responsible for physical training quit. They neither could nor wanted to stand for the way they were treated or the methods that were used. Even among us referees, we were silent outwardly about our thoughts and tough criticism of the setup. If I or any other referee had criticized the setup publicly, it would have been like saying that one wanted to abort the journey towards the World Cup in Brazil. Within UEFA, I felt safe and calm after Euro 2012. I knew what position I had there. But when I landed in Zurich and put on a FIFA jacket for the first time, I was somehow diminished. I immediately got the feeling that someone said to me: "You mean nothing, you know nothing and have nothing to contribute here." I don't know where it started, or why. Maybe it was when Massimo Busacca during one of the initial theory lessons several times called me Martin in front of everyone and I didn't dare to correct him. Instead, I went up afterwards and carefully pointed out that my name was Jonas and not Martin, whereupon he irritably replied: "Of course I know your name. Why do you ask?" It wasn't the time to insist that he had called me by the wrong name for an hour.

Or was it perhaps after I and some other referees had been scolded by Busacca for taking too long to do a theory test. Maybe it was the feeling of inferiority when I had greeted politely but quickly been dismissed by President Blatter.

I returned home from my first FIFA course with mixed feelings. I was very happy that the nine days were over, and that the journey towards the World Cup in Brazil had begun. But I wasn't sure I wanted to be part of it. I hated my own unusual uncertainty, the nervousness I felt, Busacca's moody temper and the practical training.

After Euro 2012, I had thought that I would need to get better at the political game and create stronger relationships with those who ruled.

Getting a good relationship with Busacca and Blatter felt out of the question, they were too different from me in leadership and personality. I had to seek other allies, and continue to deliver results in the matches I got to referee. My successes during the recently concluded European Championship had shown the world that I had the capacity to lead the biggest matches, even if I myself partly still had an unpleasant and slightly bitter aftertaste when I was sent home without refereeing the knockout match that I had been promised, and which I thought I deserved. I and my team had come to the Euros as one of the last selected referee teams, but when we left the tournament we were ranked considerably higher. At the same time, I knew that almost all twelve Euro referees also had the right age to be able to come to the 2014 World Cup, and we could thus not automatically advance in the ranking through referees quitting. To get to the World Cup in Brazil, we would need to be at least top nine in Europe. Countries like England, Spain,

Italy, France and Germany would, however, have one team each - and then we competed for the four places that were available for referees from the other countries.

I knew that we would need to perform at the top during the entire time up to the World Cup to have a chance of being selected. Maybe we could manage one or at most two missed situations - otherwise the possibility of reaching the tournament in Brazil disappeared.

My team also needed to change before the World Cup effort. My first assistant referee from the summer's Euros, Stefan Wittberg, would turn 45 the following year and therefore he was no longer an option. My assistant referee, Mathias Klasenius, was more or less obvious to become the first assistant referee in my team. Partly because we had camped together for a long time, partly because he had the right background, age and since June also good experience and great success from a big championship. Finally, I decided that I wanted Daniel Wärnmark in my team as an assistant referee. Daniel felt like the right person. He would put in all the time that would be required for us to make it. The increasingly tough physical tests would not be any problems at all for him and above all, with his honest personality, he would dare to challenge me, speak up and make me a better referee. Moreover, we of course enjoyed each other's company on a personal level.

The journey towards Brazil kick-started with the friendly match between the super clubs Barcelona and Manchester United at Nya Ullevi in Gothenburg. It was low-tempo, goalless and friendly. With one exception. After half an hour, United's tough midfielder

Paul Scholes forgot that it was a friendly match, and made an ugly challenge on Sergio Busquets. A yellow card was obvious, it was very close to a red. Wayne Rooney looked apologetically at me and stated that Scholes probably didn't know what a friendly match was.

It was a star-studded affair, which helped me build experience and contacts - not only with the players, but also with the leaders. Already in 2003, I had as a fourth official for Anders Frisk been involved when Manchester United met Glasgow Rangers in the Champions League, "The Battle of Britain," the newspapers had called the match. Nine years later, the charismatic and legendary Alex Ferguson was still manager of Manchester United. Young, inexperienced and a bit nervous, I had gone into United's dressing room as fourth official in 2003. One by one I examined the players' equipment before I went up to Alex Ferguson to greet. Ferguson's merits as manager for Manchester United were unmatched by any other coach. The team won, among other things, the Premier League thirteen times, the FA Cup five times, the UEFA Champions League twice. I had the impression that Ferguson wasn't a person you made small talk with, who didn't appreciate quick jokes and funny comments - rather a bit angry, grim old man who basically hated referees and wasn't afraid to take conflicts with players he didn't appreciate. I knew it was a real tough guy I was approaching in the dressing room. Ferguson met my gaze. He looked at me, examined me from top to toe and reached out his hand and asked a bit gruffly where I came from. I replied that I came from Sweden, from Luleå. He said he had no idea where that was, but that he loved Gothenburg. That's where he had won the Cup Winners' Cup with Aberdeen in 1983. The final had been held in the city and the opponent was Real Madrid. I was taken aback by his talkativeness and curiosity, and we continued to talk for a good while.

Nine years later, I met the same Ferguson in the culvert under Ullevi's stands before the friendly match. He didn't recognize me, but of course I knew about him, about his history and that I was now meeting him again - but this time in his favorite city. I sought eye contact with him and went up and introduced myself, asked how it felt to be back in his favorite city and at his lucky stadium. Sir Alex looked surprised and appreciative, and admitted that he remembered that he had talked to me about it before but that he didn't remember what I looked like. The week after the super match at Ullevi, I had been invited to Frankfurt by the German Football Association to referee the friendly international between Germany and Argentina - the same teams that less than two years later would play the World Cup final against each other in Brazil.

It was the second week in a row that I refereed world stars in all twenty-two positions. And the second week in a row that Leo Messi, the world's best football player, was on the pitch. This time in the Argentine national team, as captain. I had refereed Messi on a handful of occasions before, but never before had he been captain. Now I had a good opportunity to try to build a more personal relationship with the short, Argentine ball genius.

"Leo, we have to stop meeting like this," I said in broken Spanish when he came up first in the player tunnel. "What do you mean?" he asked. "Last week we met in Gothenburg, this week in Frankfurt, where will we meet next week?" "In Barcelona, then?" he said and smiled. The first match we refereed on the way to Brazil, in the World Cup qualifiers, was in Glasgow, Scotland against Serbia. Yet another match in the city where my career was about to end three years earlier after a catastrophic match in the Champions League with threats, hate, doubt and anxiety in the aftermath.

When we landed in Glasgow on a rainy afternoon in September, everyone knew what had happened last time I was there and how weak my performance had been then. I started at minus and would need to be better than ever before to win the trust of the players, leaders and supporters.

But I was strengthened by my successes in recent years and had now reached a point in my career where I more and more didn't care what the surroundings thought about me. I read fewer newspapers and took in less and less of what the surroundings had for opinions about my performances. The kick-off was early. Already at 3 PM local time in Glasgow, and we left the hotel just before one. The streets were already then filled with singing supporters who pilgrimaged towards Hampden Park. It was impressive, although the most striking thing was how incredibly drunk some of them were. Despite someone perhaps falling asleep on the way to the arena, almost fifty thousand spectators made it there. The atmosphere they created during the match was among the mightiest soundscapes I've experienced in my career. The match itself became boring and uneventful and ended 0-0. Glasgow Rangers player Steven Naismith, whom I had missed giving the clear penalty three years earlier, played in the national team and after the match he laughed heartily when he thanked me for the match: "Well, Eriksson, at least you did not fuck up this time." At the review after the match, however, it was just the same Naismith who created a great uncertainty in the assessment of my performance.

TV images behind one goal showed a replay in the beginning of the match when Steven Naismith hit the Serbian defender Srdan Mijailovic with a straight elbow. It happened at a time when the Scottish goalkeeper was holding the ball, behind my back. The elbow came completely unexpectedly and without any provocation at all.

The English observer clearly saw on the TV images that I was looking the other way, and he also realized that neither I nor my colleagues could be expected to keep our eyes on the area where the situation arose.

Although we in the team had missed a clear red card, we escaped criticism in the subsequent report. We were lucky.

Autumn 2012 and spring 2013, I and the team managed to line up flawless performances. For the second year in a row, I belonged to Europe's eight best referees when I was again selected to referee a quarter-final in the Champions League, this time Málaga against Borussia Dortmund. Also in the Europa League, it became a semi-final for the second year in a row. This time with the return match between Chelsea and FC Basel. We felt fantastic and had a nice atmosphere in the team before the match in London.

But on the morning of match day, we were reached by two incredibly sad news that shook us all.

First, we found out that one of our closest referee colleagues and his wife had suffered a great tragedy when their newborn son had died shortly after birth. The joy we had felt over him and his wife finally having their first child was immediately changed to an enormous sorrow, a hopelessness and a feeling that football after all didn't mean very much.

When we had received and taken in the tragic news and together tried to put words to it, the next blow came. During lunch we read that AIK's goalkeeper Ivan Turina had passed away.

The same day we were to referee the decisive semi-final in the Europa League, I and my colleagues received two extremely shocking death notices.

It wasn't someone close to any of the members of the team who had been affected, but it was a close colleague and his family who had been affected - and then AIK's great, happy and thoroughly nice goalkeeper Ivan Turina who had suddenly died, thirty-three years young. Everyone in the team was a parent and had small children, and could relate to the bottomless sorrow that our colleague and his wife had been struck by. And Ivan Turina's death shocked us enormously, not just because he was a fantastic person, but just as much because he was our age, an elite athlete and a family father. When I was alone in the hotel room for a few hours of rest and preparation, thoughts were spinning. I asked myself how I could even referee the match later that same day considering that so much had happened that had affected me during the day.

I was sad and felt desperate and empty inside. A referee becomes during a long career good at shutting off their emotions on the pitch, not letting things that have happened or happen outside the pitch affect the performance and the difficult decision-making that one should carry out during the matches. I dare to go so far as to say that the best referees have just that quality - to go into a bubble of focus, concentration and not being affected by anything else for ninety minutes. I had for all years trained to shut off my emotions inside the lines of the pitch, to be strong, not be afraid, affected by the importance of the match, audience shouting or personal things that affected me outside the pitch. That's exactly what I did that Thursday in early May at Stamford Bridge. I shut off my emotions, went into a bubble and barely heard the crowd's cheers before the match. My decisions were perfect, my feeling for letting play go on and blowing the whistle at the right time received much praise afterwards from our Portuguese observer.

After a good dinner, I finally ended up in the hotel room, alone.

It's a strange feeling to suddenly close the door, be alone when you just a few hours earlier were in the middle of the pitch with nearly forty thousand screaming supporters in the stands. When the door closed, I felt how my bubble of concentration, adrenaline and the theater I had played during the evening was punctured.

I sank down on the floor. Out of relief that the match was over and that it had gone so well, but also because of sorrow over the death notices I had received during the day and of gratitude that both I and my immediate family were healthy and doing well.

I actually wanted to call home, talk to my wife, chat with my children, but now it was after midnight. I would have said how much I loved them, how important they were and how grateful I was that I was healthy and got to live my dream. When Bosse Karlsson called me a few days after the semi-final in London, he was in high spirits. The grade from the match had come, 8.4, and both I and Bosse were super satisfied. And Bosse hinted that the season might not be completely over for me yet. A few weeks later, the Champions League final between Borussia Dortmund and Bayern Munich would be played at Wembley, and the Europa League final between Chelsea and Benfica would be decided in Amsterdam. I felt my pulse rise, it had not occurred to me that I could already be considered for refereeing a final in one of the two finest tournaments. I wondered if Bosse really thought I could be considered for one of the matches. He replied that he didn't know anything, but if one looked at the grades, he meant that there was no referee who had been better than me the past season.

Depending on which referees had refereed the semi-finals in the Champions League and which teams were left in the tournament, I realized that in practice there were only two candidates to referee the Champions League final - Italian Nicola Rizzoli and myself. I could honestly say that my competitor was a considerably better referee than me, had more experience and above all merits from refereeing big finals such as the Europa League final in 2010. But if one looked at the matches of that season, I knew that no one could beat my grades. Rizzoli had also only refereed one match in the knockout stage - and I four. My grades were maximum all the way, while the Italian's only match, a round of 16 in the Champions League between Málaga and Porto, had contained some controversial situations that I suspected had led to a failing grade. Regardless of what grade Nicola Rizzoli had received in that match, it was still set up for him to referee the final - having only one early match in the knockout stage between two less known teams that would hardly reach all the way was often an indication that UEFA wanted, believed and hoped that they would be able to give the final to the referee later on.

Besides all this, there was one more thing that pointed to why Nicola Rizzoli would get the final. He came from the most important and powerful football country of all: Italy.

Not only in terms of population and football merits was Italy a big country. Also in the corridors and meeting rooms, where the decisions about the most important selections and final referees would be discussed, the boot-shaped country had for several years created an extremely strong position with people in all the powerful positions that affected all important decisions, were responsible for and approved all important referee selections.

Besides referee chief Pierluigi Collina, UEFA's competition department was led by Giorgio Marchetti, also from Italy. He in turn reported to UEFA's highest official, the General Secretary, who in 2013 was Gianni Infantino, also with an Italian passport. At the very top was President Michel Platini. He was certainly French, but both his parents were of Italian descent. And Platini had also been at Juventus during his heyday as a player.

Before the Europa League final in 2010, there had been much talk in referee circles that Michel Platini had demanded a referee whose language he understood. That final was namely the first to be refereed with the new five-referee system that Platini himself had instituted and saw as the future of football. The UEFA President wanted to be able to sit in the stands and follow the communication between the referees, and that fact had possibly played a part in the choice of Nicola Rizzoli as the final referee.

Despite all this, I still hoped, a bit naively, youthfully and hopefully, that my performances and good grades the past season would give me the chance to referee the final. And if I as expected wouldn't get it as referee, I hoped to be selected as fourth official. When the call came on the morning of Monday, May 20, it was as expected not positive. It was Rizzoli who would get to referee the match. And I hadn't been selected as fourth official either. That role went to Slovenian Damir Skomina. I accepted somewhere that I didn't become referee in the final, I saw Rizzoli as a step ahead of me in quality and capacity - even though my last season had been stronger than all other referees at the highest level. However, I was extremely disappointed that I didn't even get the chance to be fourth official. Just like in the semi-final at Euro 2012, it was Skomina who got the assignment as fourth official before me. It stung deep inside. I was disappointed for a few days, but then looked forward to my upcoming assignments, there was a Junior World Cup coming up and then a new season where big matches probably awaited. In an attempt to cheer myself up, I told myself that it was just as well not to get a Champions League final already as a 39-year-old, what would I then have left to aim for in the coming six seasons? At UEFA's course that started the autumn of 2013, I met some high-ranking members of UEFA's referee committee. We chatted relaxed and informally over a cup of bitter conference coffee about the previous season. In confidence, one of them told me that Skomina had probably got the final as fourth official because he spoke Italian. That thing with language and nationality had played a role once again. For the second year in a row, I missed a good month of the fantastic but short Swedish summer - including the children's school graduations and Midsummer Eve. Although I looked forward to finally refereeing a World Cup, it was with mixed feelings that I boarded the plane to Istanbul for the Junior World Cup in Turkey. An important step on the way to refereeing a World Cup was to participate in one of FIFA's other big tournaments the year before the World Cup. It was said that all fifty-two referees on the way would do at least one tournament each, and ten referees had been selected for the Confederations Cup in Brazil, which was played at the same time. There, the already certain referees were selected, those that FIFA was more or less convinced would get a place in the World Cup.

The next tournament in order of priority was the Junior World Cup. Eight European referee teams were selected for it. We were happy to be one of them, and left Sweden in mid-June for what would become thirty days in Turkey.

It was tough to again leave my wife and my children for a longer period, but the bad conscience for that I had to force away. I couldn't go around in Turkey feeling bad for not being at home - that would have been like saying straight out that I wanted to fail.

I knew that the family at home was doing fine even if they missed me, just as I every morning missed being by their side. I cheered myself up and compared myself with other fathers who commuted weekly, had jobs that took them far away for long periods, pilots with tough schedules and people who were forced to take jobs in other countries. Moreover, I got to do what I, after my family, loved the most and which gave me joy and a constant smile on my lips.

In June 2013, it was very turbulent in Turkey and the Swedish Foreign Ministry even recommended for a period that Swedish citizens not travel to the country. The unrest in Istanbul had begun just weeks earlier, and spread quickly to the largest cities in Turkey.

It created concern. One of the groups also played their matches in the city of Gaziantep in southeastern Turkey, just a few miles from the border with Syria where a full-scale civil war was ongoing. I had to lie to my family that I wouldn't be considered for that group.

The first fourteen days of the Junior World Cup, Massimo Busacca was not present in Istanbul. He remained in Brazil at the Confederations Cup, and it was extremely noticeable in the atmosphere. The deputy referee chief, Manuel Navarro, was now the one on site with the highest responsibility. His completely different, positive, encouraging and happy leadership style made everything change for the better. Some instructors who had previously been quiet and almost shy blossomed out. They took space, dared to express their opinions, which made us referees also step forward and be able to have opinions. During the first two weeks, we all got a picture of how good it could have been in the group without referee chief Busacca.

The tournament became a very positive experience for me and the team.

Our first two matches went excellently: Chile-Egypt in a thirty-five degree Antalya, followed by the European super meeting between Spain and France in Istanbul. We showed that we had understood FIFA's message and interpretations, adapted our running patterns and refereed at the top of our capacity. Mathias and Daniel also showed their best sides, and we as a team received much praise for our physique, strength and speed. Somewhere in the middle of the tournament Busacca landed in Turkey, and suddenly an icy wind swept in and through the group. All instructors who had lived up, been active and really been an important part of all referees' development, their participation was now as if blown away. It was also noticeable among the referees, everyone became quieter, more buttoned-up and cautious. Besides the atmosphere deteriorating, I also experienced that the performances became worse when Busacca had arrived. The mistakes and incorrect decisions increased - or was it perhaps that all mistakes and errors were just pointed out much more often? That I and the other referees suddenly felt worse than earlier in the tournament? All referees in the tournament first refereed two matches each. Thereafter, there were eight matches left that would be distributed to the referees who had performed best during the two initial matches. At least 15 of 23 referee teams would leave Turkey, disappointed and with dashed hopes. I and my team absolutely could not be one of them. We were underdogs, new at this level, came from a small and unimportant country and had to belong to the top in Turkey. It was our only chance to impress FIFA in general, and Busacca in particular.

First, the referees for the four quarter-finals were announced. We didn't get any of the four matches. Italian Rizzoli, who had refereed the Champions League final, got as the only European one of these. I felt both hopelessness and restlessness. We had been waiting for news about getting a match for over two weeks. It wasn't really such a long time to wait, but when you every day have to train, prepare, listen to theory and be engaged and prepared for the next match, without knowing when it is - then time passes slowly. One of the things I had taken with me from Euro 2012 was that in all tournaments, periods of boredom occur, long straight stretches where you just wait, without goals or a match in sight. During that time, it easily becomes a bit of friction in the team, you get tired of each other, become a little more irritated and long for home. It's not at all strange. Eating all meals together day in and day out, training together, then hanging out in each other's rooms until you go to bed, eventually creates a little chafe, no matter how much you like each other. If you have a match ahead of you, it becomes easier, then there's suddenly a goal and a purpose for why you are thousands of kilometers away from home.

Wise from this, I had realized before the Junior World Cup in Turkey that we as a team needed an injection, a person who halfway into the tournament gave us new energy, changed the dynamics and helped to keep our mood at the top. In the autumn of 2012, I had met Gunnar Söderström, who was then a PT, naprapath and mental coach for various athletes and teams. He was an energy bundle without equal.

Therefore, I had asked Gunnar to bring his treatment bench and come down to help us in Turkey. I had booked and paid for his flight ticket and hotel room myself, of course completely without FIFA's knowledge. We were namely forbidden to bring friends or socialize with acquaintances during our assignments for both UEFA and FIFA. When Gunnar showed up in the hotel lobby, we didn't say a word. Only when we got into his room could we greet and hug him welcome to Istanbul. Gunnar could treat our tired and worn bodies with massage, acupuncture, rehab training and stretching. He naturally also broke up the social pattern we had unintentionally fallen into and changed the group dynamics. Gunnar offered music quizzes, stories and laughter. When he left five days later, I and the team had recharged with new energy, our bodies had received individual treatment and were in top shape - and suddenly not so much time remained before we could get to referee our next match.

Now four matches remained in the tournament, and far too many referees fighting for the remaining assignments. It was with extremely great nervousness in my body that I entered FIFA's big debriefing and presentation of the referees in the semi-finals on the afternoon of Monday, July 8. Time passed very slowly, the air in the conference room stood absolutely still, sweat was beading on my forehead and I felt how my light blue shirt became darker from the sweat running down my back. The first semi-final was handed out: France against Ghana. We couldn't get to referee that, theoretically, because FIFA in the tournaments tried to use a principle of neutrality. It was applied a bit when it suited, especially at the beginning of the tournaments, and in short it meant that when teams from different continents met, the referee could not come from any of those parts of the world. If, on the other hand, two European countries met, for example, it was perfectly fine for the referee to also come from Europe. In the case of France-Ghana, FIFA followed its neutrality principle: "Nawaf Shukralla, Bahrain," Busacca called out. The next semi-final was Iraq against Uruguay - an assignment that was made for one of the seven referees from Europe who were left in the tournament. Busacca spoke again: "Jonas Eriksson, Sweden," he roared. I looked up and received the applause in the room a bit cautiously with a moderately happy smile. I didn't dare to cheer loudly or hug my colleagues, because I knew that our selection meant that a bunch of other referees would now have to leave Turkey.

After all the congratulations, I managed to slip away and get up to my room. I called home and announced what was perhaps even more important than that I had gotten another match, that I now knew when I would come home.

The semi-final became another bull's-eye for the team. Since we knew that Busacca was watching the match, it was good that it went to extra time and that we during 120 minutes plus penalty shootout got to show ourselves from our best side.

One year remained until the World Cup in Brazil, and I knew that six months remained until the referees would be selected sometime in January. I was on the right track, had a whole year of matches without a failing grade, confidence at the top and a physique that was constantly getting better.

That I started the autumn by refereeing the Super Cup final between Bayern Munich and Chelsea in Prague was another feather in my cap. It wasn't just a match between the German giants and winners of the Champions League and the English big club, winners of the Europa League and with the biggest transfer budget in the whole world. It was above all the super coaches' meeting, the deep enemies Pep Guardiola and José Mourinho's first meeting since they had left Barcelona and Real Madrid respectively a year earlier. It was noticeable in the atmosphere on the pitch, and at the bench. It was about more than a Super Cup final to determine Europe's best football team - fourth official Stefan Wittberg had to work hard to keep emotions in check. Especially in the final stages of the match, in the 85th minute, at the score 1-1 when Chelsea's midfield star Ramires came in late in a duel and recklessly, on the verge of brutally, tackled Bayern Munich's Mario Götze. It was such a tough tackle that it could have been a direct red card - but I wasn't completely sure about the intensity and therefore gave a yellow card to Ramires. It was his second in the match, and therefore it was a sending-off anyway. Mourinho went completely crazy on the bench, shouted at my fourth official and refused to accept the sending-off. The play resumed quickly nevertheless. As always after a sending-off, the minutes immediately after were hectic with enormously much emotion, but after a few minutes of overtime I could blow the final whistle.

Actually, my difficult, challenging assignment should have been over now. In a normal match, the final whistle would have meant that we were done for the day, but since this was a final, it had to be decided, and the result 1-1 had not determined a winner in the heat in Prague. All referees are different, but we have one thing in common: everyone hates extra time. It's overtime work without any extra compensation. Moreover, there is a significantly greater risk that strange situations arise during the thirty minutes of extra time when all players are more tired, more easily make basic mistakes and as a consequence make incorrect decisions in the game. And if as a referee you make a questionable decision or make an obvious mistake during extra time, the media interest becomes much greater than if it would have happened during the regular match time.

Thirty minutes remained, and it didn't matter that we had done a fantastic job during the first ninety minutes, shown seven correct yellow cards and, not least: dared to send off Ramires for his second yellow card during the match. We had five minutes together as a team to eat a little, drink, discuss our tactics and any adjustments we should make in the team.

Immediately after my final whistle, I hear how my fourth official Stefan Wittberg shouts loudly in the communication system, as if to warn us. It's Mourinho who is on his way towards me to tell me what he thinks of my performance. He is angry and his body language is almost aggressive. He scolds me for ruining the match for them and says that I'm a referee who shouldn't be allowed to referee at this level.

All my years as a football referee have taught me that I should never take criticism personally or become upset or angry when a person - whether it's a player or a manager - criticizes me. Therefore, I respond to Mourinho with calm body language, and a voice that is low-key and anything but angry. I thank him for his feedback but ask him to go back to the bench and take care of his players, since we still have two times fifteen minutes left to play. Then I walk calmly and composedly away from there. Mourinho goes back to the bench after a while.and calmly from there. Mourinho goes back to the bench after a while.

I see his eyes. They are black with anger. I gather my team. We are quiet, serious while we catch our breath and recharge. I myself drink sweet and sickly blue sports drink, eat half a banana and stretch my calves a bit cautiously. I know that we all hate extra time, but it's about embracing the situation, to think that what happened is the best, to instill courage in yourself and each other and build up a feeling that we won't miss anything at all during the last thirty minutes. I pep my team like this and joke despite the seriousness. When I start to prepare for blowing the whistle to start the match again, suddenly one of the goal-line officials, Stefan Johannesson, says that he urgently needs to go and pee. It has been hot in Prague during the day and he has drunk a bit too much and hasn't had time to go out to relieve the pressure earlier. In this situation, some referees would probably have become irritated and complained about their co-worker. But I choose to take it lightly.

While Stefan unobtrusively slips out and does what he must, I delay the start. We in the team, who are the only ones who understand what's going on, giggle contentedly when Stefan is back in place and I can blow the whistle to start the extra time. During my years as a referee, I became more and more convinced that it's not possible to be one hundred percent concentrated and serious during an entire match. To be able to endure the enormous concentration required during the most important moments, I always had to give myself and the team energy by joking, laughing, being relaxed and trying to disconnect from the important task we after all were in and had been given the responsibility to handle. After that, I and my team could quickly switch up. Go from laughter and fun to seriousness and full concentration. In a second, where it was required, everyone was in the right mode - without us having to remind each other that now we should indeed be prepared and concentrated. The incident in Prague when Stefan needed to pee was such an occasion. When I finally blew the whistle to start the extra time of the Super Cup final in Prague, I didn't dare to smile or laugh despite what had happened just before. If I had done that, it could certainly have been intentionally misinterpreted by Chelsea in general and José Mourinho in particular. Even more so after the Belgian superstar Romelu Lukaku missed Chelsea's last penalty and Bayern Munich therefore won the Super Cup final 5-4. After the match, we referees, as always in big finals, had to step up on the podium first of all and receive our personal gold medal from the final from UEFA's potentates. The words from UEFA's Swedish honorary president Lennart Johansson warmed the most. His big, warm hand squeezed mine. He held on to the grip, looked me in the eyes and said: "When you see you on the pitch, you become proud of being Swedish and sitting here in the VIP stand. Thank you and congratulations, Jonas." As a referee, there is no final to win - reaching a final is as far as you can get. And Lennart's support and fine words made me happy and a feeling of satisfaction spread in my body. In the dressing room, the boss knocked. Pierluigi Collina had selected us for the match and it was in his hands our future fate when it came to big matches in Europe lay. I, who a few minutes earlier had been the boss of the world's best football players with an obvious natural authority and led them with an iron hand, was suddenly transformed into a little boy in first grade whom the teacher was just about to give the final grade. Collina was in brilliant mood, gave me a high-five, patted me on the shoulder and praised me and the team for the performance. He said that the sending-off was crystal clear, that it could even have been a direct sending-off and that I shouldn't listen to a word of what Mourinho said at the press conference. He ended by commenting on my weight: "I do believe you've lost a few more kilos." Collina left the room and the Russian observer came in and the praise continued. It was also nice but didn't really matter. That Collina had seen us live for the first time since Euro 2012 and threw superlatives at me was the best grade we could get. UEFA's General Secretary Gianni Infantino, who a few years later also became FIFA's president, also came in and congratulated us on a "fantastic match". But a few rooms away sat a disappointed José Mourinho and slaughtered me and my performance at the press conference. And not only I was attacked by Mourinho, but also UEFA. The Portuguese considered that the European association over the years had systematically disadvantaged his teams. The Portuguese's criticism threw a little damper on my joy. I knew that his words could set strong forces in motion and the first call afterwards went to my family at home: "Hello, darling! Yes, the match went well, but it was a bit lively afterwards. So if someone rings on the phone and you don't recognize the number, don't answer. And if someone knocks on the door, don't open, but call the police." I thought that I and Mourinho would thereafter always have a strained relationship. But his criticism was actually not directed at me as a person, at the father, the friend, the man, the son or the brother Jonas. The edge was one hundred percent directed at me as a professional, at me as a referee, at the decisions I had taken that this time had gone against his team.

It's important as a referee to understand that the scoreboard often governs the involved players' and leaders' feelings and attitude towards a referee's performance.

When we finally left the arena in Prague, José Mourinho stood staring at me. He clapped his hands theatrically and gave a thumbs up in a greeting that dripped with sarcasm.

During the autumn, I began to understand that a World Cup place was within reach for me, but that it was the last matches that would decide everything. There was an indicator on the way to Brazil, a watershed that I looked forward to, but at the same time feared like nothing else: the eight playoff matches that would decide which four nations would snatch the last European places for the World Cup in Brazil. I remembered what had happened to Martin Hansson after he and his team had missed a match-deciding handball in a playoff match. Now I found myself in the same situation as Martin had been in four years ago. I was torn. Part of me didn't want to referee a playoff match at all - there were only risks with it, only problems and opportunities to fail. Another part of me wanted the confirmation that I belonged to the top eight in Europe. If I would also get a return match, it would be like proof that I belonged to the top four, since the best referees almost always refereed the return matches.

I had looked at the four playoff matches, and could immediately remove one of them for my part: Sweden against Portugal. I could probably also remove Ukraine-France, for surely a Swedish referee wouldn't get to referee France four years after what happened with Martin in 2009. Iceland against Croatia was also not particularly suitable for a Swedish referee considering that Lars Lagerbäck was the national coach for Iceland. Then there was only one conceivable match left: Greece against Romania.

When Bosse Karlsson later called to give me advance info on how the selection had gone, he told me that I had gotten a match. And a return match too.

I therefore assumed that it was about Greece-Romania. But Bosse corrected me. We were not going to Romania. And not to France, Ukraine, Croatia or Iceland either, it turned out. Besides the European playoff matches, intercontinental playoff matches were played at the same time between teams from Latin America, Asia and Oceania. I quickly realized that we had gotten one of those matches.

Bosse announced that we would referee the match between Uruguay and Jordan at the legendary Estadio Centenario in Montevideo. It was an eight-day long journey from departure to return, and a fantastic honor that I as one of four European referees had been given the trust to referee one of these matches - which were counted as more difficult than the European playoff matches. When Jordan and Uruguay played their first match in Amman, on November 13, I and my colleagues sat glued to the TV at home in Sweden to study the teams, the players, the tactics, the atmosphere and the feelings between the nations. It was in a way crazy, but also a fantastic privilege to get to move over twelve thousand kilometers, fly for twenty-five hours, to come to Uruguay and there for seven days as a full-blooded professional prepare for an assignment that was extremely important. In place in Montevideo, we were very well taken care of by our hosts and really got to see the best that Uruguay had to offer. We ate the most fantastic food that could be offered, drank good wines, experienced a day trip to the super luxurious Punta del Este, saw wild sea lions play in the water at South America's easternmost point, bathed in the Atlantic but at the same time trained carefully and prepared professionally.

It was said that there were sixty-two thousand spectators at the arena where the world's first World Cup in football had been played in 1930, that it was sold out to the last seat. But it felt like there were considerably more people present, and when we asked one of the local organizers if it really was true, he told us that all military personnel, police and people who worked for the state got in for free if they came there in uniform, and that they were not counted in the official attendance figures.

The player tunnel at the stadium in Montevideo was considerably smaller and more compact than at all the modern European arenas I had refereed in before. The players didn't fit on the same side, but had to be divided. I and Mathias stood on the side where the home players of Uruguay crowded, and Daniel and Stefan were responsible for Jordan - but we couldn't see each other, the only communication was through our headset.

It was visible that Uruguay was extremely confident of victory, it was just ninety minutes of waiting to really get to celebrate the World Cup place in Brazil. That it was relaxed and playful was shown among other things by Edinson Cavani, the great home star who had played in Napoli, Paris Saint-Germain and Manchester United. When he came out from the dressing room, he had a small child in his arms. His son looked scared as he sat on his father's arm and wide-eyed observed the surroundings. When we went in on the pitch and the stands exploded in a mighty soundscape, the little boy started to cry and Cavani had to hand over his son and focus on playing the match. Another world star who was on the pitch was Luis Suárez. The skilled Uruguayan was also football's "bad boy", a cheater, dirty player who was most notorious for having bitten other players on several occasions. At one point, Suárez also fell a bit too easily in a duel with a Jordanian. I stood close to the situation and I waved him up, let him get up and since I was a decimeter taller than him I held him close to me, but not too close. At arm's length I looked at him with ice-cold eyes and said in my simple Spanish: "Not tonight, not with me. Do you understand?" He looked down, didn't say a word. Then I smiled, fired off a smile and said with warmth in my voice: "Thank you for listening. Soon the match is over and you get to celebrate the World Cup place. It will feel better without a yellow card." Suárez looked up again and smiled.

Just my ability to be able to vary my mood, my facial expressions and my body language was a quality that helped me become a good referee. To be able to show my stern and cold gaze, to a second later transition to a warm, happy and broad smile.

When I blew the final whistle in Montevideo, Luis Suárez, Edinson Cavani, Diego Forlán and the entire arena could celebrate Uruguay's advancement to the World Cup. After the match, I and my colleagues could breathe out in the worn dressing room that hadn't been renovated since its inauguration almost a hundred years earlier.

We were glad that we hadn't ended up in focus this time either, that our observer had written a nice grade that lifted us one step closer to new matches a few hundred miles north for the summer of 2014. After I found a large cockroach in my suit pants, which almost scared me to death and gave my colleagues the best laugh of the trip, we could celebrate the match and success with a good dinner and a good drink. A week after the match in Montevideo, I was to end the season with a match that, when I got it assigned, gave me an extremely bad feeling. I didn't want to referee this match, I wanted to leave it if possible. It wasn't that it was a decisive match, nor that I had a match so soon after returning from Uruguay, nor was it any of the teams separately that created the problem: Juventus or FC Copenhagen. It was the teams together that created my thought of leaving it. As a referee, you are always responsible for declaring which teams you don't want to referee for various reasons. With some regularity, you filled in for UEFA and FIFA a so-called Integrity declaration where you noted which teams or nations you could not or did not want to referee, and for what reason you wanted to avoid these teams.

In my case, there were two teams that I had written down. Partly my favorite team since I was five years old and in my first football school was assigned a team that I would belong to for the entire first week: Nottingham Forest. With red shirts, a cool logo, a name that was mentioned in Robin Hood (the sheriff came from Nottingham after all) and the fact that the club appeared a few times a year on Tipsextra made Forest my team.

The other team I wrote down I added much later. In my Integrity declaration in 2012, I wrote for the first time that I could not, would not or should not referee Paris Saint-Germain. Not at all because that team in any way had my sympathies, it was more because I wanted to be professional and avoid situations where I could end up in a suspected conflict of interest situation.

The background was that I in 2003, when I was sales manager at IEC in Sports, got to know the club's Qatari president Nasser

Al-Khelaifi. The bearded president and I were the same age, our firstborn children were daughters and born at exactly the same time, we both liked sports, and working with TV rights we both saw at that time as a dream job. During my time at IEC, I often traveled to Doha in Qatar and negotiated and sold rights to Al-Khelaifi, who at that time was a high executive at the newly started channel Al Jazeera Sport. But we were not just business acquaintances but had become friends even privately. Nasser visited me on several occasions in Stockholm and I was even invited to his wedding in Doha in January 2006. After Al-Khelaifi became president of PSG, our contact ceased. Partly because I had already left the rights business, partly because I realized that the contact and relationship with Nasser could create situations where my neutrality, integrity and objectivity could be questioned. Nasser also understood that regular contact with a top-level referee would be inappropriate. Our contacts ceased, even though we ran into each other in various contexts afterwards. None of the teams I was to referee in the autumn of 2013 were on my integrity declaration. Nor had I had a history with any of them that could affect their view of me or my view of them. Still, it felt wrong that the last match before the World Cup selection would be Juventus against FC Copenhagen in Turin.

The reason for my reluctance to referee the match was Euro 2004. Before the last round of group C, where Sweden, Denmark, Italy and Bulgaria played, the first three mentioned teams had a chance to advance and take the two knockout stage places. Even if Italy won as expected against Bulgaria, both Sweden and Denmark would advance if they played a draw with two goals or more, i.e. at least 2-2.

The Italians were already resigned before the match and claimed that the Scandinavian countries would arrange the match and play 2-2 so that both advanced to the knockout stage.

I myself sat in the stands at Estádio do Bessa in Porto that evening and celebrated when Mattias Jonson made it 2-2 in the final stages of the match. Sweden and Denmark advanced to the quarter-finals on more goals scored. And Italy was sensationally eliminated. The rage in Italy was complete. They considered it a clear example of a fixed match - in Italian a biscotto. And the Swedes I talked to were just as sure and completely convinced: the match was absolutely not fixed. To understand the Italians' dead-certain thoughts that the 2-2 result was predetermined, it requires not only background knowledge about Italian football, but also about the country and culture in general. As soon as a possibility of a biscotto appears, Italian media and the general public become engrossed and obsessed with the plot and intrigue they sense is behind it all. An Italian referee told me that in his home country, they sense a conspiracy behind almost everything. "We Italians believe that there is always something behind," the referee explained. "Our distrust of referees comes from the fact that we in Italy have corruption, poor trust in our politicians and in the state, not to mention the political system in general." As one in a country looks at its political system, at the state, at democracy - so one also looks at football referees. As a referee, you become an extension of the political system, of the social climate that prevails and a mirrored image of how people respect the state and its representatives. In Sweden, even if it changed during the twenty years that I refereed football at the highest level, it is completely different. We have, more or less, no corruption within our state apparatus. In addition, we have a relatively great trust in our governing politicians (although it has decreased), in our political system and our democracy. This also means that we basically trust our football referees, that they do their best and even if it sometimes goes wrong, we don't automatically believe that there is a conspiracy behind the mistakes. In nearly five hundred elite matches in Sweden over twenty years, I have received lots of criticism and been confronted by angry supporters for (what they think are) incorrect decisions that I have made. I have been threatened, called the most vile and degrading things - but I have probably never been accused of being corrupt, bribed or intentionally influencing a result. My experience as an international referee is completely different. As soon as I started refereeing internationally, insinuations appeared that I was bribed, corrupt and that the match result was predetermined. I was a referee and therefore suspected, hated and despised.

The match in Porto, in June 2004, had thus according to the Italians been a typical biscotto, a perfect example of a fixed match, even though afterwards there was no evidence whatsoever that the match had been fixed in any way.

The tag sat deep in the chest of all Italian football supporters. Even though nine years had passed, the feelings remained, the hatred and suspicion against Sweden and Denmark. Not separately necessarily, but together our countries formed a large red-white and blue-yellow cloth for all Italians.

Therefore, it was uncomfortable to be selected for an extremely important and directly decisive match between Juventus and FC Copenhagen.

Just Italy against Denmark. With a Swedish referee.

When I found out about the selection, I immediately called Bosse Karlsson and told him about my feelings, that in my opinion it was wrong that I should referee the match, that it was a suicide mission - especially just six weeks before the selection of the referees for the World Cup. It almost felt like UEFA wanted me to fail.

Bosse called and checked with Collina. He got the answer that the Italian was extremely aware of the situation, but that the selection was right. I should referee the match. I realized that it was just to face the facts and try to turn a potential setback into the opposite. I thought that I had at least been professional and reacted to the selection.

Instead, I focused on the fact that I had done a great job last time I was in Turin, and that it would be fun to come back there. This time I would be extra careful not to smile or seem happy when I talked to any of the Swedish players in FC Copenhagen, nor spend more time than necessary with the Swedes. It was about not increasing the suspicion that I knew the Italians had towards me and my team from the second we entered the arena. As always in Italy, we were escorted by aggressive police cars to the arena. With the blue lights on, the police kept the traffic away to ensure that the referee team would be in place on time. Everything went smoothly until we had just arrived at the mighty Juventus Stadium. The police who were driving in front of us suddenly stopped, stayed put and we had to wait for a while. We looked at each other in the car and wondered what had happened. Had there been an accident? After a minute or so, we heard shouts and screams from the tunnel where our cars were to drive down. At the front of the barriers, we saw a gang of an estimated few hundred supporters of the home team. As we drove past, they leaned forward towards the cars, shouted loudly and clearly showed with their fingers what they thought of us in the referee team. At the same time, everyone chanted loudly, hatefully and in time: "Due-due, puttana madre." Two-two, your mother is a whore. The home team's supporters had not forgotten what had happened nine years ago. I don't want to think afterwards about what would have happened if FC Copenhagen had won the match. If I had blown two penalties for the Danes and Juventus had been eliminated from the Champions League. Would I have come out of there alive? What would my life have looked like after that? Would the dream of refereeing the 2014 World Cup have remained just a dream? Now it became exactly the opposite. Juventus won the match 3-1, and the Italians got two penalties with them. The first when FC Copenhagen back Lars Jacobsen handled the ball, and the second when Olof Mellberg wrestled down Fernando Llorente. Both penalties were clear and didn't create any major discussions. Olof Mellberg, who otherwise with his hot winner's skull used to question decisions, just turned and walked away without saying a single word. When I after a few minutes of overtime blew the final whistle on the year's last match, my colleague Stefan Johannesson shouted drunkenly and happily in the communication system: "Merry Christmas, Merry Christmas!" There was admittedly a month left until Christmas Eve, but I could now take Christmas leave from football with twenty-one straight international matches over eighteen months with maximum grades, without a single major mistake.

It was fantastic, a completely amazing record that I understood many of my competitors had difficulty living up to. I now dared to seriously dream of a place in the World Cup, even though I didn't quite believe in it. I continued to train and prepared meticulously. I barely drank alcohol on New Year's Eve, trained harder than ever and ate no candy or sweets after New Year's Eve. Seven weeks after the match in Turin, the email came. Fifteen days into the new year, at 08:24, I read the email on my mobile phone on my way home after dropping my daughters off at school. CONGRATULATIONS! At yesterday's FIFA Referee Committee Meeting you were selected to participate at the 2014 FIFA World Cup Brazil ... I shouted loudly and cheered to myself. Then I went home to my wife and told her the news. After that, the phone rang incessantly all day.

All my hard work, my job and my sacrifices over so many years had paid off. I was one of twenty-five referees who were selected for Brazil - and in the absence of a Swedish national team, I and my team would be the only Swedish participants in Brazil. I was Sweden's eighth World Cup referee of all time, and looked forward to a magical summer.

The World Cup Dream in Brazil

Of the eight Swedes who had officiated World Cups since 1934, there were essentially two categories when it came to performance, at least in terms of how the world perceived them and how their legacies were shaped. Either you weren't remembered at all, you were invisible, not associated with a championship or any decisive mistake - that was the best rating you could get. Or you ended up in the history books for being involved in one or more controversial situations during a major tournament. In this context, it didn't matter if you had actually made the right call or if FIFA supported the decision you had made. It's always the media and the public who determine whether a referee has failed or not. Among the seven Swedish referees who had officiated World Cups before me, there were several who hadn't been involved in any major controversial situations or been vilified in the media. Who remembers, for example, Sten "Stabben" Ahlner's match in the 1958 World Cup? Or Bertil Lööw's participation in the 1966 World Cup? Or the brilliant Ulf "Utta" Eriksson's two flawless matches in the 1978 World Cup? A tournament where Eriksson, after his performances, was a potential candidate for the World Cup final - but where an Italian beat "Utta" to the world's finest assignment. Or who remembers Erik Fredriksson's fine performances in the 1982 and 1986 World Cups? Almost no one. For when you ask people or Google his name, Fredriksson's legacy will always be about his performance in the 1990 World Cup when, in the match between the Soviet Union and Argentina, he missed a clear handball by Maradona on the goal line from just a few meters away. Bosse Karlsson's caution, which was correct but given to the wrong player, in the Argentina-Nigeria match in the 1994 World Cup is what's always associated with his name - despite having had a fantastic career with finals at the highest level and several flawless big matches in Europe.

Ivan Eklind perhaps got the worst legacy of them all. Eklind had only been refereeing football for eight years and international football for two when he was selected for the World Cup in Italy in 1934, which didn't become an ordinary football championship but instead a propagandistic event orchestrated by the Italian fascist dictator Benito Mussolini.

The then twenty-eight-year-old Ivan Eklind from Solna was entrusted to referee both the semi-final and final of the tournament, which even then should have been impossible as it gave one referee far too much influence over the result. Italy played in both of Eklind's knockout matches, and the Swedish referee tolerated major unfair play and provocations from the Italians, who also won the tournament.

The Italian victory left a bitter aftertaste. It wasn't just the Czechoslovakian final opponents who felt that a larger number of inexplicable decisions had all gone against them. Many claimed that Mussolini had used undue pressure to get the Swede to referee in Italy's favor, and that Mussolini himself was behind the selection.

Eklind and Mussolini had, among other things, been seen at a shared dinner, which today would of course be completely impossible, and during the Italian national anthem before kick-off, the Swedish referee had given the fascist salute. In Italy, Eklind was remembered as "The Count of Rome", despite being banned for life as a referee for his actions during the championship. After submitting a protest, the punishment was lifted as his guilt could never be proven, and Eklind went on to referee three more matches during the 1938 and 1950 World Cups. Few talked about those matches, though; everyone remembered his two matches in the 1934 World Cup, which came to define his entire legacy. Given the history, perhaps that legacy was well-deserved. A referee's career can be ten or twenty years long at the highest level, contain tens of thousands of correct decisions, but what we are remembered for can be one mistake or a single controversial situation where we as referees actually made the right call. When I, eighty years later, during the spring of 2014, prepared myself for the World Cup in Brazil, part of me wanted to make history and referee a World Cup final, to be the first Swedish referee to have a flawless tournament and be trusted to officiate football's most important match. Another part of me was terrified of being forever associated with some incorrect decision that would haunt me for the rest of my career.

I knew that was the price that came with being a football referee at the highest level. The better the matches, the more money involved, the more people watching, the more an eventual mistake or controversial decision would cost. Yet one always wanted the biggest matches, because the reward became ever greater. You didn't think about the risks. Just like a Formula 1 driver who wants to drive faster or a mountain climber who just wants to reach higher all the time. No one thinks about the car crashing or falling from a peak. The focus is on the positive, on what gives adrenaline. When I was selected for the World Cup in January, I talked to my wife and explained that this year would be special, that I would probably be away for nearly one hundred and fifty days. With her and the rest of the family's fantastic support, it was always easier to travel away, and to come home. Any guilt and shame for not being at home during homework, school graduations, birthdays, parties, midsummer celebrations or when the children were ill in February never came from the family - only from myself. I had always believed that thorough preparation yielded the best results - whether it concerned training, equipment or studying rules, teams and tactics. With the experiences from Euro 2012 and the Under-20 World Cup in 2013, I had also built up insights into how I could most easily handle being away from my family for six or seven weeks, how my colleagues and I could stick together, have fun and not wear on each other, how we maintained our energy levels and most importantly: how we managed to be at our best when it really mattered. I knew that I was now a significantly better referee than in previous championships - that I was good at being at my best precisely when it mattered and that I thought I had understood and could handle parts of the political game.

I travelled to Rio de Janeiro extremely well-prepared. With me, I had brought my own pillow, a large and heavy bag with medicines and other items from the pharmacy, eight pairs of well-worn and tested shoes for training, running and matches on all surfaces, as well as a large bunch of newspapers, books and DVDs to kill much of the downtime while waiting for new matches.

The weeks before departure were extremely intense considering everything I had to accomplish from a referee's perspective: training, preparations, Spanish studies, planning, refereeing Allsvenskan matches and not least a series of interviews. I was Sweden's only participant in the summer's World Cup, the first World Cup referee since 2002, and therefore almost all media wanted to meet me, do interviews, take pictures and write reports, and without exception, I agreed.

I'll willingly admit that I thought it was fun, that it gave me a kick to talk about myself even though it took an extremely long amount of time. Moreover, I knew that once in Brazil, I wouldn't be allowed to give any interviews at all. But above all, I realized that I had a fantastic opportunity to make refereeing more popular in Sweden by agreeing to talk about our difficult job, create interest from more people to want to try the world's hardest job (as I called it) and maybe get some players, leaders, parents or spectators to realize that there was a person behind the referee, a human behind the decisions who always did their best. Then I had secretly promised to record a "Summer on P1" that would be broadcast five days after my return from Brazil. I was proud as a peacock, honored to have been asked - but hadn't realized how much time it would take to write a script, and tried to record in parallel with all my other preparations. But most importantly, I tried, with emphasis on tried, extra hard to be the world's best husband and father during my last weeks before the trip. I did my best to spend time with the family, to be present at my daughters' football training, watch dance performances, read bedtime stories, cook, do homework and pick up and drop off at school. We also went away for a few days to Denmark and Legoland to do something fun before dad would be away for a longer time. The last evening, I went around the house and hid several presents and scratch cards that I could then arrange treasure hunts and other fun things for my girls with from Brazil.

I set off at dawn, sneaking out like a soldier on a mission so as not to wake anyone, standing alone outside the house in the warm and sunny morning for a few minutes before the taxi at 5:00 AM swung up and I headed towards Arlanda and Brazil. As I stood outside the house in the silence, it was with mixed feelings. But once I had sat down on the plane and fifteen hours later checked into the hotel, I had disconnected my emotions to instead focus all my attention on the World Cup with great joy and confidence. On the long flight across the Atlantic, I thought through what the World Cup had meant to me throughout my life. I closed my eyes and thought through where I had been every four years since 1982 when my first World Cup memory was created. I thought back to what I had been pondering right then, what dreams I had had and how I had felt. I realized how much my life had changed at least every four years. Thinking through all the World Cups that I myself had memories of was like taking a journey through my own life, and how much the tournament had meant to me over the years. Twice before, I had been to the World Cup myself. First in 1990 in Italy, which I visited with my father and which left such deep impressions of what a World Cup could be despite the Swedish national team's fiasco. And then the 2006 World Cup in Germany, where I got to see Zidane's brain fade in the crazy World Cup final's extra time from a VIP stand. I was there together with the Qatari Nasser Al-Khelaifi, with whom I had just finalized a rights deal. A bit away in the stands sat my Swedish referee chief Bosse Karlsson, who was a referee observer in the final refereed by Argentine Horacio Elizondo.

But now it was June 1, 2014. In a few hours I would land in Brazil, and in eleven days the World Cup would begin and I was on site: ready to make history myself.

We were a total of twenty-five referees who had been selected for the World Cup. Everyone had brought two assistant referees, so that was an additional fifty people. There were also eight reserve referees, each with an assistant referee. Or support duos as they were called.

They were there as fourth officials, and as reserves if any of the seventy-five first selected referees should become injured.

With instructors, technicians, administrators and management, we were nearly one hundred and twenty-five people in total in the referee group at the referees' base camp Barra da Tijuca, about twenty kilometers outside Rio de Janeiro.

The tournament that the whole world sat down for every four years was called a World Championship. But the name itself was partly incorrect because it wasn't necessarily the world's best nations that played the tournament - rather teams from all over the world.

The teams had qualified for the World Cup in their respective confederation which roughly corresponds to the world's continents. Only a certain number of countries within each confederation could thus reach the World Cup. If one were to make a distribution based on where the best national teams were found, the tournament would look different. In reality, Europe and South America were extremely underrepresented in the World Cup in relation to how good the football was on those continents.

Personally, I had no problem with this. I thought that a World Cup should be played with teams from all corners of the world - even if it didn't always mean the thirty-two best teams.

However, the political involvement in who would referee the best matches in the tournament was harder to accept. Of course, Europe should have more referees in a World Cup. There was no doubt that the referees from UEFA were the foremost, best trained, most experienced and above all those who had the most routine to handle big matches week in and week out, with lots of audience and the world's best players on the pitch. Of course, all participating teams deserved to have the best referees officiate the most important matches, regardless of which confederation they came from. Just because teams from all over the world participated didn't mean that the referee selection had to look the same. Referees should be selected on merit, quality, competence, experience - not on which passport one had or which confederation one belonged to. It should be a matter of course. Just ask those who during a major championship have been "afflicted" by a politically appointed referee who then proved not to be up to standard and through one or more strange decisions decided their tournament. Ask an Italian what he thinks about the Ecuadorian referee Byron Moreno's straight through poor and questioned performance in the 2002 World Cup when Italy lost to South Korea. An Englishman what feelings the Tunisian referee Ali Bin Nasser evokes after he approved Maradona's handball against England in the 1986 World Cup - or for that matter the outrage against the Uruguayan assistant referee, Mauricio Espinosa, who didn't see that Frank Lampard's shot against Germany was at least a meter over the goal line in the 2010 World Cup. Or perhaps a German supporter's reaction to the linesman, Azerbaijani Tofik Bakhramov, who firmly claimed that England's ball was over the goal line in the 1966 World Cup.

Therefore, it is not unimportant to point out that one can and should of course be able to reach the World Cup, referee major championships and important matches even if one comes from a less successful football country like Luxembourg, Gambia or Seychelles. Only performances, quality and competence should determine who should referee the matches.

Just like the twenty-two players on the pitch, all referees deserved to be judged equally and given the same chances.

This of course also applies to referees from large, powerful, important countries with representation in world football's finest rooms, in committees and boards. All too often, referees with the right passport were prioritized and selected for the tournaments and once there for the most important matches.

That was wrong too, of course. The right person for the right assignment - always. Regardless of which passport you have. We were in place in Brazil eleven days before the first kick-off. The closer we got, the more nervous all referees became. The speculation was in full swing: who would get the extremely important and symbolic opening match between Brazil and Croatia? Given FIFA's neutrality principle, everyone expected that the most experienced referee who didn't come from Europe or South America would get to referee the opening match. FIFA stuck to the neutrality principle as long as there were sufficiently good referees available - and in the opening match, it would be impossible for FIFA to claim otherwise.

Therefore, it was also the Japanese Yuichi Nishimura, with experience from the 2010 World Cup, who got the honorable task of refereeing when the whole world was watching. Unfortunately, it still became an opening match to remember, but not thanks to sparkling football, nice goals or a dramatic match - but for Nishimura's performance.

Everything started pitch black for us referees. All headlines the day after were about the referee and the two situations that really stood out in Brazil's favor. Partly an elbow in the first half that gave the home star Neymar a yellow card, but which could just as well have given a red since it was intentional and with force, partly a penalty to Brazil at the score 1-1 that was incorrect. Nishimura thought that the Brazilian striker Fred was pulled down in the penalty area by a Croatian defender, but the replays showed that the attacker made the absolute most of minimal contact.

Moreover, Nishimura had disallowed a goal for Croatia when the Brazilian goalkeeper was fouled. Quite correct, in my opinion, but it only put even more focus on the referee's poor performance. Everything had gone against Croatia - everything had gone with the home team, the big favorite Brazil. In retrospect, I have understood why Nishimura awarded a penalty for Brazil. It had nothing to do with Brazil as the home nation, nothing to do with the crowd pressure or that he disliked Croatia. It was all the practical training that we had been forced to undergo that had created far too trigger-happy referees. That training was about blowing the whistle. The training players were almost always given instructions to create situations that we referees should then act on. Even if you weren't sure it was a penalty, you should blow. The more often you blew for penalties, the more praise you got. And when the players on a few occasions were given instructions to dive instead, they did it so poorly and obviously that it was easy to see the difference. Everything was actually exactly the opposite of how it is to referee football in reality. Refereeing football means that you basically shouldn't actually blow for a penalty - especially not in a World Cup and even less in an opening match - if you're not completely convinced and sure of your decision.

But Nishimura and the rest of us had in the weeks before got another behavior ingrained in our spinal cord and as a result, he awarded a penalty when he saw a light hand on the shoulder and a Brazilian player who exaggerated the contact in a realistic way.

After the opening match, the mood in our referee base camp outside Rio de Janeiro sank. Everyone understood that it had been a less than good performance, that we as a group had received quite a bit of criticism and that going forward there was extremely little room for any mistakes or questionable decisions.

Usually when referees came back to the hotel from an assignment in another city, there were high fives, hugs, congratulations and laughter.

But not when Yuichi and his team came back from São Paulo. They snuck in, sat down a bit in the shadows and kept a lower profile than usual.

I went up to them and shook hands. I didn't want to lie and say how good he had been. I thought it was better to be honest, but didn't want to avoid talking to the team altogether like some others did. Massimo Busacca had been present at the match in São Paulo, but was back already the next morning. He was in a bad mood, brief, stressed and more irritated than usual. As ultimately responsible, it was his reputation and job that were at stake. And it had started with a disaster. Nishimura was now completely frozen out, ostracized and almost isolated in FIFA's eyes. Very often, he and his team were picked out for special training - they had to jog around without any particular focus. After June 21, Nishimura and his colleagues were joined in the freezer by New Zealander Peter O'Leary and his team, who made an equally controversial performance in the match between Nigeria and Bosnia. Also a Colombian assistant referee, Humberto Clavijo, who incorrectly flagged off two goals for Mexico against Cameroon met the same fate. He was removed from his team and didn't referee any more in the tournament. But Clavijo was lucky - Mexico still won 1-0 and the focus in the media fell on other things than his mistakes. It took over two weeks before I talked to Nishimura for the first time about what had happened during the match. We ended up next to each other on the bus on the way to the Maracanã stadium where we were going to see Ecuador-France, and talked quietly about what had happened, so no one else would hear. The Japanese told me that Busacca had come down to the dressing room at half-time and shouted and carried on, without Nishimura understanding what he meant. After the match, he hadn't received a word of feedback from anyone within FIFA. He was ostracized and alone. There was no one who cared about the person behind the referee, how he felt and how he could come back. There were people within FIFA who cared, who were human, who asked how you were doing, but with a leader like Massimo Busacca at the helm, the good leaders didn't get to take much space - and the culture within the organization became worse and worse all the time.

We referees were increasingly viewed as a commodity, a product, without understanding that we had feelings, a need to receive praise or a comforting or encouraging word when things had gone to hell. There was hardly anyone who saw the human behind. No one who valued the work before the World Cup - it was only performance that mattered. If you didn't deliver, you didn't exist. That hardly made the referees better, rather more insecure and thus worse.

After a few days, FIFA had its first review for all referees where they told us what they thought about a number of important situations. In typical FIFA manner, nothing that was shown was clearly or directly incorrectly handled by the referees. This included all of Nishimura's questionable decisions.

The strategy was: admit no mistake, defend it as far as possible.

Massimo Busacca insisted that there had indeed been contact between the players at the penalty in the opening match, even if it was minimal.

This unwillingness to admit mistakes made us quickly internally assign Busacca a new nickname in line with Baghdad Bob, the Iraqi minister who during the invasion of the country in 2003 had insisted that they were not losing the war: Brazil Busacca. But FIFA's ostrich mentality also resulted in the reviews becoming extremely unclear and theoretical. For less confident and experienced referees, who might not always be very good at English, it meant great risks that they would misunderstand, or not understand at all, how they were expected to act. But at all costs, it was important to avoid criticizing the referees' performances. If FIFA directed any kind of internal criticism towards decisions and thus towards the referees, they would simultaneously admit that they had prepared them and trained them incorrectly, and also selected the wrong referees for the tournament. So it was best to never criticize the referees' performances, neither internally nor externally. FIFA and the referees never made mistakes - that mentality was incredibly deeply rooted in the organization's leaders. It absolutely didn't set the stage for becoming better and developing. On the contrary. The tournament had begun - but all days during our last two weeks had looked the same, so we began to feel restless and wished that something would happen. While referees began to travel out for matches, we remained at the hotel in Rio de Janeiro with the same routines every day. Wake up at seven, immediately drink half a liter of water, fill a new bottle with water and electrolyte drink and then go out and wake up the body with a few kilometers of nice walk together with Mathias and Daniel along the beautiful beach.

Then back to the hotel, eat breakfast, up to the room, apply sunscreen, pack the bag, down to the bus, every day for security reasons take different routes to the training facility, train for just over two hours, pack into the buses again, take yet another new route back to the hotel, hurry to get to the hotel's elevators to not have a hundred people standing in line before, up to the room, shower and shave every other day, eat lunch, drink a cup of coffee and then attend a several hours long theoretical lecture by Busacca.

For me, leadership is about being a role model. That is, acting in the same way as you tell other people to act.

To practice what you preach. Massimo Busacca absolutely did not live up to those guidelines, on the contrary, he was hypocritical and demanded one thing from his surroundings - and then acted himself in a completely different way.

Of course, mobile phones were forbidden during our long, theoretical sessions. Everyone probably understood that. But once, during the more than six weeks we were in Brazil, someone among the hundred referees had forgotten to turn off the signal on their mobile phone. It rang loudly, and although the referee quickly turned off the sound, Busacca reacted immediately by snorting, sighing and making a sarcastic comment that the World Cup apparently wasn't an important enough reason to turn off the signal on one's mobile.

During a lecture a few days later, a mobile phone rang again. Everyone held their breath, which poor soul was going to get a telling-off this time? Busacca glared at us in the audience for a short second, before he realized that it was his own phone that was ringing. He took it out of his pocket, looked at the display and then said: "This is very, very important, I need to go." Then he went out and left the stage empty. After a minute, he was replaced by another person who tried to gather up what was left of the presentation. Busacca always demanded full attendance from everyone in the entire FIFA team, including physical coaches, instructors and masseurs. During the most technical parts, it was almost ridiculous that those who were not referees or instructors should sit and listen to everything that was said - what would a Brazilian masseur do with several hours of discussions about assessments, running or interpretation of the handball rule? But Busacca insisted. For him, it was important that everyone was always present. He demanded total silence and full attention from everyone present in the room.

But when someone else was talking, which admittedly didn't happen very often, other rules applied. Busacca could answer or make calls, talk loudly with someone else without respect for the person at the podium.

Of course, we speculated in the team about what our first match would be. As always in my mental preparations, I hedged my expectations and hopes. Regardless of which match FIFA had assigned me, I would still have said it was the best match we could have gotten. I was so happy, grateful, charged and ready to accept anything to make my World Cup debut. I wanted to referee early, but not too early. I wanted to referee good teams, but not too good. Preferably well-known European teams, but not too strong nations that could go far in the tournament. The only thing I knew was that I wanted to leave our camp in Rio de Janeiro and instead travel away for three days - change food, environment, hotel, city and surroundings. We needed it after almost two weeks with exactly the same routines daily. It was Friday morning, the day after the tough opening match when the Japanese referee Nishimura had blown a wrong penalty in favor of the host nation. The mood in the referee group was not at its best, everyone felt the seriousness and how tough the coming days would be. When I came down to the reception, FIFA's deputy head of referees Manuel Navarro, the in comparison incredibly respectful, kind, friendly and warm Swiss, was looking for me as the referees slouched off to the buses that would take us to Friday's training. He asked me to follow him for a moment. We went a bit to the side so no one would hear, and then Manuel congratulated me and told me that I had a match on Monday in Natal: USA vs Ghana. The reason he told me this already now was that I and the team would have to travel immediately after it was announced on Saturday. I had to promise not to tell anyone else before then. The selection of all matches became public two days before, and the practice was that the referees who would travel from Rio de Janeiro left the day before to the match venue. But because our flight to Natal was long, over three hours, FIFA wanted us to travel already two days before, that is, the same day as the selection was officially announced.

Almost all referees had seen that Manuel had taken me aside, and understood that I had received some special information. Therefore, most people looked at me a little extra when I a minute later entered the bus as the last person. But I couldn't say anything yet. So I walked through the entire long bus with a warm and wonderful feeling spreading in my body. When I sat down at the back next to Mathias and Daniel, I tried to act cool, not smile or look happy, but it didn't go so well.

After a few seconds of attempted poker face, I told them which match we would referee on Monday. Three days after the news, I blew the whistle for our World Cup debut in a Natal that upon our arrival on Saturday had welcomed us with a tropical rain that never seemed to end. It had been pouring for several days, but the forecast for our kick-off was clear and warm: close to thirty degrees despite the match starting at 19:00.

I remember the day before and the match day itself as if in a daze. A sense of unreality lay over the fact that this was the football World Cup and it was actually me of all people who would referee the match. I became almost feverish at the thought that FIFA had given me the responsibility and trust to referee with the whole world's eyes on me. That it was also the USA was special. Not because it was a particularly big football nation. But the USA was a world power, a football country of the future, and I knew that the match would be followed by nearly twenty-five million TV viewers in North America alone. It felt strange to see hundreds of military personnel guarding our hotel, to ride with a crazily overdimensioned police escort to the arena and see thousands of people standing along the road cheering. When as a referee you find yourself in football's absolute finest room, at the best matches and biggest arenas, you enter a bubble of concentration where you really shut out all feelings that you don't need to make the right decision in each of the 5,400 seconds that a match lasts.

I think you have to have been a referee to understand the feeling of loneliness you feel - despite having people around you all the time. How for a limited time you disconnect everything that isn't essential for one reason: to be able to make the right decisions, not be pressured, stressed or influenced. I loved getting into the bubble, to step by step enter that almost meditative feeling that was created and as a result of which I neither saw nor heard the audience. I can miss the feeling of managing to keep away thoughts that I could actually fail. I never thought about the fact that everything I said was constantly being recorded and that my bosses, whether they were called Busacca or Collina, could listen through everything I had said on the pitch whenever they wanted. When I refereed football at the highest level, I entered my own world where nothing could affect me. The USA's football-loving then Vice President and current President Joe Biden was in Natal to combine a little football with political meetings, but hadn't even had time to enter the VIP stand and sit down before Clint Dempsey gave the country the lead after just thirty seconds - one of the fastest goals in World Cup history. I could hardly believe my eyes. My life's first whistle in a World Cup final tournament was for a goal. I have, apart from my first whistle, very few memories from the match. As usual, it's fragmentary still images that remain in my cerebral cortex. The first image is a situation in injury time of the first half when Ghanaian Sulley Muntari comes in late and tackles American Jermaine Jones. When Jones falls to the ground he is irritated, and as a reaction he flicks with his feet which then hit Muntari in the head. According to the rulebook, it can, theoretically, be two red cards. One for the tackle and one for the feet that then, even if unintentional, hit Muntari's head. It might have been a bit too strict, but it should be at least two yellow cards. And a free kick to the USA, since Muntari started it all with his tackle. In my ear, my assistant Daniel shouts loud and clear: "YELLOW CARD, you must warn them." I know that Daniel is absolutely right in principle.

But at the same time I hear in my head Massimo Busacca's voice which for weeks has preached that we shouldn't warn if we don't absolutely need to and definitely not show red cards if it isn't our last resort.

Muntari quickly gets up and leans down irritatedly towards the lying Jones. Muntari is just about to take a stranglehold when I make a lightning-fast decision - I choose to try to solve everything with a large portion of self-confidence and presence, even if it's completely wrong according to the rules.

I place a calm and cautious hand on his shoulder to show that I see what's happening. He calms down, interrupts the stranglehold and instead starts to hold his head which hurts. I don't know what I'm saying, but it's words that calm. And when Jones gets up, a number of other players come there to mark their presence, but they too quickly calm down.

If I'm to single out any moment from my career that I'm most satisfied with, it's what happened in Natal after forty-five minutes.

Even if I did wrong, seen to how the rulebook is written.

If the selections of referees in FIFA are political, then the selection of fourth officials takes another step down into the political quagmire. Our fourth official in the match was called Norbert Hauata and came from French Polynesia. He was the world's nicest and kindest guy, but whether he had the competence to be at a World Cup I wasn't quite as sure about. Partly he lacked experience from international football in general, partly assignments as fourth official in particular. The football aspect was one thing, a much bigger problem was our communication and Norbert's inadequate English. Since we in the team during the match would speak Swedish with each other, and only during short moments and seconds switch to English to give instructions or ask questions to Norbert, we knew that the stress and the high volume on the pitch would probably mean that we would have to speak both quickly and forcefully. Likely, Norbert wouldn't keep up, and therefore we had decided before kick-off to keep him out as much as possible, only when it was absolutely necessary would we include him in the discussions. Part of the fourth official's role is to communicate with coaches and leaders on the substitute benches, answer questions and provide information - so we understood that language would be a problem since both benches were English-speaking. Therefore, we had decided that Mathias, who was the assistant referee closest to the benches, after we had talked in our communication equipment would check with Norbert and really make sure that he had understood what we said. Still, it goes wrong at the end of the match, and it could have been a disaster for us.

After the first matches in the tournament, we had understood that FIFA quietly thought that the referees had been a bit too stingy with added time, that we shouldn't be afraid to add the time required. Of course, we shouldn't make up extra time, but rather round up a minute than down.

With FIFA's thoughts in our heads, we approach the end of the match.

We would preferably blow the whistle directly after ninety minutes to avoid anything that could negatively affect our first World Cup performance. But we need to add at least a couple of minutes.

Should we settle for three minutes as the heart and brain want? Or should we take FIFA's opinions into account and round up a minute? We reason for a few seconds, and in the team come to the conclusion that we will add four minutes. It's a bit much, but we can argue for it - moreover, we know that FIFA supports us in our reasoning, if needed.

I call on Norbert and announce our decision. After several dubious replies back and forth, I think the decision has gotten through to him but I still feel a bit unsure. I ask Mathias stressfully to really check that Norbert has understood how many minutes it's about. When I hear that Mathias for the fourth time repeats the number of additional minutes, I breathe out. But when Norbert goes up to the sideline and shows his board with the added time, the number five still lights up on the screen. The American bench with head coach Jürgen Klinsmann at the forefront goes completely crazy - and starts shouting at Norbert and Mathias. They're leading their World Cup premiere, had hoped for three minutes of added time, were ready to accept four minutes, but five minutes is way too much.

The rulebook doesn't take into account misunderstandings, language barriers and colleagues from French Polynesia with poor English. So when the fourth official has shown the added time, it can be increased by the referee, but not decreased. We must play five minutes - even if it's completely wrong, and contrary to our decision.

I try to stay calm, not get upset at Norbert or waste energy on what I can't influence. Now we're going to play five minutes, and it's just to hope that nothing will happen during the last minute of the match - because then Klinsmann and the USA will rage, the time will be scrutinized and everyone will realize that it was crazy with so much added time. Then our World Cup debut would become a fiasco with a match-deciding mistake. But fortunately, nothing happens. The USA holds on and when I blow the final whistle, I feel an enormous pride, joy and tiredness in the almost thirty-degree heat. All players from both teams thank us, and we leave the pitch without anyone throwing anything at us, shouting at us or even thinking about the referee team. In the player tunnel, we meet Joe Biden and his entire entourage, on their way down to the USA's dressing room. He is pleased and radiates joy after the opening victory. We are also satisfied and when we close the door to our dressing room, we can hug, cheer and play some music. We take our time drinking sports drinks to recover, stretch, fill in reports, respond to the first messages from home and enjoy the feeling that we have gotten away with a match in the World Cup without anyone talking about us. Then we can finally leave the dressing room and drive back to the hotel with the same enormous police protection as when we traveled to the arena a few hours earlier - even though it hadn't been necessary. This time we could have walked back to the hotel in the warm Brazilian evening.

 We eat the late dinner at the hotel in the only open restaurant. Only a handful of people are present, and we sit down, order a salad, pizza and a beer. I'm not really very hungry, that feeling usually always comes first when you start eating after having completely emptied yourself for a few hours.

It's calm and nice in the restaurant, we can talk and the music is just right. But while we wait for our food, a bunch of American supporters come in and completely take over the restaurant.

We consider whether we should leave the premises immediately, and take the food with us to the room - so as not to end up in a situation where we could be accused of celebrating the victory together with American supporters. But we decide to stay.

Our dinner becomes a kind of practical test of the motto that "a good referee is not seen". We eat our pizzas, dessert, drink coffee and none of the hundreds of Americans look at us, want to talk to us or make the slightest hint of recognizing us.

Coming home to our base camp after a successful match was like standing in a shower of praise, getting pats on the back, kind words and meeting constant high fives.

Massimo Busacca, on the other hand, always had difficulty giving praise. He was hard to read, said nothing special but congratulated us briefly on the match and asked: "Did you enjoy it?" That was his way. We had to get praise from others.

We knew somewhere that we would get another match after our acclaimed performance during the first match day. We sat out the second round, other referees were in action with both good and less good results, but we continued to train with focus and did everything we could to endure the tedium that came with the practical training.

But apart from the training, which I still despised, everything was dreamlike. The food was good, the weather brilliant and I and the team thrived together, the body was in top shape, we had done a fantastic first match and moreover we got to see all the matches played at the classic Maracanã on site.

We traveled an hour before kick-off with our bus directly from the hotel to the arena, again with a generous police escort so that we avoided queues. Once there, we stepped out, went straight into the VIP section, ate and drank well before, during the break and after the match - and then went back to the hotel. Visiting FIFA's VIP section at a World Championship is a spectacle. There, the world's potentates from the organization mingle, sponsors and more sponsors who pay millions of dollars to have their brands associated with the world's largest sporting event, TV personalities, rights holders, football profiles, politicians, actors, people with too much money ... and then a bunch of referees who are free from assignments.

The luxury is in abundance, the food lavish and is not only changed between matches but also during matches. The dishes served are different before, during the break and afterwards. You leave neither hungry nor thirsty from the arenas. The sponsored beer is free, the wines expensive and the ice-cold champagne served is from Moët & Chandon. The seats included are the best, directly outside the VIP lounge where well-dressed hostesses show the way if you can't find your way to your seat.

During one of our visits to Maracanã, we were to see Spain meet Chile.

I, Mathias and Daniel stood in a corner with a plate each and looked at the spectacle in the VIP lounge. But at the same time as we laughed at how crazy everything was, we enjoyed being as far as you can get from our everyday life in Sweden with life puzzles, grocery shopping, lawn mowing, pickups at school and a constant problem with staying home with sick children. In the middle of the buzz, we suddenly noticed that something happened that changed the dynamics in the room. A person came in and created an enormous commotion. People went there, shouted, took pictures, asked for selfies and were completely beside themselves. It was very strange, because in these VIP rooms you hardly raised an eyebrow if Franz Beckenbauer sat down at the table next to you or Gary Lineker had a beer at the bar. The person who created the commotion remained in the far part of the room, and more and more people drifted there. Then I saw three people who immediately revealed who it was that had made people go crazy - Helena Seger and the sons Maximilian and Vincent glided through the room, completely unnoticed, sat down at a table and started eating and drinking. The boys wanted ice cream and sat there with an ice cream cone each.

Left standing was the mighty Zlatan Ibrahimović whom people flocked around. They took pictures and autographs, wanted to chat or just hang in his presence. Of course, as a referee, I can envy big stars like Zlatan who actually play football and don't referee, who score goals, who can become heroes, who get supporters to shout their names and who, even if it's least important of all, earn insanely much more than a referee. But when I see Zlatan who can barely move a step, and his family sitting alone in solitude a few tables away, I realize that I would never want to swap lives with Zlatan. That everyone wants a piece of him, all the time. To always have to think about at least trying to be nice and accommodating. If he and his family are so watched here, in a closed VIP lounge at Maracanã, how is it then when he goes out on the town? Stays at a hotel? Eats at a restaurant? After that evening in June in Rio de Janeiro, I often think back to Zlatan every time someone asks if I wouldn't rather have been a world-class player. I realize how much I love being in the middle of the pitch, at the big arenas among full stands and shouting supporters, right among all the world stars. How much I enjoy being challenged and making the difficult decisions. But I also understand that I even more love that after the match and the end of the workday, I completely disappear from people's consciousness.

When I stand there and observe how Zlatan is courted, I suddenly hear a voice calling me in the VIP lounge. I look up. It's an old acquaintance, a person I have intentionally tried to avoid in recent years due to the conflict of interest that our respective roles can create, Nasser Al-Khelaifi, the president of Paris Saint-Germain, that is, Zlatan's boss.

We hug each other, talk quickly and intensely about what has happened, how we are doing, how big our oldest daughters have become, how quickly time passes, that it would be fun to see each other some other time at another occasion when I'm no longer refereeing football and when a World Cup match isn't around the corner in a few minutes. Meanwhile, the circus around Zlatan continues in the other end of the room. Two days later it was Midsummer Eve. Celebrating the finest and brightest holiday without my family and instead with my referee colleagues abroad had become a necessary tradition. The year 2014 was of course no exception, and after the usual training on Midsummer Eve we danced around a FIFA flag, sent home the film and wished everyone a happy Midsummer. After that, we quickly went to the hotel, showered and changed before we skipped the usual lunch buffet and instead waited for the room service that had been ordered in detail a few days earlier. Just after one o'clock there was a knock on the door and in came the puzzled serving staff carrying various platters and bowls with boiled potatoes, strawberries, whipped cream, boiled eggs and some butter in small packages.

When the staff had gone out, we complemented what had already been served from our packing from Sweden: herring, crispbread, Swedish snaps, packaged salmon. Plus the purchased beer from a nearby store that Daniel had efficiently and discreetly smuggled up to the room in his backpack. Then we celebrated Midsummer in as traditional a way as we could, even though I on that day and evening longed extra much for my girls in Sweden.

Two days later we set course for our next match in Brasília. Just a few days earlier, Busacca had read out our upcoming assignment as the last of seven assignments presented at the time. We had almost given up the thought of a new match when the nonchalant Swiss, a bit listlessly read out the assignment that all referees dreamed of: Cameroon vs Brazil.

We were to referee Brazil. In a World Cup. On home soil, in the capital Brasília. We had been entrusted to referee a home nation in the great national sport, a Brazil that were favorites to win the tournament, who had won the Confederations Cup the year before, who had won the most titles of all nations through the ages and who were now going to play their hundredth World Cup match.

The match against Cameroon was also fateful. Brazil needed to take points to avoid risking being eliminated and preferably they should win to get the easy path to the final that everyone had already planned for. Brazil's first match against Croatia had as mentioned led to big discussions about Yuichi Nishimura's performance, that he should have given possible advantages to the home nation, that FIFA at all costs wanted Brazil to advance. Therefore, our selection was extra honorable, but at the same time risky. Refereeing Brazil was mined territory, a high-risk project, a ticking bomb that could detonate if we made a controversial or questionable decision - it didn't even have to be incorrect. As strange as it sounds, I loved it. The greater the risk, the more important match, the bigger kick afterwards. I longed for the kick-off, looked forward to the challenge, to all eyes being directed at me, to a tough match. I had decided in advance that I would manage it, regardless of what happened during the match, and I was already looking forward to the enormous feeling that I knew would follow afterwards.

The headlines in Sweden made both me and my family proud. "Eriksson referees Brazil's big match", wrote Aftonbladet, and Expressen made a special front page for Luleå that ended up on mom and dad's fridge: "Luleå referee Jonas Eriksson gets dream match in World Cup." I was scrutinized in Brazilian media before the decisive group stage match. I was called the millionaire and apart from my private finances, my height and previous decisions were discussed. None of that I read or took in. However, we noticed that the match and our selection were written up. At the hotel in Brasília, we were recognized in a completely different way. People shouted, pointed and cars honked at us on our morning walks. We usually waved happily back, even though we didn't understand a word of what people said.

We left the hotel one hundred and twenty minutes before kick-off in two cars, surrounded by a bunch of police in cars and motorcycles for security reasons.

On the way to the arena, there were people everywhere. Estádio Nacional Mané Garrincha towered up like a circular spaceship that had landed right out on the Brazilian highlands where the capital had been built sixty years earlier.

Already upon arrival at the arena, it was almost full in the stands. When we ninety minutes before the match started to change, we heard the audience faintly chanting: "Brasil, Brasil, Brasil!" We understood what discharge awaited. Shortly after, we got the usual briefing from FIFA regarding the security situation. We were told that it would of course be full, hardly any supporters from Cameroon, the remaining seventy thousand spectators all supported Brazil. No order problems were expected - if Brazil won and advanced, that is. Otherwise, there was a risk of riots. Not just outside the arena, but maybe in all of Brazil. I, Mathias and Daniel looked at each other. We didn't need to say that this was the most important match in our careers, that this was when it mattered, that we had to perform at the top when the whole world was watching and that despite the pressure from the home nation we would referee as neutrally as usual.

In retrospect, I don't think I understood how important the match was and how crucial my performance was for the entire tournament and for my own future. Maybe it was lucky. When I look back at the World Cup in general and Brazil vs Cameroon in particular, I understand how much was at stake, what forces were at play and what could have happened if I had had a bad day at work.

I wouldn't have been able to move freely, would have received death threats against me and my family, with the greatest probability been sent home to Sweden immediately and my future career as a referee would have received an irreparable blow.

But no such negative thoughts are in my head before the match.

Just thoughts that in less than two hours I will be sitting in the dressing room and then will be able to enjoy a performance that hopefully went unnoticed by everyone.

When the Brazilian captain Thiago Silva comes forward and greets cordially, I feel fantastic. In the pictures I see afterwards, I am smiling, happy, calm and confidence-inspiring when Silva welcomes me to his home country and we chat in the player tunnel.

From inside the arena, I hear AC/DC's fantastic power song "Thunderstruck" at full volume. I get goosebumps and shiver. I long until I can take the players out onto the green grass and a few minutes thereafter blow the whistle to start the match. The music stops and then I hear the rumble. The roar and screams from seventy thousand people who simultaneously cheer, whistle and shout. After a few seconds, the audience changes and I hear the chant through the concrete walls: "Brasil, Brasil, Brasil, Brasil!" At a given signal, we begin the march in. First down the stairs, then over a flat surface that is maybe ten meters long, and then we take the twelve steps up towards the green pitch. We are forced to walk slowly because Brazil insists that all players walk in time and keep their left hand on the shoulder of the player in front. It doesn't bother me at all, instead I get to enjoy a few extra seconds in what is perhaps the loudest moment in my entire referee career.

I'm first up of all from the steep stairs, I know that the whole world is watching me right now. I take a few steps, look up at all the spectators and hear how they scream. I take the match ball and for a short second I close my eyes and imagine that all this cheering is for me and my colleagues. When I then look up, I smile broadly, I have no memory of that but I see it on the TV images afterwards. I do remember, however, what I thought when I looked up at the stands. That everyone had put on their Swedish national team shirts to support the Swedish referee team.

It was a yellow arena as far as the eye could see, and I imagined for a second that we were on home turf, that everyone in the stands was our supporters and convinced myself that we had ninety fantastic minutes ahead of us.

FIFA has a rule that says that only ninety seconds of each country's national anthem should be played before the matches. For Brazil, which has an intro, without singing, which in itself is thirty seconds and a national anthem that is considerably longer than that, FIFA chose to stop the national anthem after the first verse. But that didn't stop either players or audience from continuing to sing without music. I stood still and shivered. I have never experienced a more powerful backdrop, I was taken and I dare promise that those who were present got a memory for life.

The closer we get to kick-off, the more I enter my bubble of concentration. The first free kick is already after thirty seconds. The one who creates it is one of the most powerful players I have ever refereed - a muscle mountain of almost ninety kilos, distributed over one hundred and eighty centimeters and with the most fitting nickname I have ever encountered. Givanildo Vieira de Souza, or as it is written above number 7 on the back with clear letters: HULK. The nickname comes from his physical playing style, from his power and speed. He is extremely fearless and immediately at the start of the match sets full speed on the home team's right flank. The only way for Cameroon to stop Hulk is to literally wrestle him down, and that's exactly what happens in the first minute of the match. The Brazilian is pulled down in a good position, and I could easily have shown a yellow card - but I solve it with a free kick and a warning. I can see that I look confident in my decision, that I seem convincing - but when I see the situation afterwards, hear how the audience screams and puts pressure on me, I can wonder how the hell I withstood the pressure. The noise level is crazy, and becomes even higher as the Brazilian players constantly, at every whistle and stop in play, turn towards the audience and with their arms urge them to scream and cheer. When Neymar after fifteen minutes gets a light push from the Cameroonian full-back Allan Nyom, it happens outside the pitch when play is stopped, the audience explodes. Again I stand against them, even though I can of course warn Nyom, I choose to give the Cameroonian a proper telling-off instead.

So after seventeen minutes it happens. Neymar makes it 1-0 for the home team, and a whole nation and everyone in the audience cheer. I have never experienced anything like it. Then the match hangs in the balance. The home team loses its aggressiveness and allows Cameroon to step up onto the pitch. The "Indomitable Lions", as the national team is called, first hit the crossbar and a minute later Cameroon equalizes to 1-1. For ten nervous minutes the audience falls silent. The home heroes lose initiative and self-confidence. Is the catastrophe about to happen? Is Brazil about to be eliminated? Will Mexico or Croatia overtake the huge favorites? The players feel the seriousness, there are more misplaced passes, more free kicks and Brazil becomes more and more cautious.

But then, right before half-time, Neymar scores 2-1. I can see the relief in the faces of the players, the coaches and the 65,000 spectators. I feel relieved too. Not because Brazil is winning, but because the match is going smoothly and without major incidents. I'm satisfied with my own and the team's performance in the first half, but hopefully my leadership in the first half has helped me on the way. Even if most things have gone well, there is one thing that grates from the first forty-five minutes. What the players in both teams have been most upset about are the balls - several players have complained about the air pressure in them, and on numerous occasions they have demonstratively thrown them away and had them replaced. Our routine was that the balls left in the dressing room should always be checked by the fourth official ninety minutes before kick-off, and then fifteen minutes before the start of the match be handed out to the person responsible for the balls. The reason we referees want to keep the balls during this time is that the home team, which is responsible for the balls, can otherwise choose to let out air and play with intentionally too loose balls or alternatively pump them harder. We ask our fourth official, Svein Oddvar Moen, if he really checked the pressure in the balls. He answers that he absolutely did, but Daniel, the one in our team who has the best eye for details, looks doubtful. He takes out his own gauge, inserts it into the match ball that I brought from the first half and says shockingly: "But hell, we only have 0.4 bar in the ball." It's far too little. A football should have an air pressure corresponding to 0.6-1.1 bar, and at elite level the value usually lies closer to 1.0.

But air pressure can also be measured in the unit psi, and on a normal gauge you see both scales. Svein has simply read wrong, looked at psi instead of bar and chosen to empty the balls of air before kick-off. We have played a half in the World Cup with far too loose balls, rather resembling a bunch of beach balls without steering and control. Svein runs a bit shamefacedly out to the chief of the balls and makes sure that they are pumped up to the right levels before the second half. After that, we in the team have learned to always check the balls ourselves to avoid ending up in the same situation again. When we have solved the problem with the balls and go out for the second half, I just want the match to be over. After five minutes we see Brazil make it 3-1. After the Brazilian forward Fred's goal, the match is more or less decided, but I can't relax yet. I must not miss a warning for any of the three Brazilian players who already have a warning and thus risk being suspended in the round of 16, and an incorrect penalty can nullify my chances of getting to referee another match in the tournament. Therefore, I am still in my bubble and on my toes all the time, running at maximum when needed, concentrated even when the play is a bit slower and more cautious. When after four minutes of added time I can finally blow the final whistle, I allow myself to breathe out. I lower my shoulders, look up at the stands, see all the spectators in the yellow ocean and hear for the first time their song and cheers outside my bubble. What I don't know right then is that Brazil has won the group on goal difference - that the goals the team has scored have been decisive for "Seleção", as the national team is called, to advance with the placement in the group that everyone expected, with the future draw that everyone wants to see. I don't want to leave the pitch. I try to stay extra long on this warm evening and enjoy, take in the atmosphere, hear the audience hail their heroes and shake hands with all the satisfied players. Neymar who was substituted in the second half comes up to me. His upper body is bare, well-trained with clear tattoos. Over his shoulder hangs a sweaty Cameroonian national team shirt that he has exchanged. He shakes hands, and laughs lightly when I wish him good luck in the tournament. And not only the winners come forward and thank. Even the eliminated Cameroon's big star, the tall Stéphane

Mbia, gives me a high five and a sweaty hug, which feels okay since his team just lost the match. A step behind comes the hirsute David Luiz. He looks almost exactly like the character Sideshow Bob in "The Simpsons". Even though I like him, I absolutely don't want a hug from him. I want to referee the home nation one more time in the tournament, and then it's less good to have been too friendly and hugged. I stop his hand in the middle of a high five, say some words of praise in English to him and Luiz responds with a wink and a pat on the shoulder. As a referee, you can never win a match or score a goal, but closer to a victory than the feeling I had in the dressing room afterwards I'll probably never come. When I finally become completely alone, minutes after almost a billion people have seen me in action - it can't be described, it must be experienced. I sit down and a few seconds later my colleagues come walking. We gather in a sweaty and long group hug, and breathe out. Our Norwegian fourth and fifth officials, Svein Oddvar Moen and Kim Haglund, come into the dressing room and we hug again. We are so happy, satisfied and full of adrenaline. We can't sit still, we want to celebrate the performance with song, dance and even more hugs. Usually we put on happy and positive Swedish music after the matches. But now we want to celebrate together with our Norwegian friends. But which song suits everyone? What happy, Swedish-Norwegian songs can all five of us sing? We ponder, search on Spotify, before someone cracks it: "Play 'La det swinge', for God's sake." The winning song in Eurovision 1985 with Norwegian Hanne Krogh and Swedish Elisabeth Andreassen starts, and there we dance around and sing along. Five men in their forties with bare upper bodies, filled with energy and adrenaline. The song goes on repeat and we sing louder each time it starts. The third time the song repeats, we interrupt in the middle, because we have received unexpected visitors.

We have played such loud music that we haven't heard that there has been a knock on the door, that a person has snuck into our dressing room and is now standing wide-eyed looking at our strange Nordic war dance.

"You seem to enjoy", says Samuel Eto'o and laughs.

The Cameroonian striker, the legend who among others has represented Barcelona, Inter, Chelsea and not least for two years Russian Anzhi Makhachkala, where Eto'o was then the world's highest paid football player.

Now he has just finished his fourth World Cup, and also his national team career, he tells us. This is his last international match and he wonders a bit apologetically and pleadingly if he could get the match ball.

I lie and say that we unfortunately didn't bring the match ball in from the pitch, but that he otherwise would of course have gotten it. Because in my bag is already the ball, which I intend to keep. It's my memory, from my World Cup match. Eto'o instead has to ask for a ball in the room next to ours, where the chief of the match balls sits and he is guaranteed to have better luck. After the match, the only thing that clouds our joy and fantastic feeling is Brazil's 3-1 goal that Fred headed in after David Luiz's hard cross. It's a tight offside, but Mathias is perfectly positioned, cool and chooses not to flag.

When the replay images come, the TV production freezes the image correctly when the ball is played, but what goes wrong is where the line is drawn, the line that shows the world's TV viewers if Fred was on the right or wrong side.

Since David Luiz and the ball are in front of the second last defender in Cameroon, the line should actually be drawn from the ball's most offensive point - not at the second last defender's most defensive body part.

Simply put, it means that the line that the whole world's TV viewers see clearly shows that Mathias, and thus I as responsible, have made a big and match-deciding mistake. And TV viewers were not lacking. Just in Sweden, nearly 1.3 million people watched SVT's broadcast and in total, the estimate was that just under a billion viewers followed the match in some way.

Several TV channels and newspapers prove not to be sufficiently knowledgeable or source-critical, and have therefore followed the line that FIFA has drawn. We receive harsh criticism in several media. We see the images ourselves in the dressing room on Mathias' mobile phone. For a few seconds I have a lump in my stomach: Was it wrong? Has our decision affected the match? It didn't matter that it was my assistant referee who made a mistake in that case - it would affect me just as much.

Mathias is always confident in his decision, but really irritated, even angry, at FIFA for drawing the line incorrectly. We sigh, know that we have done right - but also that the media in ignorance will criticize me and Mathias for the decision. It matters less that FIFA the day after issues a press release where they correct where the line should be drawn, and thus prove us right - the error is already established for those who followed the TV broadcast. We leave the arena an hour later, drive the fifteen minutes by car to the hotel and wherever we look, people are celebrating with dancing, singing and happy faces. We arrive at the hotel with our police escort, security guards check that everything is calm in the lobby before they give the all-clear for us to go in. Even there a celebration is going on, a bit more subdued than out on the streets, but still. When we walk through the reception in our suits, people stop, turn around and wonder curiously: who was that? Someone shouts loudly: "Árbitros!" The referees! A spontaneous applause breaks out, and I smile a bit embarrassedly on my way to the elevator. We go up to our rooms, I go into the room and take off my uncomfortable suit, change into something more relaxed. It's too late to call home to the family. It's now almost nine in the evening local time, and thus well after midnight at home in Sweden.

I send some quick messages to my wife, my children and to my parents in Luleå. We'll talk tomorrow, I think, as I leave the room and knock on the door to Daniel's room.

There we hug our only supporter in the stands - Gunnar Söderström. He had, just like for the Under-20 World Cup in Turkey a year earlier, arrived incognito and during today's match secretly sat in the stands and cheered us on.

When Gunnar came to Istanbul and with his presence changed the dynamics in our group, it gave us new energy in an incredibly positive way. Therefore, we had decided that we would do the same thing in Brazil.

In secret, just like the year before. We were 23 days into our stay, had as a dream to stay for another 21 days until the final was played - so Gunnar's energetic addition, halfway through our journey, once again became an enormously important boost for us. But Gunnar is not allowed to join for dinner. We eat it together with our observer from Rwanda, we get some kind words of compliments about our performance, drink some ice-cold and sponsored beers on the outdoor terrace and enjoy our greatest success in our careers. When we the next day returned to the referee headquarters in Barra da Tijuca, Massimo Busacca was more angry than happy. It was as always clearly visible in his body language. Praise was not to be thought of, he barely greeted when we came back to the hotel. Italy had been eliminated from the tournament after losing in the directly decisive match against Uruguay, but maybe it wasn't the result that bothered the referee chief the most. In the match, referee Marco Rodríguez had missed that Uruguayan Luis Suárez had bitten Italian defender Giorgio Chiellini in the shoulder. It should have meant a red card, and apart from that mistake, an Italian player had, a bit too easily, been sent off already after 58 minutes.

The referee's performance and decisions had affected the team that had then been eliminated from the tournament and then it became all the more sensitive. Now it wasn't just any country that had been affected - it was the incredibly powerful and boot-shaped neighboring country to Switzerland.

But it wasn't just that match that bothered Busacca. He was irritated about many other things and other people, especially a person with almost the same surname as me: Ericson, Niclas in first name.

Swedish Ericson from Alingsås was namely director of FIFA's TV division and thus chief of all sales of rights, production and service and the one who ultimately, at the top of the hierarchy, was responsible for ensuring that the TV production did the right thing and for example drew an offside line in the right place.

"They have one job, and they fail at it. Now the whole world thinks we made a mistake, which we absolutely didn't", said Busacca when we had a review of our match in Brasília in front of the whole group. Mathias, on the other hand, got no praise at all for having managed the difficult situation.

When the group stage was over, all the referees had for the first time a completely free day. FIFA therefore arranged a joint excursion to the mountain Corcovado, where the thirty-eight meter high, mighty Christ statue Cristo Redentor stands at the top.

Actually, I hated joint excursions, social contexts where you were forced to experience things together. I always preferred to do things when I wanted to, at the pace I wished, but a smooth and quick police-escorted bus through Rio de Janeiro in rush hour traffic made me choose the arranged tour. I have an incredibly hard time enjoying, stopping, owning the moment. I'm never really satisfied when I stand still, want things to happen all the time, that there should be something around the corner or that you should be in motion in some way. When queues arise in connection with the visit to the mountain, this becomes clear. My colleagues and I try to get down from the top in a smoother way and avoid the queues. Everything is governed by my restlessness. It's troublesome, it makes me not even in Brazil at a World Cup, in the midst of the highlight of my football life, able to enjoy, relax and take it a little easier. Instead, I want to move forward and be in motion on the way down from the mountain. After a long walk down the slopes, we just make it to the buses and can return to the hotel.

During the weeks in Brazil, I also took the time to talk to the FIFA representatives, especially the Swiss in Blatter's entourage, when I ran into them. I was careful to go up and greet and talk about weather, wind, currencies and the World Cup, about everything or nothing, about Sweden and Switzerland.

Mathias and Daniel sometimes got tired of me spending time on what they occasionally thought seemed to be meaningless discussions with Swiss old men, but I was convinced that it could help us get bigger matches to play with in the political game.

A referee colleague who had done major championships for FIFA before had told that Blatter's entourage influenced him in a number of issues and that it could matter if you as a referee took an interest in them. So to play along in the political game, I spent time on them throughout the tournament. I'd rather talk to one person too many than one too few. Rather shake hands with a person twice than not at all. It didn't matter that I didn't know what the person was called, I have a good face memory and could easily remember where and when I had met a person before.

At each new selection, I sat on pins and needles. Nervous, tense and expectant to be selected for our third match in the tournament. But since all five remaining round of 16 matches at least on paper required a non-European referee for neutrality reasons, I thought it was over.

Therefore, we had low expectations that one of the two last round of 16 matches would be assigned to us or any other European team - Switzerland played in the first round of 16 and Belgium in the second. We slouched into the room at the last second, sat down in our usual places, were extremely relaxed and not at all prepared for us to actually be able to get one of the matches. When the last of the round of 16 matches was to be selected and Massimo Busacca read out my name, we could only grin: "Argentina-Switzerland, Eriksson, Sweden." Until that second, Brazil's meeting with Cameroon, five days ago, had been the most important match of my life. That was no longer the case. Now the most important match of my life was in front of me, more precisely in forty-eight hours. Alone in the room I could cheer loudly, dance around and jump around. I looked at the clock and realized that the family at home in Sweden was still awake, so I called them immediately. It probably wasn't the match itself that made me happiest, it was the kick-off time. The match would be played at 1 PM local time, which meant 6 PM at home in Sweden and then the family could for the first time watch the match together in front of the TV. Or parts of the match rather, because for our daughters who were then five and eight years old to sit still for ninety minutes and watch football,

I had no great hopes for that. Just that they could see me for a few minutes felt like my biggest win as my two previous matches had started as late as midnight and 10 PM, which had meant that the girls had been sound asleep on both occasions. When I told them about my match they cheered loudly: "Hurray, we're going to see dad referee the World Cup, how fun it will be. We'll eat ice cream and cheer for you." We were going to referee a round of 16 match in the World Cup. We thus belonged to the top ten in the world with a knockout match. We also knew that the final referee was often chosen among the referees who had refereed best in the round of 16 matches. Another positive thing was that as a referee you didn't want the team you had refereed earlier in the tournament to advance to the final. Then you could be removed as a potential referee due to not being able to influence the same team's results too many times. Now there was still a great possibility that the team of Argentina and Switzerland that won the match could then be eliminated in the upcoming quarter- or semi-finals. And if the winners should still go all the way to the final, it was still two matches between us refereeing them and a possible final. Refereeing the same national team in both quarter-final and final was not likely - but round of 16 and final was definitely a possible scenario. We in the team had gathered in good time in the lobby before our departure to São Paulo. When we gathered like this, there would always come a bunch of colleagues, wishing us good luck and saying a few encouraging words on the way, which also happened this time. Many colleagues were of course disappointed not to have been selected themselves to referee a round of 16 match. A larger group of referees would also be sent home after our match which was the last round of 16. But it didn't show, most in the referee group were generous with praise and well-wishes. However, these were qualities that the highest chief, Massimo Busacca, completely lacked. In the middle of the encouraging farewell from colleagues, the deputy referee chief Manuel Navarro came down to the reception. He wished good luck, heartily and sincerely, but said at the same time that Busacca wanted to talk to us in his office. We knocked, stepped in and were all a bit expectant and curious about what the highest chief wanted with us. When we entered the room, Busacca's gaze was almost a bit irritated and already before he had opened his mouth his body language screamed: what do you really want? When he finally spoke after a good while, we were astonished: "You might be satisfied because you have done what you think are two good matches in the group stage, but one thing you should know: for FIFA and in the world you haven't proven anything yet, not one bit. You are nothing. You have incredibly much left to prove." Then continued a several minutes long harangue where the conclusions were that we weren't really good at all, that our round of 16 match really was a match where it was up to proof, that we needed to show the world that we were worthy of the selection.

Not a single kind word, nothing positive, nothing encouraging or good luck before we left the room. Completely shocked, we looked at each other when we had walked out into the lobby. We had almost gotten a telling-off, but above all we had been told that we were useless, that we hadn't proven anything at all for FIFA, that none of our previous matches had any significance.

Even though I disliked the Swiss referee chief before, I knew that from that moment I really deeply and sincerely despised Massimo Busacca and his leadership. To be so stupid and selfish and such a bad leader that you think you can get a referee and his team to perform better by belittling, criticizing and putting them down on the way to the most important match of their lives.

It was good that we had each other in the team and together could mostly choose to laugh at Busacca's idiotic attempt to bring us down already before the match - and with humor and a large portion of self-confidence instead try to turn it into an opportunity. With a clenched fist in the pocket, we would show everyone, including Busacca, how good we really were.

After almost two hundred international matches, I know that certain assignments just flow, that everything goes extremely easily and nothing messes up. There are clear similarities that it's then I have performed the very best. The energy is then not spent on irritation, anger and frustration - but all focus ends up on the task that is in front of you and the decisions that need to be made. And then there are matches where most things go wrong in the build-up. The round of 16 match between Argentina and Switzerland in São Paulo became such an occasion. It started with Busacca's horrible and belittling talk before departure. It continued with extreme queues to the hotel from the airport. That we had a police escort didn't help, the rush hour traffic in Brazil's largest city with 21 million inhabitants was not to be trifled with and it took a long time before we finally reached the hotel. At the hotel, we understood from our referee host that we couldn't train at the match arena as planned. It was an important routine for me, to get to test the communication equipment, run on the grass, test the shoes, check the dressing rooms and visually see an arena so that you felt more at home when it was game time a day later. It was too far there and also too much traffic. They had instead fixed one of the official training arenas that was closer to the hotel for us.

I was dissatisfied, but experience has taught me that there's no point in wasting energy on things that don't go as you have planned, especially things that you can't influence. When we arrived at our reserve arena, we started the warm-up in playful forms. The temperature was perfect, as was the grass pitch, and the body felt in top shape during the first ten minutes. Then a bus rolled into the arena with a bunch of workers, as well as a larger wagon with a strange, large container on. The workers went out onto the grass pitch, despite us five training on one of the long sides, and one by one they then put on a mask each and pulled out a long hose from the container. Then the men in masks started to spray the green pitch with something that looked like a pesticide of some kind.

Kindly, but firmly, I went up to the referee host and pointed out that we wanted to train in peace, without pesticides, and that he had to solve the problem for us. But the chief of the pitch was stronger and higher in the hierarchy, and his orders from the highest level were clear: the pitch must be sprayed now, because in two days the winners of Switzerland-Argentina will train here.

It didn't help that I tried to call the deputy chief Manuel Navarro - he didn't answer anyway. So we had to abort our session, perhaps the most important day before training we had had in our careers.

Apart from the training, which I still despised, everything was dreamlike. The food was good, the weather brilliant and I and the team thrived together, the body was in top shape, we had done a fantastic first match and moreover we got to see all the matches played at the classic Maracanã on site.

The referee host was stressed, probably felt that I and the others were starting to lose a bit of our patience. After a few calls, he could happily announce that he had indeed found a new training pitch, not at all far from where we were. It was free and would indeed not be sprayed tonight.

After another twenty minutes' car ride, we arrived at an arena that was certainly nice, but it had significantly more focus on athletics than football. The grass that we were to run on in our studded shoes was definitely not grass, other than in patches. I became more and more frustrated, but I kept that to myself.

We made the best of the situation and laughed at it all. The training was, more than usual, light-hearted and we had together a common goal: that no one would get injured. That goal we at least fulfilled.

The kick-off in the round of 16 match was already at 1 PM, which of course was extremely early for us who in for example

Champions League were used to starting the matches at 8:45 PM - almost eight hours later. This meant that the build-up and planning became completely different, not only for the match day but also for the day and evening before regarding food, drink, sleep and tactics. We realized that we would need to leave the hotel at 10:30 AM for a journey that with police escort and closed roads would take 45 minutes, arrive at the arena no later than 11:15 AM, have time to test our equipment, have a briefing with FIFA staff, change, warm up lightly in the dressing room to Mathias' playlists, go out to warm-up at 12:15 PM, be back in the dressing room at 12:35 PM, there have ten minutes for the last own preparations, stand in the tunnel at 12:47 PM. Two minutes later the players would come out. At 12:53 PM it was time for the walk-on to the FIFA anthem, then national anthems, handshakes with the players, coin toss and then kick-off exactly - without exception - 1 PM. So from 10:30 AM, our schedule would be in the hands of FIFA. Usually, with a kick-off at 8:45 PM, there was always time in the hotel room in the afternoon. Then you could relax, pack the bag and sleep for a few hours. Now it was different. With a record early departure, we only had time to wake up, eat breakfast and then go to the arena. So the night's sleep was more important than ever. Therefore, we ate an early dinner, as early as we could after having traveled around half of São Paulo in our hunt for training pitches. Then the goal was to get a good night's sleep and start the day with a joint, proper breakfast at nine o'clock.

Immediately after dinner, I went up to the room, packed the bag for tomorrow and after brushing my teeth I lay down in bed. I was a bit curious if I would be able to fall asleep this early, and how the night's sleep would be. A bit worried, because all my thoughts during every waking second had been focused on tomorrow's round of 16 match. I quickly felt that I was tired, and without me having time to think that I would soon fall asleep, I was asleep. But then suddenly I woke up with a start. It was then I realized that I had actually fallen asleep, and immediately became a bit irritated that I had woken up, or rather been woken up. But what the hell was it that made me wake up after only four hours of sleep? What was it that was making noise and thumping from the room next door? I heard a man and a woman talking loudly to each other in Spanish or Portuguese. It was hard to perceive clearly. What wasn't unclear at all was the mood between the two. The conversation was very irritated, at times they screamed at each other - usually she at him. Now and then someone threw something hard on the floor or wall. Suddenly I was wide awake and saw that the clock on my mobile phone showed 3:15 AM. In ten hours I would referee the most important match of my life, in just over five hours the alarm would ring for breakfast. What if I wouldn't be able to fall asleep again now? I tried to ignore the Norén-like drama in the room next door.

But the fight escalated. Now the man and woman were constantly screaming at each other. For ten minutes I lay and listened to what was unfolding in room 801 at the Renaissance Hotel in São Paulo. Then I called the reception. I asked them with as calm a voice as possible, so as not to stress myself up, to send up security personnel to the room next door.

I hung up the phone and remained lying and heard the continuation of the fight. Both persons now sounded totally crazy at each other, in undiminished tone they screamed louder and louder until suddenly there was a hard knock on their door.

After that I heard a loud discussion with a few more people involved, a loud scream first from the man and then from the woman.

The man screamed loudly in pain, the woman more in horror. Then it sounded like a wrestling match took over room 801 and after a minute's noise I think the man was carried out by the hotel's security personnel and the woman was left alone, crying. After that it became completely quiet in the room.

I remained lying in the darkness and kept my eyes closed. I breathed deeply. It took a while before I finally could fall asleep again. But at 4:47 AM I woke up again. Something was making noise at the door, I heard that it rustled and sounded like someone was trying to break in.

I quickly turned on the light, sat up. Then I heard brisk steps continue down the long corridor. I got up and went to the door to see what had happened. Then I saw a rather thick envelope, just big enough to contain a bunch of bills, pushed under the door. Immediately I thought that someone had tried to bribe me, that in the envelope lay a larger amount of money with a clear order to let one of the teams win. I bent down and picked up the envelope. Tired and groggy I realized in the same moment as I lifted up the envelope that I of course shouldn't have picked it up. Now maybe I removed some fingerprints, I thought worriedly.

I looked at the logo in the upper left corner. "Renaissance São Paulo Hotel." Who wanting to bribe the referee takes an envelope from the hotel you're staying at? I therefore quickly tore open the envelope. Luckily there was no wad of bills, but instead a letter that was folded a number of times to fit in the envelope.

When I read what was written in the letter I could breathe out and relax. But in the same second I became a bit irritated. It was a message that they had sent up security personnel to the room next door and now apologized for what had happened. It was signed by a reception manager who surely only meant well, but who now had woken me up a second time.

When the alarm finally rang at 8:30 AM, I wasn't at all as rested as I had hoped. Twenty-five minutes later Mathias and Daniel knocked on my door, we always gathered there before we went down together to meet the others. Partly to check how everyone was feeling, partly to sync that we had thought right about clothes and dress code.

Four hours later I stand in the green referee shirt for the day in the player tunnel under Arena Corinthians. I don't feel any tiredness at all, the body is alert, the head clear, the pulse reminds me that in a few minutes I will start the round of 16 match between the light blue and white striped Argentina and the all-red Switzerland.

I hear early the sixty-five thousand spectators who are in the stands. Unsurprisingly, most of them support Argentina, given the geographical proximity. But the "most important" spectators come from Switzerland, FIFA's home country. Of course, President Sepp Blatter sits with his entourage in the stands.

Argentina is the first team to come out from their dressing room. It's all world stars that I've met before in the Champions League who come forward and greet: Leo Messi, Javier Mascherano, Gonzalo Higuaín and Ángel Di María. One player is however a bit more hesitant, he stands a few meters away and doesn't seem to seek contact.

It's five months since I awarded a penalty and sent off Manchester City's center-back Martín Demichelis in the Champions League. It was a controversial decision that he hasn't forgotten, even though he today plays in the same team as Leo Messi who was the one he fouled on that cold Tuesday in February.

With only two minutes left to an uncertain penalty shootout, the Swiss right-back Stephan Lichtsteiner fumbles with the ball in midfield in a duel with Argentine Rodrigo Palacio. The Argentines are ruthless in their transition, and eight seconds later the ball is in the net. Ángel Di María has given the team the lead and celebrates wildly in one corner.

In the goal stands a tired Stephan Lichtsteiner and mopes. Over his clumsy and poor action and over his disappointment that the dream of a World Cup quarter-final is now probably gone after Argentina's leading goal. When we blow the final whistle no one can complain about us.

When we blow the final whistle no one can complain about us. We have not influenced the result, no one talks about me after the match. I and the team have once again peaked our form, and via the referee observer from Paraguay we get a message in the dressing room from Busacca, that he is very pleased with our performance. We are back at the hotel already at 5 PM, and can enjoy an early dinner together. After that, we remove ourselves from the official FIFA representatives, go up to the room and with the help of room service we order up caipirinhas to celebrate our performance. We celebrate and recover at the same time. We accelerate and brake at once.

When I sit in the room and enjoy with a large drink in my hand, I simultaneously have the thought that it might soon be a match again - my yellow compression socks envelop my tired calves.

When we traveled to Brazil exactly a month earlier, we had as a goal to referee two matches and saw it as a bonus to get to referee in the knockout stage. Now we were there. We had refereed three matches and all had gone extremely well. We were in a dream and none of us wanted it to end. That night I was spared marital quarrels in the room next door and notes under the door. I slept like a baby. With the round of 16 matches over, there were only eight matches left, and twenty-five arbiters were no longer needed on site. Before what FIFA called the release, Massimo Busacca held a long speech about how good the referees had been in the tournament, how small the margins had been, that they would have gladly kept all the referees and how satisfied all teams, players and leaders had been with our performances. That no team was disappointed with the referees was pure lies. There had been many good performances - but also a bunch of decisions and rulings that had affected individual teams.

Brazil-Busacca was at it again.

When the list of the referees who would be sent home was read out, and I could state that I didn't belong to them, the referees were selected for the first quarter-finals that were played two days later. I didn't get a match, but became the fourth official in the European super match between France and Germany at Maracanã. It was fun to get an assignment, I thought, and nice to avoid traveling again when we had just come back to the base camp. Then I didn't think more about it, but at dinner the same evening one of the most experienced referees came with an exciting theory about the reason why I had gotten that match. FIFA was thinking of me as a potential final referee, he meant, and then they wanted me to have had a match at that arena. The thought had not previously struck me, but now when he said it, a hope and a thought was lit. Could I be considered to referee the final? Being a fourth official was an honorary assignment, but absolutely not usually particularly difficult or challenging. I had a good relationship from before with the national team coaches Joachim Löw and Didier Deschamps, and could spend ninety minutes in the sun at Maracanã while my Argentine colleague Néstor Pitana without a single word of English, French or German led the match with a smile and a clear iron hand. The day after the assignment as fourth official in the European super match, we had training in the morning, then free time to be able to see both remaining quarter-finals Argentina-Belgium and Netherlands-Costa Rica. The first we saw on TV, but when the second was to be played we all three felt like moving around a bit, not sitting at our hotel and watching it together with a bunch of other referees. I wanted to meet people, see and experience the World Cup beyond police escorts and cordons. I was free, wanted to drink a beer and for once not be the always so watched referee with a strict agenda. I went down to the FIFA staff and ordered without problem a private FIFA transport from the hotel in Barra da Tijuca to Copacabana - the four kilometer long, iconic beach in the middle of Rio. During the World Cup there was a fan zone, where supporters from all over the world gathered and watched the matches on big screens. The car dropped us off and we agreed that the driver, who got my mobile number, would pick us up half an hour after the match was over.

If someone should recognize us, we had agreed to deny that we were referees and immediately leave and go to the hotel.

But no one noticed us, and instead we could enjoy an exciting match, with a beer in hand. I got to feel what it was like to be a supporter at a World Cup, and I enjoyed it. But as the match approached its climax, I discovered that my mobile phone was no longer in my shorts pocket. I looked around, went down on my haunches in the sand, searched in all pockets, asked Mathias and Daniel if they were joking with me and had taken it. After a minute's intense searching, I realized that I had been robbed. In the enormous crowd, it was probably not at all difficult for a pickpocket to fish it up. It felt humiliating, troublesome and exposed. It was an unpleasant feeling that someone had taken advantage of my inattention. A bit of my good mood disappeared when I had to spend the entire extra time on the phone with

Sweden to block my SIM card. But I only had myself to blame. With mixed feelings I received a few days later the message that we would not get to referee any of the semi-finals. I was sad that we didn't get a match, but at the same time it meant that the hope that we would get a final lived on for a few more days. I was again selected as fourth official, now for the match Netherlands-Argentina. Together with the Turkish team, led by one of my closest referee friends, the fantastic Cüneyt Çakır, I got three calm and pleasant days that shortened my wait until Friday, July 11, the day when the final referees would be selected. When we for the last time left the training facility that Friday, people came up and said they believed in me and my team for the final. I got to sign autographs and pose for selfies with the players and leaders who had helped with the practical training for almost seven weeks. After the semi-finals, there were twelve referees left in Rio, but of these we knew that several were not relevant for more matches. We could on our own reduce the list to five, six referees who could be relevant for the last matches. I was one of them. When we went into the room where the final referee would be presented, I had steeled myself. I hadn't thought a thought about how happy I would be if it was me who was selected - but rather prepared myself that it wouldn't be me. All to not be too disappointed. I was on the other hand not at all worried about refereeing the final itself, if I should be selected. I would fix that. I was just worried that it wouldn't be me who would get the honor of refereeing it.

On the way into the room, the Brazilian referee colleague came up to me and put his arm on my shoulder. He congratulated me ahead of the selection. I shivered. Was he right? Did he know something already now? He was the home referee and maybe knew more than we others. We sat down in our places and waited for the announcement. The heart was pounding. Harder than before all matches I had ever refereed. The representative for FIFA read from his paper the details about the match before he came to the referee. But instead of my name I heard: "Nicola Rizzoli, Italy." Applause broke out. I sat close to Nicola in the room and was among the first to be there and congratulate Nicola and his team with a heartfelt hug each. He, if anyone, deserved to referee the final as a skilled referee and a decent person. But I was still a bit surprised. He had refereed Argentina in the group stage and in the quarter-final against Belgium. And now a third time in seven matches - could that have happened to a referee from a smaller country than Italy? No one knew exactly how the process looked when FIFA chose their knockout stage referees. It was never talked openly about what criteria FIFA used to choose referees: what qualities were required, how much nationality decided, how lobbying affected the whole thing or if and how the match grades were counted. What should mean most was of course quality and competence - but the decisions were always made behind closed doors and communicated without any motivation or explanation. Everyone involved knew that political influence affected which referees got to referee the foremost matches. Coming from the right country was a big advantage. Having powerful people on your side, preferably members in boards and committees, could be a decisive advantage. And being friends with the FIFA president and his staff could also be what decided.

Seen to history, you generally have to come from Europe or South America to be selected for a World Cup final. Of all twenty finals, eighteen had been refereed by referees from the powerful continents. In particular, you should come from the politically strong countries Argentina, Brazil, England, France or Italy. Referees from these countries had refereed sixty percent of all finals through the ages. Or take the five most recent finals that have only been refereed by referees from three powerful countries: Italy, England and Argentina. Coming from a smaller nation and reaching a World Cup final is possible, but extremely unusual. The now deceased Danish great referee Peter Mikkelsen told me at a FIFA course what had happened when he had been in the form of his life as a referee during the 1994 World Cup and there was talk of a World Cup final for him. The referee committee and the then general secretary, Sepp Blatter, wanted Mikkelsen to referee the final, but FIFA president João Havelange instead chose Hungarian Sándor Puhl in a political demonstration of power.

After the negative final announcement and our first congratulations to Nicola, we went up to our rooms, slammed the door in disappointment. I then called up my wife and my children and told them that I had finished refereeing. I felt despite our successful performances in the championship like a loser. My greatest comfort was that I would soon be home with my girls.

When we didn't get to referee the final, we didn't want to stay in Brazil to see the match on site either. We wanted home as soon as it was just possible.

At the earliest the day after would it be possible.

When the Italian final referees prepared for the match with a physical check, we instead took a caipirinha each on the hotel's rooftop bar, while the sun slowly went down over our World Cup adventure. Then we continued out into the night. Finally, we could go out without a thought of the next match. It was a wonderful feeling of joy and freedom, combined with an insane emptiness and disappointment. It became an evening where I don't remember everything that happened quite clearly.

We have been given tips to go to a fantastic combination of bar, nightclub and disco outdoors. The guards want to see identification, and none of us had thought to bring that. We understand that it's not about an age check but that it's a security routine that you need to leave your passport or ID card at the entrance. For a while it looks like we won't get in, before Mathias solves the whole thing by taking out his mobile phone and showing some pictures from the match in Brasília to them. The guards laugh and start shouting to each other, pointing at us, taking pictures of me and the others and then the person in charge says that they make an exception for us, that we are warmly welcome and will get the best table in the place. Inside the nightclub, we by chance meet a Swedish guy from Värmland. He has traveled around in Brazil all alone during the World Cup, and we talk about all sorts of things over a drink. Suddenly he says: "Damn how proud one has been as a Swede here. What referees we have had here in the World Cup, totally incredibly skilled." Then he takes a sip, looks up and asks us: "And you guys, what have you done here in Brazil then?" A minute later he has realized with an open mouth that it is precisely we three who are the Swedish referees he has been so proud of. Right there and then I realize for the first time that I may have made some Swedes proud back home, that we may have made the referee profession a bit more popular, even though we are now mostly crushed over not getting the final.

We came home to the hotel towards dawn. Tired and tipsy we lumbered through the lobby and managed to stop the elevator just before the door closed. In it stood another loser. Tired, depressed and not entirely sober.

On the way up to the eighth floor we shared the elevator with football legend Ronaldo, "the elder". The retired Brazilian had only three days earlier, when Germany pulverized Brazil with 7-1, lost the title as the World Cup's all-time top scorer to German Miroslav Klose.

As a person, I don't find it easy at all to cry. I keep myself even outside the football pitch all too often in an emotional bubble where I don't let my feelings show or affect me.

But when I, thanks to my wife's film of the event, can travel back in time to Sunday, July 13 and see how I, at home in Sigtuna, sneak up and surprise my children - then I get goosebumps and tears in my eyes.

When they cry with joy, with shock, and crampingly hug me as if they think I will disappear I realize the truth.

I'd much rather be home with my girls than referee the World Cup final at Maracanã. When Nicola Rizzoli at 9 PM Swedish time blows the whistle to start the 2014 World Cup final, I'm half asleep and couldn't care less about free kicks, penalties, yellow and red cards or political selections. I'm just so happy to be home and I don't know if I ever want to travel away again.

The Promise in Berlin

My World Cup success made an impact, which was noticeable in everyone I met - players, managers, colleagues and observers. It motivated me to try to live up to the increasingly high expectations, both at home in Sweden and internationally. At the same time, my team and I had just experienced the biggest football tournament there is, and it wasn't entirely easy to recharge. It was four years until the next World Cup - an eternity in an active sportsman's career. On the way there, a European Championship in France awaited in two years, nearly one hundred and fifty matches along the way, surely sixteen tough running tests, nearly six hundred travel days, at least one major FIFA tournament, numerous days in the classroom with the unsympathetic Massimo Busacca and insanely much meaningless practical training at FIFA courses.
I hesitated. In four years I would be forty-four - my children would by then have become nine and fourteen years old. If I fully committed to refereeing in the next World Cup, I knew I would miss a lot of important time with the family: school graduations, football training, dance performances, Midsummer celebrations, not to mention all the fun everyday events. Would I have the energy for it? Would my body hold up? Suddenly I understood those elite

athletes who immediately after an Olympics can't talk about the next big competition four years later, that it involves so incredibly much time during which one must perform at the top, work with one's body, have the energy, stay healthy, injury-free and maintain the complete passion to constantly perform at the highest level. When we talked about the future in the team, we knew it would be a while before we would experience such a maximum experience and kick as we had in Brazil in the summer of 2014. But we needed new goals on the way forward. It was extremely important that we were in sync together, that we knew where we wanted to reach, and we had therefore put common words to the vision that would make us endure all the travel days and put in all the effort and training needed for us to be one of the world's best referee teams.

The overall goal was to reach Euro 2016 in less than two years. Eighteen referees would be selected for the tournament, and since we already before the 2014 World Cup belonged to Europe's nine best referees, it felt like a highly reasonable goal, hardly even a challenge. Therefore, we set the bar much higher. I had always been a performance junkie - a thrill seeker. A person who seeks success, first place, the ultimate challenge, the coveted and elusive dose of the key player in the brain's reward system - dopamine. For me, a life without achievements and kicks would be insanely boring. Like a confined and dark room without either oxygen or light, like a football match without a ball or a life without a family that loves me and that I love. The day I didn't reach further than during the previous season would mean a failure - even if I still belonged to the absolute top. For me, it was always about trying to get a little better, work a little harder, reach a little further and thus get an ever larger dose of the performance drug I was constantly seeking each year. Otherwise, I might as well quit and do something else. Eventually, Daniel, Mathias and I agreed to set a high goal, which was also realistic after having refereed a semi-final in the same tournament: we would referee a Champions League final in 2015 or 2016. This became an incredibly strong goal image for all our training, matches and travels. Every time it was heavy, tough and the wind was blowing against us, we would have the goal image of getting to referee at the Olympic Stadium in Berlin 2015 or San Siro in Milan 2016. We also had a personal email to me from Pierluigi Collina where he once again congratulates me on my excellent performances in the World Cup. We felt we had support and confidence. I had already in 2013 touched on the thought of getting to referee a Champions League final, but realized that the Italian Rizzoli took precedence. In 2014, it felt completely fair that the skilled Dutchman Björn Kuipers got to referee the final. But for the coming two years, there wasn't exactly a swarm of current candidates.

UEFA's top group was undergoing a change, some sure bets quit for various reasons and several skilled referees came from countries that usually played both semi-finals and finals in the Champions League. This meant that it was an advantage to come from Sweden, which was never involved in those contexts. Moreover, there were already four referees in the group who had refereed a final, and by tradition, you don't get to referee the same final twice.

There were six, seven referees that I thought could be relevant for the final in Berlin. When I saw the names on the list, I realized that I was at least as good as the other referees, had just as much routine and felt that we had about the same confidence from UEFA. What was clear, however, was that I came from a small and unimportant country.

I competed with referees from large and powerful countries like Spain, England, Germany and Turkey, although there were also referees from smaller countries like Slovenia and Serbia. Against them, I at least knew that I was fighting on the same terms.

After the World Cup in Brazil, I knew that I was approaching almost thirty matches in a row with a maximum rating from the observers. Hardly any of my colleagues could show the same numbers. If we just continued to deliver, I knew that UEFA couldn't ignore us, regardless of our Swedish passports. The final at the Olympic Stadium in Berlin would be played on June 6, Sweden's National Day. I saw it as a positive sign.

My World Cup also echoed elsewhere in the world. Suddenly I was personally invited to referee important international matches around the world. And even though it was of course difficult to fit into my tight schedule, I was flattered and the performance junkie in me chased adventures and kicks. That's why I and the team said yes to refereeing, among other things, some league matches in Qatar Stars League and a super cup final in Kazakhstan.

The trip to Kazakhstan was a special experience. The invitation to referee the Super Cup final between FC Astana and FC Kairat had come from the national federation, via Collina and UEFA.

Given the severe cold in Astana, the temperature was never above minus twenty-five degrees during the four days we were there, the match would be played under a closed roof at the only arena in the country that could handle such matches.

Before the match, our hosts and local fourth officials warned that there was a risk that our important communication equipment would stop working during the match. If the country's president, Nursultan Nazarbayev, came to the arena, his security forces would knock out all digital communication, including our equipment.

Nazarbayev had been president of Kazakhstan since the country's independence in 1991, among the longest periods in the whole world that a non-royal person had ruled a country. Through elections that made FIFA appear both transparent and democratic, he had managed to retain absolute power and led an authoritarian regime that had been accused by a number of human rights organizations of violating fundamental human rights.

Sure enough, Nazarbayev showed up at the arena after fifty minutes of play and all our communication equipment was knocked out. Not being able to talk to each other was special, but we fell back on the basic principles of frequent eye contact, always having the game between me and my assistant referees and clear but discreet signs to guide each other. After the match, we remained down on the pitch, when someone suddenly turned on music at full volume. After a few seconds, we recognized the song and were surprised to hear the theme from the TV series "Dallas". Someone nudged us and pushed us towards the steps leading up to the stands. We were apparently going to receive a medal from the president. I took the lead. The feeling of walking up to the VIP stand, receiving applause from the audience and a medal from the authoritarian president while the theme from "Dallas" was played at full volume was surreal to say the least. How sport in general and world football in particular is used and exploited by dictatorships and states as a tool to promote political ideals or messages is of course neither an unproblematic issue nor something that can be swept under the carpet. Societies that do not treat all people equally in terms of gender, ethnicity, sexual orientation or religion gladly use international sports as a way to promote trade, improve international relations or occasionally as a way to distract and soften up the world's criticism in other areas. The phenomenon of countries with human rights deficiencies arranging large sporting events in order to wash their reputation clean even has its own word nowadays: sportswashing. That the 2018 Football World Cup was awarded to Russia, that the 2022 championship went to Qatar and that the 2022 Olympics were placed in China were three examples that of course really brought the discussion to the fore. In addition to those countries, there were a number of other nations that I regularly visited as a football referee and which consistently persecuted minorities, dissidents and banned independent, critically examining mass media.

In one camp are those who advocate boycott one hundred percent, complete isolation of countries and no exchange whatsoever, in the other corner those who mechanically argue that sport and politics don't mix at all and that one should do exactly as one has always done.

I stand somewhere in the middle. I don't believe in isolation and rejection of countries that are not exactly the same as the country I come from or do not have the values that I grew up with. There are few people who can raise issues on an agenda, like sports personalities when they really take a stand. They can get people to listen and sometimes influence more than politicians, economists or royalty. On the other hand, it usually works very well to isolate states in terms of issues other than sports such as trade, goods, investments and access to capital. Look at South Africa in the 1980s, where the isolation eventually forced the apartheid regime to the negotiating table. But I don't believe in traveling around to dictatorships and states that oppress people, standing up and shouting, holding up banners and then never traveling there again and trying to influence from a distance. As always, it's about daring to talk, saying what you think, telling how we have it in our countries, but doing it in the right way, with the right voice, at the right time, with the right timing and in the right forum.

As a referee, I was completely forbidden to make political statements in any direction, just as I couldn't have sympathies for a club team or a nation I refereed. But when the opportunity arose in the right forum, whether I was in Kazakhstan, Turkey, Saudi Arabia, China, Qatar or Russia, I could always talk about Sweden and our view on equality. On the fact that girls can both play and referee football with the same obviousness as boys do it. That we have referee courses where girls and boys are trained together, with the same instructors and the obvious fact that the best female referee in Sweden today finally has the same conditions as the best male referee. About our daughters who quite naturally and without making it a gender issue both play, referee and coach football in Sigtuna IF.

I talked about our high Swedish taxes, but also about what we get out of the money in terms of healthcare, education, care, social safety net, infrastructure and how there is an idea that together we move society forward.

I could talk about the obvious that in the same way that all twenty-two players on a pitch are judged by the same rulebook, everyone in a society should be judged equally regardless of gender, ethnicity, sexual orientation or religion. I gladly spoke about the importance of organizing collectively (even the elite referees in Sweden have their own interest organization), that together you always become stronger and not least how important it is to speak up regarding issues of work environment. Of course, I could have said no to all assignments I got in countries that, from my personal point of view, did not treat all people equally regardless of gender, ethnicity, sexual orientation or religion. But how could I really draw a line there? Was it okay to referee a cup final in Kazakhstan? How did I reason about refereeing a World Cup qualifier in Belarus? Should I referee Russia at Euro 2012 in Poland, but refuse to travel to Russia for a Champions League match the same year? Was it okay to travel to Turkey in 2013 during the unrest at Taksim Square to referee France against Spain in the Under-20 World Cup, but wrong to referee the club team Başakşehir in a Champions League qualifier because the country's president Erdoğan obviously had sympathies and connection to the team? There were many questions to ask oneself, but not particularly many easy answers. I was also the only referee at European top level who had a national break from November to March. My competitors in the hunt for refereeing playoff matches in the international cups had league matches during this period where they could hone their form. Should I then say no to refereeing matches in for example Qatar, Turkey, Saudi Arabia, Kazakhstan and Spain, while the chiefs at UEFA encouraged me and my colleagues to prepare as well as possible? I accepted if someone thought I shouldn't have refereed any of the matches. I knew at the same time that I always followed my employers' guidelines. Where there were matches that I was allowed to referee, I did it. Where I was assigned to referee matches, I did it. When they required me to prepare with matches abroad to keep in shape and be relevant for the finals I dreamed of, I did it.

Then it wasn't always the case that my highest chief within UEFA set a particularly good example.

The mantra for us referees was simple and well-rehearsed if one should eventually end up in a situation where bribes or irregularities occurred: recognise, resist, report. That is: detect, resist, report. If I had discovered something suspicious, or been offered some form of bribe, it was my absolute duty to report it to UEFA or FIFA. While the importance of independence and high ethical standards was emphasized by UEFA, Collina and other members of UEFA's referee committee worked in parallel as consultants on referee issues for various national associations. Some of the nations that used this were among others Romania, Georgia, Ukraine, Turkey, Greece, Cyprus, Russia, Kazakhstan and Bulgaria. Common was that these countries generally had a substandard referee activity, often lacked representation at the highest level within UEFA - and were willing to pay large sums for foreign help. Sitting on two chairs and taking compensation from different sources was not at all forbidden but rather established within UEFA, although it of course involved a great risk of conflicts of interest.

Since July 2010, Collina had had a, to say the least, gilt-edged job contract to help Ukraine reorganize and structure the referee activity that had long been plagued by questionable decisions, corruption and major scandals. It had gone so far that the president of the Ukrainian league, Vitaly Danilov, the year before Collina's appointment had asked the then UEFA president Michel Platini to send a commission to the country to "clean up the sport", which was plagued by fixed matches and other corruption.

Pierluigi Collina's assignment in Ukraine began at the same time as he also became the highest chief of UEFA's referee department and was responsible for coaching, training, classification and selection of referees for all of Europe - including those in Ukraine. The reason for his extra job in Ukraine was hardly a passion for developing refereeing there, the main reason was probably money. Collina earned, according to reports, over five million Swedish kronor per year. A high salary, especially considering that he didn't spend more than a few weeks per year on site in Ukraine. The hopes were high that Collina's presence would change the system fundamentally and develop the referees. But from the start, he received a lot of criticism for being on site far too rarely. Collina needed an assistant, a wingman, a right hand on site in the country, especially considering that he himself was there so rarely. That's how his Italian colleague Luciano Luci came into the picture. A former referee in Serie A, from Tuscany like Collina and a personal friend of the bald referee chief for a long time. Collina even handed over the title of chairman of the Ukrainian referee committee to Luci. It is of course an extremely difficult question to measure or purely objectively put into words how much better, or worse, the Ukrainian referees have become with the Italian's leadership. The only way to give a sense of it is to see what ranking, that is, in which categories, the referees have qualified in the 2010s. That ranking is done twice a year by UEFA. And of course, Collina himself had all the possibilities to influence the ranking.

When Collina took over in 2010, he cleared out six referees and put in six new ones. After that, things went upwards in the categories. Four out of six referees were moved up one or in some cases several categories. During Collina's years as responsible, there were eight occasions when the referees took a step up - and only on one single occasion was a referee moved down a category.

Above all, two Ukrainian referees made meteoric careers and climbed quickly in the UEFA ranking. Either they were exceptional talents or they had an advantage of having Collina as chief both nationally and internationally. Regardless, it's interesting to see what fantastic international development the

Ukrainian referees had during Collina's years as responsible. And equally fascinating is it to look at how the development immediately stagnated when he left the assignment. Now, a number of years later, the Ukrainian referees are back at the same level as they were before he started his assignment for the country.

Is there then no control function that can prevent conflicts of interest and situations of bias within refereeing? The answer is unbelievably no. It is up to those involved to speak up, step away from decisions where they might be sitting on two chairs - but it doesn't happen very often.

Because it is partly very established that you have several roles, partly so much money involved for the people who have dual positions, so no one speaks up and challenges the structure or demands that it should cease. While Collina sat on two chairs in Ukraine and UEFA, other employees in UEFA were in similar situations. The Scot Hugh Dallas was for a period responsible chief for the Greek referees, and even other members of the referee committee took assignments from smaller associations.

Like a shy teenager, I tiptoe behind him. My heart starts to beat a little faster, I notice that I'm breathing more heavily, a bit higher up in the chest. My reaction is actually crazy. I'm forty-one years old, married and have two children, have earned enough money to not need to work more in my life. I'm one of the world's best referees. I have no problems lecturing Cristiano Ronaldo, taking conflicts with Zlatan, being ice-cold and tough against Leo Messi or telling off Neymar if the situation requires it. I don't get nervous about refereeing twenty-two egoistic, cheating world stars in front of eighty thousand spectators in the stands and several hundred million TV viewers. But in Pierluigi Collina's company I feel nervous and maybe even insecure. It might have to do with my inferior position, that I know how cynically he can handle the people he doesn't appreciate or dislikes (even though I'm currently on his in-list), or it might have to do with his power, that he is the only person who stands between me and my goal - a final in the Champions League.

    We go and stand outside the hotel entrance, and I'm quiet. I have decided in advance that it's Collina who should lead the conversation, but that I should be clear, ask questions, be honest and tell about my disappointments in recent weeks. We make small talk for a while before I tell him that I'm a bit disappointed that it's not me who's going to referee the match to be played in Berlin the day after. Collina looks at me, nods understandingly and says: "It could just as well have been your final this year. It was details, very small margins. It was a flipped coin that landed on the wrong side for you." I nod, a bit as if I accept the fact that I've received praise and confirmation, but that chance made Cüneyt get the final instead of me. Collina puts his hand on my shoulder and looks at me with his eyes that just then are both kind and warm and says: "If you just continue as you've done in recent years, it's undoubtedly your final in a year. Then it's you who referees, no one else. Am I being clear?" I don't know what to answer. I've got the confirmation I wanted, I know that I was second this year, but that I'm the given number one next year - if I just continue to deliver. I smile, feel warm inside and am so happy about the total confirmation that the most powerful person in the referee world gives me that I almost forget an important question. When I've actually said goodbye I ask why I didn't get the final in the Europa League either. Collina looks at me, he's silent for a few seconds, as if he's searching for a good answer. Then he says: "Jonas, you're not a referee for the Europa League. You're better than that. You should have the big final, right? Atkinson got it because he's from England, a country that often plays finals. Moreover, he's approaching the end of his career, while you have yours ahead of you." I can't get a sound out, more than nodding happily and showing with a thumbs up that I obviously agree. If I got to choose a single club team final it would be the one in the Champions League, all other finals pale in comparison.

I hurry up to the hotel room to text my two closest colleagues Mathias and Daniel. I know that they put in as much time as I do, are just as passionate, dedicated, serious and become just as happy as I do about successes, and just as disappointed, sad and frustrated when we're maneuvered out in the political game.

The final in Berlin became an experience that I as a fourth official could enjoy from the area between the benches. But all the time there was now after the talk with Collina another arena and a new date in my thoughts: San Siro in Milan - Saturday, May 28, 2016.

There and then I would referee my final in the Champions League.

All people need vacation. A time to recover, sleep in, do other things than what you do during the rest of the year, travel away, have time with the family, relax and recharge the batteries. As a referee at the highest level I had quite a lot of free time, in terms of hours, but my free time was never longer and continuous, and above all it didn't occur when the schools were closed.

The Allsvenskan always starts early in April and is played until mid-November. The annual course is arranged in January-February, and the closing course is held at the end of November. December is a somewhat free month, if you're a referee in Sweden at the elite level.

As an international referee at the highest level, the season is exactly the opposite. The initial course is in August, then the season continues from that month until May when the final finals are played. Then championships are played at senior level in June and July every even year and every odd year either Confederations Cup or Junior World Cup. I was never free. There was always a match in front of me, a tournament to aim for, a running test to pass, a rule test to nail and a final to long for. It took its toll, not just physically, but also mentally. To always try to be the best and perform flawlessly, to always be hungry for new matches, to have the energy to analyze the matches you did and recharge for new ones. Not to mention always having enough energy to handle the criticism that I as a referee received in connection with assignments. When my career had really taken off in the summer of 2012, I ran into a hamster wheel that actually never stopped spinning. For three years there was no talk of any real time off, any cohesive vacation, opportunity to really recharge the batteries, log out and think about something other than training, matches and tournaments.

The summer of 2015 finally came a championship-free period in June-July. But there wasn't particularly much time off for me. I took my family and my wonderful mother-in-law to the west coast of the USA for a few weeks of well-deserved road trip, but after two days of rest, it started to itch in my body and I began a training period that was significantly harder than any I had gone through before.

Certainly there were days when the body was tired and screamed that it wanted to rest. But as soon as I thought about my final in the Champions League I got energy, speed and power to train hard, even if I was on vacation and maybe should have rested. Our youngest daughter Milla liked that dad was with us on a longer vacation, together with the family. Even though she was only six years old, she had learned that I was usually away during most of the summer holidays. One day in San Francisco she asked: "Dad, when you referee you're the boss of all the players. You decide over everyone, right? But dad, if you're now the boss of everyone and decide. Why don't you make sure to be free in the summer and be together with us instead, like this summer?" I was speechless, got tears in my eyes and explained that I would soon be home every summer, but that for a few years ahead there would be more summer holidays when dad traveled around to various football tournaments. As a referee I always wanted to referee the most important matches where as much as possible was at stake: a title, a promotion, a league victory or maybe even talk about a club's future being at stake if the team lost. Often it was also in those matches that there was the most prestige, emotions and a clear rivalry between the teams and players. Not always, but usually all those ingredients were present when there was a derby between two clubs. A derby is a match between two teams from the same city or nearby cities. Most meetings have economic, historical, political, religious or social overtones that - besides the match itself - add an extra layer of rivalry. I was sitting in the car on the way from Landvetter to Halmstad, just before lunch, Friday, September 18 and planning the near future together with Mathias and Daniel. We had some intense weeks ahead of us - with almost exclusively important and decisive derbies. The same evening we would referee the fateful match Halmstad BK-Falkenberg where a loss for the home team would most likely mean relegation. The Thursday of the following week we would referee Elfsborg-IFK Göteborg, a match that could confirm Blåvitt's first place and definitely hang off Elfsborg in the top battle. Our derby triple would then be concluded on Sunday with Hammarby against AIK, where AIK had to win not to lose ground in the top battle. Our three matches in ten days would then be crowned with Champions League a few days later: Juventus against Sevilla. Not a derby, but still a good conclusion to some of the most intense days I had experienced. On E6 at the exit to Kungsbacka my phone rang. A +20 number was shown on the display. I hesitated to answer, but was too curious to let it be. At the other end was a man who said he was calling from the Egyptian Football Association. He had got my number via mutual friends at the Qatari Football Association and wondered if I wanted to come and referee the country's big derby between Al-Ahly and Zamalek, who would meet in the cup final in Cairo on Monday. They expected nearly one hundred thousand spectators on site. I was tempted, but the match was only three days away. And we now had an extremely intense match period with four matches in thirteen days - could we manage and have time for a fifth match in that time? Was it even possible to solve practically? I hung up and ten minutes later I got an email with all the information. First I verified that it was genuine by calling the switchboard at the Egyptian Football Association and asking for the person who had emailed. It checked out. He was who he claimed to be.

Purely theoretically I calculated that we could manage it. Departure Sunday, match on Monday, home Tuesday and then match in Borås on Thursday.

First I made a quick call to my understanding wife. She heard from my enthusiastic voice that I wanted to go, that I had gotten excited about the thought of getting to referee the Egyptian cup final, and as always I was grateful that she supported me, even though I understood that it meant that I would be away for another three days in an already extremely intense period.

Then a call to my boss, Bosse Karlsson, who I had to keep informed about my plans. He too was as always understanding.

He knew what I got excited about, understood the pride I felt over having received a personal invitation and that it would be a memory and an experience for life to referee such a match.

On Friday afternoon, before I at Scandic Hallandia lay down to sleep as preparation for the evening's fateful match, I emailed the

Egyptian Football Association and confirmed that we would come and referee the hyped cup final.

But first there was another match that mattered. I always took pride in being present and focused regardless of which match I was currently refereeing, regardless of what challenges were tempting after that. When the match at Örjans vall in Halmstad was over we slept well. We flew home, repacked our bags and then set off towards Cairo for an enormous adventure.

When we board the flight that will take us to the Egyptian capital we stand out among all the older tourists who are going down to see Cairo's sights and cultural treasures. We are four men of the same age, all over one hundred and ninety centimeters tall, all with identical Adidas bags, all dressed in jeans, shirt and jacket. When we sit down in the seats the flight attendant comes up and asks us what we're really going to do in Cairo. I don't always want to tell who we are, to avoid talking football during the hours on the flight, so I choose to look down. But one of the colleagues answers honestly and nicely that we're going down to referee football, the Egyptian cup final, Al-Ahly against Zamalek. The flight attendant gapes widely and freezes: "Oh, I'm sorry for your sake. Those matches usually mean war and chaos, you know that, right?" We smile at each other when we get this first indication of how sensitive, big and important match we have in front of us. On the flight down I read more about the teams and the match in the book When Friday comes. Football, war and revolution in the Middle East and realize even more what a veritable powder keg we're heading to.

We're going to referee two of the African continent's most successful clubs, which also have the same city as their home. Traditionally, Al-Ahly's supporters are seen as belonging to the working class, while Zamalek is said to be supported by the more affluent social classes.

Al-Ahly is the big brother, with a clear lead over Zamalek in both head-to-head meetings and titles, and is statistically the world's second most successful club in terms of international titles, behind Real Madrid. The ultras movements in both clubs played together a major role in the uprisings around the Egyptian spring in the early 2010s, but the supporter groups in the clubs also tended to be able to clash with each other in connection with the derby matches. In February 2012, five hundred people had been injured and seventy-two supporters of Al-Ahly killed in connection with riots after a league match in the port city of Port Said. After that, the Egyptian league had been stopped for over a year, and when it started again it happened without spectators. When spectators were finally, in February 2015, again allowed on a larger scale in the arenas, the next catastrophe occurred when twenty-two supporters from Zamalek died. It happened outside a stadium in Cairo after the police had shot tear gas at the supporters and panic had broken out - and it had occurred just seven months before our visit. On match day we prepare on our own at the hotel. We're told that the match will be played without an audience, for security reasons, because they fear riots. Even exactly where the match will be played is secret, so that the supporters won't have time to gather outside either. Therefore, it's announced only a few hours before kick-off that the match will be played at Petrosport Stadium, a smaller arena that only holds sixteen thousand spectators. Even though there's not supposed to be a single spectator at the arena, there are more police present than I've seen at any other match before. The cordons start maybe a kilometer from the arena, and then we're stopped at least ten times at different checkpoints and at each stop have to open the door, show our accreditation and tell who we are.

Finally our minibus stops in front of the entrance to the arena, almost two hours before the match is to start. From the moment we leave the bus we're constantly followed by a cameraman who documents every step we take - except when we're inside our dressing room. Moreover, we constantly have two people by our side who we don't really know who they are. They follow every step I take. After a while they even become more numerous.

Soon we have almost ten people who speak Arabic, loudly and noisily and seem to be discussing important things.

After half an hour we understand that it's representatives for each club who are marking us. The fear that one team will be able to influence us in some way is so great that each team constantly has a person following us. If one team comes in with a second person, the other team also fetches an additional person, as if to maintain a balance of power in our dressing room. It's almost parodic to see, and after a while I choose to - honestly, kindly, clearly and firmly - tell them with a smile that I appreciate their company, but now we must prepare for the match and I ask them to leave us alone, whereupon the room is finally emptied. The heat at kick-off is striking. It's thirty-two degrees and the humidity is noticeably high. The match is tough and intense, and my task resembles a cook's at a stove that has a boiling pot with milk as a base. The pot wants to boil over all the time, and I have to struggle in every way to remove the pan from the stove, put it back carefully, turn down the heat, whisk around and remove the lid to try to control the match. That there are empty stands is not quite true, because there are surely a few thousand people as spectators at the match in the form of military personnel, police and other official persons who seem to have the right to be in the stands. I have to play out my entire register, use an exaggerated body language to convince the players of my decisions, run more than usual, be present and clearly show who's in charge. After ninety minutes Zamalek has won fairly with 2-0 and celebrates, while Al-Ahly immediately leaves the pitch. We referees also leave the pitch, go into the dressing room and breathe out. Slowly we start to fill up our emptied depots with food and drink, change clothes, stretch and prepare for our next assignment in Borås in seventy-two hours. Just when we're about to enter the shower, one of the hosts from the Egyptian federation comes running into our dressing room and announces that we're going to receive a prize from the president.

In a minute we've hurriedly put on our clothes adequately, except for socks and football shoes which I realize I won't have time to put on, so when I receive a medal for the cup final in Egypt 2015 from a president, I do it in flip-flops and note that match two of five in thirteen days is completed.

Despite everything, I probably didn't really understand there and then how much the match meant, that a derby match in Cairo is literally a matter of life and death and so much more than just a match with a winner and a loser. We saw it as a break, an adventure, a poorly paid excursion and something you do once in a lifetime. "I'm so disappointed in him, I never want to see Jonas again." Sweden's most capped male national team player of all time, Anders Svensson, didn't mince his words when he judged my performance in the match between Elfsborg and IFK Göteborg, my third derby match in seven days.

He was extremely disappointed with my performance, above all with a missed decision. A missed free kick in midfield, one of my three hundred decisions that evening at Borås Arena. That the play then continued for a number of seconds, and that his teammates Adam Lundqvist and Sebastian Holmén then incurred a clear penalty - Anders had time to forget in his great disappointment.

Anders had himself made it 1-0 and was on his way to ensuring that Elfsborg kept up in the Allsvenskan top battle. But when Emil Salomonsson shot in 1-1 it meant that the dream of a Swedish championship gold for Elfsborg and Anders during his last season was blown away. In the dressing room I saw replays of my most important decisions. The penalty was correct, I could defend that, but the free kick in midfield was a miss. I judged it wrong, despite having the right position. I took the bull by the horns and met journalists and others who wanted to talk to me about my mistake. Even though it felt extremely heavy at that moment to go out into the bare player corridor at Borås Arena and give an interview for TV. Composed, serious and almost a bit sad, I admitted that I might have made an incorrect judgment in the match. I stayed overnight in Gothenburg and talked to my wife at home in Sigtuna the next morning. The front page had screamed out my picture and Anders Svensson's quote about never wanting to see me again. My daughters had seen it, and my wife had had a bit of difficulty explaining why a player wouldn't want to meet dad again. I encouraged her, and my wife encouraged me. Tomorrow I would be home again and soon this intense period would be over. My phone rang continuously the day after the match. I didn't answer a single number that I didn't already have in my phone book. One number stood out. It just never stopped ringing, I had missed nearly ten calls before the same number sent a text: "It's Anders Svensson, you must call me." I basically like Anders. He's a grumpy winner's skull who sets high demands on others in his surroundings, who always wants answers to his questions and who since I first met him in Allsvenskan in 2001 had always treated me with respect and had an ability to distinguish between issue and person. I'm also not a person who holds grudges, so I wasn't angry at Anders after yesterday's comments, on the contrary I could as also being a grumpy winner's skull to some extent understand his reaction, and when I got a break I called him back.

 He immediately apologized to me, told me that he was so damn disappointed right after the match that it just slipped out of him. But that he realized that it was completely wrong of him to express himself as he did.

I bought Anders' apology, said it was okay, and promised that in the future when we met it would be forgotten on my part. I can distinguish between criticism of my decisions and when criticism is directed at my person, it was one of the reasons why I had managed to referee football at the highest level for almost fifteen years. I admitted my mistake, Anders Svensson his - and we both moved on. Today when I meet Anders we can laugh at what happened in 2015, even though Anders still doesn't really want to admit that it was a correct penalty that I awarded. Once a winner's skull, always a winner's skull. Our five matches in thirteen days, of which four intense derbies, ended six days later in Turin when after ninety minutes I blew the whistle on Juventus' match against Sevilla. I could finally breathe out and note that I would finally get to rest and be home a little. The last Saturday in October I refereed my fifth gold match in Allsvenskan. On all four previous occasions Malmö FF had won the Swedish championship, but just in 2015 it wasn't the home team that had the chance to take first place - but the away team IFK Norrköping. Refereeing a match where the gold is handed out is the most powerful experience you can have as a Swedish referee. There is enormous prestige, and the nervousness sits deep in players, leaders and supporters. At this point there was a lot of speculation before the match about whether the hung Malmö FF would go for victory, as a loss would secure the gold to IFK Norrköping ahead of the chasing rivals IFK Göteborg and AIK. However, it wasn't something we in the team put any weight on, for us it was about preparing for what would happen on the pitch and absolutely not weighing in anything other than what we saw happen in our judgment.

This day I also refereed the earliest sending-off ever in an Allsvenskan match during the 2000s. I stood right next to when Markus Rosenberg already after five minutes kneed Linus Wahlqvist in the head after a duel. It took a second before I was really sure that I had perceived it correctly, and my assistant referee Daniel could confirm that it was a crystal clear red card.

With one more player on the pitch, IFK Norrköping could win the match 2-0 and win the Swedish championship. I made a match-deciding decision, which by extension also decided where the Swedish championship gold ended up, and I was proud that we as a team had not let ourselves be influenced by the hype around the gold match but dared to referee a completely correct sending-off, regardless of how decisive it was.

The Allsvenskan season was now over, but I had more important matches ahead of me with only seven months left until the Champions League final.

I was always confident that I would be selected as one of eighteen referees for the European Championship in France. Collina's words in Berlin, that the final in Milan in May 2016 was mine if I performed well, made me sure of a place in France - above all because all matches during the autumn of 2015 had continued to give maximum grades. When the qualifying matches for the European Championship were therefore selected in November, I knew that I would get one of the eight matches that would decide which countries would take the last four European Championship tickets.

We woke up in Lviv in eastern Ukraine on the morning of November 14, charged for a match the same evening between the home nation and Slovenia in the first meeting of two. But when I had woken up, turned on my phone and read the news flow, I froze.

The evening before, Paris had been hit by a large-scale and coordinated terrorist attack with shootings and explosions at six locations in central Paris and the suburb of Saint-Denis. One hundred and thirty people had been killed and three hundred and fifty people had been injured. One of the places for the terrorist attacks was the French national arena Stade de France.

In connection with the friendly international match between France and Germany, three explosions had occurred and at least four people had been killed.

I called directly to UEFA who answered that the plan was for our match in Lviv to be played as planned, but with mourning bands on the players and a minute's silence before kick-off. Just four days later we were supposed to referee a training international match at Wembley between England and just France.

That dream experience was now of course at great risk of being cancelled, but what did a match really matter considering all the innocent who had lost their lives in a meaningless terrorist attack. The match in Lviv went well, yet another match with maximum grade, and I looked forward to being able to be free for three days instead of refereeing England against France which we coldly counted on would be cancelled. But when we had come home and I talked to the English Football Association on Sunday, the message was clear. Terror was not allowed to win. The match would be played. When I told my wife that I would after all travel to London, she didn't want me to go. She thought it felt far too dangerous. I myself was calmer, could separate the emotions from my logical thinking and knew, from all experience, that the security for me as a referee would be at its highest during the match. I managed to convince my wife and explain that we would be safe and in good hands. It ended with us traveling to London on Monday, and going directly from Heathrow to Wembley to just as usual train at the arena for forty-five minutes. If the security in Egypt two months earlier had been extreme, this took the prize. There were police and security personnel everywhere, barrier upon barrier, check upon check - before we finally were inside Wembley. We had a briefing on site with the chief of operations for the match. Usually it was about a brief of one minute with clichés and self-evidences - but now it took fifteen minutes. We got important information about how to handle certain special situations. At the end the chief of operations confidently summarized the situation by saying that tonight Wembley was the safest place one could be. Forty-five minutes before the match I met the French national team coach Didier Deschamps. We silently shook hands. I held on to his hand, looked him in the eyes and said that I regretted the sorrow. That I and my colleagues shared it with him and the French people. That football felt unimportant today, but that I was still glad that the match would be played. The French national team coach looked composed and almost a bit moved when he looked up at me, thanked and said: "Tonight we let football win." There were security guards and police everywhere in the corridors, you could hardly walk a meter without having to show the accreditation that gave us the right to be there. However, when we had put on our referee clothes no one asked anymore. The extreme security was not strange. In the tunnel before the match I met both Prince William and Prime Minister David Cameron. Together with the two national team coaches they silently laid down flowers to honor the terror victims in Paris.

When all seventy thousand spectators and the French and English national teams together sang the French national anthem La Marseillaise I got goosebumps. A few meters from me stood the French star Lassana Diarra whose cousin had been murdered just four days earlier. He looked silently down at the ground. And the superstar Antoine Griezmann stood with an empty gaze staring straight ahead. His sister had been close to being killed by the terrorists, but had escaped unharmed.

All of Wembley was dressed in French colors. And on the big screens a message was pumped out in red, white and blue: liberté - égalité - fraternité.

Freedom - equality - brotherhood.

The traditional team pictures were not taken with each team separately, but all players and referees were mixed into one single large picture to the audience's rhythmic and loud applause. The memorial ceremony was concluded with all players and referees standing around the center circle, and the announcer announcing a minute's silence in memory of the victims of the terror attacks in Paris.

When the stands cheered and shouted out their feelings after the absolute silence in the gigantic arena it was an incredible experience. Never during my thirty-one years as a referee has football united as it did at Wembley that cold, but warm, evening in November. For everyone who was present it became an evening that no one will ever forget. The 2015/2016 season didn't go a day without me thinking about San Siro in Milan, May 28, 2016 - the final that I had got Collina's promise to get to referee. During the autumn we had refereed another nine matches with the highest grade - I had now done a total of forty-eight straight matches without a single big and clear mistake. A sensationally good record that showed that I had not only been good for a short period - but for three and a half years. My path towards the final felt straight as an arrow, and only one, two or maximum three matches remained before my dream could come true.

Collina and his closest had in recent years matched the referees in the playoffs according to an informal template. It meant that a final-relevant referee maybe didn't referee particularly much in just the Champions League. If he despite everything did, UEFA often avoided the referee refereeing strong teams with a big chance for the final - to not risk that something happened on the way that could create a conflict or attract media interest. The pattern had been extra clear during the last few years. The future final referee would only referee one match in the playoff's round of 16, preferably with two little-known teams that had little chance of reaching the final itself - then the referee could be completely rested until the final or tested in the Europa League's later rounds.

That's what I hoped for. I had got Collina's promise in Berlin, and my grades pointed unequivocally straight in that direction. When I had written in the date for the final I had realized that my dad would turn seventy the day before the final which was my big and only goal. It had given me even more energy and fuel, and I saw it as yet another sign that the 2016 final really was mine. What a seventieth birthday present it could be to my dad, if he was in place in the stands when I refereed the Champions League final, I had thought.

When half the season had gone I began in my head to move myself to Milan on May 28. I checked flight times for me and the team, thought a bit loosely around our logistics, our preparation and how we afterwards could enjoy a dinner together with our invited friends. I soon realized that I would need more tickets than those UEFA would provide me with. So already in January I bought more tickets to the final in Milan via the Swedish Football Association. Only my contact person at the association knew that it was I who had bought the tickets, and I don't think she ever connected that I bought them to have a chance to invite more than two people to Milan if I should get to referee the final. With tickets secured I traveled down to the annual UEFA course on Cyprus in February. Once there I easily ran through the yo-yo test and passed the rule test without errors. I found out that I didn't have any round of 16 match in February. Probably it meant that I would get a return match in March - either in the Champions League's or

Europa League's round of 16. If and exactly which match I had I would find out only after the first meeting between the teams.

But I was at the same time extremely curious about whether Collina's words in Berlin still applied, I wanted to have another positive indication. I decided to ask a question if I became alone with him.

The opportunity came in a break when we ended up next to each other on the way out of the room. I masked my real intention by asking if it was true that I didn't have matches in February and how he viewed if I should accept going to Saudi Arabia or Qatar to prepare during that period when there were no matches in Allsvenskan. He answered that it was true that I didn't have any matches in February and that he really encouraged me to referee "real matches" abroad to be prepared for the very important matches that UEFA planned for me.

Collina looked around as if he wanted to make sure that it was only him and me. Then he told that they possibly planned to use me for the return matches of Champions League, but that everything depended on how the first meetings ended.

"If we really don't need you, then we'll try to keep you clean for coming, let's say, more demanding matches in Champions League", said Collina and winked at me with one eye, as if we had a secret that only we two knew about.

A few weeks later I could see, via the still unknown bug in FAME, that we had a match on March 16. That gave two possible matches: Barcelona-Arsenal or Bayern Munich-Juventus. None of them was preferable, because all four teams were clearly potential finalists in Champions League.

After the first match Barcelona had probably decided their double meeting - while Juventus and Bayern had played 2-2 in a tough and tight first clash. If we were to get one of the round of 16 matches then I absolutely didn't want to referee the even return in Munich.

But that's exactly how it turned out. When Bosse Karlsson called and announced that it would be a visit to southern Germany in a few weeks, I moped for a few hours before I as usual turned it into an opportunity: if we managed this match there was absolutely no obstacle left for UEFA, then we could fly directly to Milan for the Champions League final on May 28.

Even though I was a bit disappointed to be tested in such a tough match as in Munich, I was calm. I was confident with my own competence, my team and my forty-eight straight matches without a failed grade. My self-confidence knew no bounds. UEFA could put me on any assignment - without me failing, I felt.

Therefore, I wasn't particularly nervous or concerned before the match.

On the contrary, I longed for the kick-off and the atmosphere at the arena that during my career was perhaps the one I thrived best at.

The match in Munich on March 16 becomes one of the toughest matches I referee in my career.

The Italians surprisingly lead 2-0, but with seventeen minutes left the home team reduces and then equalizes in the first minute of overtime.

It goes to extra time, what I least of all wish for. And there's a lot to do for us in the team. During the one hundred and twenty minutes I blow forty-five free kicks and hand out twelve warnings - it's a war, tough, grumpy and irritated and when we leave the pitch there's only one thing, a disallowed goal, and one person, my colleague Mathias, that Juventus is angry at.

In the twenty-second minute Mathias had flagged for offside after Juventus' German star Sami Khedira had hit a lightning-quick pass to a free-standing Álvaro Morata who had scored. Morata could, after several replays in slow motion, be found to be on the right side by some single centimeter. The disallowed goal would have meant 2-0 for Juventus.

The grade for Mathias becomes failed. It's painful to see that a person who had been so phenomenally good in the match otherwise fails after having missed an offside by some centimeter that is first discovered after a bunch of replays. But such is our reality.

It doesn't help that the observer is super pleased with my performance and that I can cash in my forty-ninth maximum grade in a row. There's a fly in our Swedish ointment of joy that Mathias missed a decision, and that we therefore probably won't be able to referee Bayern Munich anymore in the tournament because you almost never referee the same team twice in a playoff. Especially not if something controversial has happened, then you're considered unsuitable to referee the same team again. Above all, I'm genuinely worried that the mistake has affected just Juventus, and that their disappointment and anger is now directed at Mathias in particular, but also at me and my name. I know from before that you can miss things, make incorrect decisions - but you should avoid refereeing against a powerful country like Italy. It can cost, because the country has had an outstanding ability to get its hands on a number of important positions in football Europe, especially within UEFA in spring 2016. We flew home to Sweden the day after. I really wished for my own sake that Bayern would be knocked out as soon as possible, but also that Paris Saint-Germain would be eliminated. It would facilitate my way towards a possible final. A week later I was glad when I angled up my laptop and saw that three dates were blocked - Wednesday, Thursday and Friday. It meant a quarter-final in Europa League. We had got the easier first match, and of the four assignments I got the two teams that were least profiled at an arena that I had always thrived at and done two good matches at earlier in my career.

Portuguese Braga against Ukrainian Shakhtar Donetsk was the perfect match for us to referee, and a last step towards a final in Champions League. And with my fiftieth straight top grade we flew home from the sunshine in Portugal and noted that it was probably clear, nothing could stop us from getting the match that we had aimed for in recent years.

I watch the quarter-finals on TV, and I silently cheer as one of my wishes comes true. Paris Saint-Germain is eliminated. Unfortunately, both Bayern Munich and Manchester City went through, but I knew that difficult semi-finals remained for both teams and they wouldn't meet each other, which meant that both teams could be knocked out.

When I knew that the semi-finals had been selected I checked UEFA's digital calendar. It still showed nothing for me, and I cheered again. Bosse Karlsson called and confirmed that I hadn't got any semi-final.

"It's leaning towards a final," he chuckled.

The four semi-finals would be refereed by the Turk Çakır, the Englishman Clattenburg, the Slovenian Skomina and then Çakır again. It was remarkable that the same referee would referee two semi-finals in the same competition. Everyone in the referee world was equally surprised, and didn't understand what it depended on. No one dared of course to challenge or ask Collina why it was so. It was speculated that someone already selected had become injured, but the discussions landed in that UEFA probably didn't think there were enough good referees and therefore Çakır got to double up.

The semi-finals ended exactly in the way that we in the team had dreamed of. Bayern Munich was knocked out, as was Manchester City. The final would be an all-Spanish derby between Atlético Madrid and Real Madrid.

With twenty-four days left until the final in Milan, the speculations were in full swing about who would get to referee it. Of the twenty-nine referees that were in UEFA's Elite category, you could easily reduce the number to the eighteen who would referee the European Championship the same summer. Then you could reduce the list further by removing those who were too new, those who were too low ranked and who hadn't refereed anything at all in the playoff, those who had refereed too poorly during the season, those who had already refereed a final and the three who had just refereed a semi-final. No matter how I turned and twisted it, there really remained only one name in my calculations - my own. I understood that Collina's proposal on who should referee the final would be sent out during the weekend, or at the latest on Monday. But already when the weekend approached, the Spanish radio channel Cadena Ser went out with a revelation that I would referee the final between Real Madrid and Atlético Madrid. A number of European colleagues sent congratulatory texts for the final. Swedish media followed suit and wrote that it was clear that I would get to referee the match. Questions poured in and I politely answered that I couldn't comment on UEFA's selection or speculations about upcoming international matches. But how I hoped that the media was right. Every waking second I thought about when the phone would ring and Collina would give me the message. The highest responsible for UEFA's physical training of referees, Professor Werner Helsen from Belgium, congratulated me on the selection in an email on Sunday. What did he know that I didn't know? I and my colleagues talked to each other several times a day, and sent messages in our WhatsApp group at least once an hour. Everyone was nervous, hopeful and jointly convinced that it would be us who got the final this time. No one else could compete with me and the team - it was our final in Champions League. A dream would come true.

But UEFA's internal system, FAME, showed nothing on the screen no matter how much I angled and twisted the computer. The phone was at the same time worryingly quiet throughout Monday. That evening we refereed Örebro SK-Hammarby IF, and I talked to Bosse Karlsson on the phone afterwards. He said he didn't know anything. A proposal should have come now. He thought it was strange that it was delayed.

I wake up early, Tuesday, May 10. It's my mother-in-law's birthday, she turns seventy, and the whole family will have dinner together at Sigtuna Stadshotell in the evening. I hope to be able to celebrate my selection at the same time. At least once every quarter hour I update my schedule in FAME to see if any shaded dates have appeared that can verify that I will referee the Champions League final, but nothing is visible. Nor does Pierluigi Collina call. The same day we have a meeting with all twelve Allsvenskan referees at a hotel in Sigtuna. Because I had a match the day before I train lightly in the morning, shower and then eat an early lunch together with everyone else. The mood is good, and I feel fantastic.

When we then drink a cup of coffee after the meal, I take out the computer and log in again and then I see that something has happened with my calendar. Some dates are shaded, three days that indicate that I am booked in May. But it's the wrong dates. It's three dates next week, when the Europa League final is to be played in Basel. The clock is 11:47 when I note that my dream has once again been crushed. I text Mathias and Daniel: "Unfortunately. The secret path shows Europa League." But I don't understand at all what has happened and why. If we weren't going to get the final, who the hell would get it? There's no one left on the list.

I want to hide most of all but in front of me I have four hours of meeting with my colleagues where the next point on the agenda is two hours of discussions about Swedish Elite Football's values work.

The Secretary General Mats Enquist is present, comes up, takes my hand and pats me and congratulates me on the final in Champions League. I mumble something inaudible in response, because I don't know how to handle it. I hardly remember anything at all of what is said or discussed during the rest of the afternoon. Only my closest friend Markus Strömbergsson, who I sit next to, knows about what I've seen in FAME. When Collina starts to call me during the course I first avoid taking his calls, as if I think I'll avoid the final in Europa League if I don't answer.

But Collina is persistent. He calls three times in half an hour.

He's used to everyone dropping everything when he calls, but I refuse to answer. So he texts that he wants to talk and that I should call him back. I refuse, I don't even answer the text, but sit through the course all afternoon without opening my mouth. When the course is over I drive aimlessly around in Sigtuna. Should I completely ignore calling Collina back? Can I who had been so sure of being assigned the Champions League final at all rejoice in a final in Europa League? Why is he breaking his promise? Finally I nevertheless take courage and call Collina back. He answers directly, sounds a bit stressed. Then he says: "Jonas, I'm glad to be able to share very positive news with you. We have decided that you and your team will referee the final in Europa League next week. It's not just any teams, as you probably know, but Liverpool against Sevilla. A match that really requires a strong referee of the highest quality. That's why we've appointed you." I who usually talk a lot, tend to be nice and ask questions am this time extremely brief, don't feel grateful at all, and am probably very clear that I'm dissatisfied with the message he has just given me. I hang up, drive on around in Sigtuna and think to myself what a false bastard Collina is. He lied to me straight to my face a year ago. And now he doesn't even have the guts to be honest and tell why I didn't get the final, and moreover come dragging with a bunch of flattery about how the final in Europa League indeed requires a really good and strong referee. A year ago in Berlin he said that I wasn't a referee for Europa League, that I was better than that. Now he thinks I should be proud of that final. Five minutes after we hung up the final referees become official in the media. The email was prepared and the news goes out directly. The news about the final referee shocks me even more. It's Mark Clattenburg from England who will referee. Certainly he's a complete and skilled referee in every way, but he refereed the decisive semi-final between Atlético Madrid and Bayern Munich. If you referee a semi-final you should according to all rules and guidelines in the referee world impossibly be able to referee a final. It has, as far as I know, only happened once before: World Cup 1934 when Ivan Eklind refereed both semi-final and final in the same championship. Moreover, the final would be the Englishman's third match out of four with Atlético Madrid in the playoff: round of 16, then semi-final and now final. That too broke against most guidelines and rules that were usually practiced. You shouldn't referee the same team on too many occasions.

The same afternoon, but earlier, Collina has called my English colleague. He first misunderstands Collina and thinks he's going to be fourth official in the final, that it's my team that's going to referee it.

But Collina corrects him.

Clattenburg first thinks it's a joke and becomes as surprised as everyone else will be a few hours later when it becomes official.

But it wasn't a joke.

Directly when the final referee became official Mark was the first who called me and told what had happened, about his conversation with Collina, that he was shocked that he was selected and not me, that he thought that I actually deserved the final and that he understood my great disappointment.

Mark Clattenburg was a skilled referee who deserved a final in Champions League, I'm not saying anything about that, but that he got to referee in both semi-final and final indicated that something didn't go as it should have done. I really like Mark, we're good friends and have always liked each other, we've been able to be honest and discuss refereeing with open cards.

When the news about the final referees is wired out to the world it constantly pings in my phone. For each signal I get more and more stomachache.

Those who know me and understand the referee world send messages and regret that I didn't get the final in Champions

League, while those who don't know me and aren't informed happily congratulate on the final in Europa League. I soon turn off both phone and all feelings. What had really happened? How could it become like this? Why had I once again been betrayed? Did it have to do with that I was from little Sweden, an unimportant country that at the time lacked representation in UEFA's executive committee? Did it have to do with that I simply wasn't good enough? That Mark Clattenburg in spring 2016 was so much better than me that he deserved to referee both semi-final and final in Champions League? Or did it have to do with that I had angered mighty Juventus and Italy by my assistant referee Mathias having missed a tight offside by some centimeter and that the Italian champions therefore had become angry and complained loudly to UEFA? Had I maybe actually been selected for the final on sporting grounds but been stopped by the ruling football politicians within UEFA? They would have their say about the laid proposal on final referee, they always did before the tournament's last and most important match. Had the Italian chiefs at UEFA simply said no? Had the most powerful person in the football world, Juventus president Andrea Agnelli, used his network against me and my team? Maybe it was after clear pressure from the club that had been eliminated and that had connections all the way to the rooms where the decisions were made? I kept a straight face and was present at my mother-in-law's seventieth birthday dinner. But I remember that the food and wine didn't taste as good as usual, and that I just wanted to go home and turn off the light. I absolutely didn't celebrate the final in

Europa League, but instead mourned yet another missed final in Champions League. My wife's words, from the kitchen a year ago after I had been rejected in both finals, played in my head when I couldn't sleep: "There may not be forces working against you, but there are definitely forces that aren't working for you." I realized that my wife was right. The painful truth made me hardly get a wink of sleep that night. I would never reach a final in Champions League. I would never be able to trust Collina again. Ever. My six purchased match tickets, intended to celebrate my dad's seventieth birthday in Milan, still lie in the drawer at home in Sigtuna today.

European Championship in France

It's Thursday, 8th June 2016, the day before the start of the European Championship in France. My colleagues and I are standing outside the dining hall door at our hotel. We're famished, having not eaten since lunch hours ago, and we're chomping at the bit to be first in line for the buffet. But we're not the only ones with that idea.

Along with nearly a hundred other officials in various capacities, we've been here since Monday, and everything is set for the tournament to finally kick off. The mood in the group is top-notch. It's relaxed, pleasant, cheerful, and jovial, as it tends to be the day before a major championship begins. After all, no one has made a single mistake yet (for obvious reasons), and all eighteen referees are still dreaming that they'll be the one to officiate the final in Paris exactly one month from now.

The actual preparations for the tournament - training, instructions, rules tests, practical assessments, and fitness tests - were all completed earlier in the spring. As a result, the past few days have been calmer, creating less stress, pressure, and anxiety than usual. This is one reason for the group's good and relaxed atmosphere. The other is that the boss, Pierluigi Collina, is in a stable and good mood. He's friendly, laughing, and seems to be in high spirits. The mood of an extremely strong leader like Collina always affects the entire group. Everyone finds it much more pleasant and relaxed when he's not around, regardless of what mood he's in. In all the years with him as boss, I've neither seen nor heard a single referee question, challenge, or ask Collina anything in front of others. When he turns to the audience after a presentation or lecture, fixes his eyes on the participants, and after a pregnant pause says in a clear voice, "Am I being clear?" you'd rather not ask any questions. Not even if you disagree or don't understand what he means.

The doors to the large dining hall open, we approach a table, hang our jackets on chairs to mark our spots. Then we move on to see what's on offer today. To our surprise, they're serving hamburgers. And grilled sausages. With a host of delicious sides. We happily help ourselves.

We're certainly not used to this type of food, as since Collina took over as boss, an almost ascetic menu has been introduced during UEFA courses and tournaments. But now we're in the gastronomic homeland, France, and Collina seems to be in a brilliant mood. Perhaps that's why we're being served the grandest feast I've ever experienced in a refereeing context, I think to myself. All the referees are like starved wolves, no one queues at the boring salad buffet, no one fetches the pasta or soup that's served every day - it's clear that everyone truly appreciates the sausages and hamburgers.

The atmosphere is at its peak, the volume high, and laughter rings out between the tables.

At the only two reserved tables, in the centre of the room, sit the members of the Referees Committee and UEFA employees. There, free beer or wine is also served to those who want it, but that's certainly not a privilege extended to the rest of us. The committee members share our opinion - that the food has become much worse since Collina took over. Therefore, tonight's generous buffet is appreciated even at the two round tables in the middle.

My team and I share a table with our Hungarian colleagues who are officiating tomorrow's opening match. We all happily eat from the buffet, and together with them, we conclude that this was absolutely the best preparation they could get for tomorrow's assignment.

Well-seasoned, grilled hamburgers of the finest beef, elegant and flavourful French sausages with brioche buns, pickled onions, French mustard, and good salad.

At the table, we collectively praise Collina for his surprising decision, as we assume it's he who's behind the decision to offer good food that we really like. Maybe it's to show that the tournament starts tomorrow, that we've had a fantastic build-up, and that dinner is like a little gift to thank us for a job well done so far.

Suddenly, Collina himself enters the room. I can see he's in a good mood, on the move, and as always, he goes to the buffet and curiously lifts the lids. He looks, scans, and ponders what to eat for dinner. But when he comes to the sausages and hamburgers, he freezes. He asks a question to the chef standing at the station, asks another, and the chef on the other side seems stressed.

From a distance, we can see how the poor chef walks away and comes back with some kind of manager. We can see Collina shouting with an exuberant and irritated body language. Most people are still eating with good appetite, and the volume in the room is high. Not many have noticed what's happening, but from our table, we can see everything clearly.

The manager looks very concerned, he's searching for someone and finally finds UEFA's head of all our physical training, Professor Werner Helsen. Werner goes over, and we can see Collina continuing to berate him.

Then Collina stands up and tries to overpower everyone in the dining hall by clapping his hands. It takes a few seconds before nearly a hundred people notice him. The room falls absolutely silent, and all eyes are on the Italian. No one can miss that he's angry. Really angry.

He begins by saying that a mistake has been made. A big mistake by those responsible and the kitchen who have erroneously served hamburgers and sausages. The biggest mistake, however, is that we've all eaten what was served.

"Do you really think the players who are going to play matches in the Euros are sitting and eating hamburgers and sausages, do you think that? You are very unprofessional," the Italian shouts. Then he leaves the hall as quickly as he came. With brisk steps, he disappears. The silence is still total. No one says anything, no one touches their plate, no one chews, drinks, or moves at all. Even at our table, the silence is complete, until my colleague Markus Strömbergsson says: "I liked the sausage, at least. I'm going to have some more." Then he gets up and slowly walks to the buffet and takes a sausage and a bun. Everyone looks at him, most with respect for daring to be himself, for daring to do exactly what everyone would like to do.

After a while, I too go and get another hamburger.

And slowly, slowly, everyone realises that Collina isn't coming back to the dining hall. At least not for a while. Soon a queue forms as nervous referees and members of the Referees Committee are back helping themselves to the buffet again. But not everyone dares to come forward to continue taking food. Some don't dare for fear that Collina will return.

At the table, after the meal, we sat for a long time and enjoyed the tournament's tastiest meal. Several referees came over, thanked Markus for his courage and laughed that he was the first person who dared to go up and take more food. And it wasn't just the referees who thought Markus had shown courage. Several members of the Referees Committee also came to our table and expressed that they thought Collina had overreacted and handled it completely wrong.

During the next four weeks in Paris, not a single sausage or hamburger was served at the Barrière l'Hôtel du Lac.

Euro 2016 should have been Michel Platini's greatest triumph. Previously, the former great player had won the Euros as a player on home soil, and now France had been given the honour of hosting the championship again, with Platini as UEFA President. But when the tournament kicked off, Platini was suspended from all football-related activities and wasn't even allowed to be at any of the Euro arenas.

World football's largest organisation, FIFA, had been in freefall after the scandals that had erupted days before the 2014 World Cup. The English newspaper Sunday Times had then, in several articles, been able to prove that a former member of FIFA's Executive Committee had paid several million dollars to gain support for Qatar's 2022 World Cup campaign.

A year later, at the end of May 2015, the FBI conducted a dawn raid on the five-star Baur au Lac hotel in Zurich, and sleepy FIFA bigwigs were led out one by one. The raid became the starting shot for the biggest scandal of the century in the sports world - where FIFA's dubious handling of TV rights, match tickets, and allocation of major championships would be scrutinised for several years to come, and where numerous individuals would be indicted and forced to leave their positions.

During the autumn, justice also caught up with the two who ruled the football world: Sepp Blatter and Michel Platini. First, both were suspended for ninety days by FIFA's Ethics Committee after suspicions of a monetary transaction in February 2011 from Blatter to Platini amounting to 17.2 million Swedish kronor. Both of the accused claimed their innocence and appealed the verdict.

While Platini was suspended as UEFA President, he was replaced by the Referees Committee's elected chairman, Spaniard Ángel

María Villar Llona. But the acting UEFA President was himself in hot water and had his own problems. In November of the same year, he was forced to pay a fine of 25,000 Swiss francs and was simultaneously warned by FIFA's Ethics Committee for failing to cooperate in an investigation into the bidding process for the World Cup in Russia. Later, Villar Llona would also be arrested, suspected of embezzlement and corruption, and leave all his positions within UEFA and FIFA.

Platini and Blatter fought hard to counter the accusations against them. The explanation from the bigwigs regarding the payment was that it concerned a salary payment for the work Platini had done for FIFA in 2002, nine years earlier. Others claimed it was a direct payment to Platini for him to refrain from challenging Blatter as president during the FIFA Congress in 2011. But the transaction lacked an agreement or documentation, and their appeal was rejected. FIFA's Ethics Committee decided to suspend both Sepp Blatter and Michel Platini for eight years from all football-related activities. The two most powerful figures in the football world were suddenly gone. Sepp Blatter was replaced by UEFA's former General Secretary Gianni Infantino, and Michel Platini by the Slovenian lawyer Aleksander Čeferin. But on the referee side, everything remained the same. Collina continued to rule in UEFA and Busacca in FIFA - despite the fact that the bosses who had once hired them were now banned from all football for eight years.

I was actually extremely neutral upon arrival at the Euros in early June. I felt numb about missing out on a final again, sad that I couldn't feel confidence in those who governed, and realised that there would always be political forces that I couldn't influence.

I travelled down to do my best, to referee as well as I could and not care about what I couldn't influence. Of course, I dreamed, like the other seventeen referees, of getting the final on July 10th - but I also understood that it wasn't a realistic thought, after everything that had happened in recent years.

I was, however, in fantastic form, had a team that was Europe's best with Mathias and Daniel as assistant referees and with Stefan Johannesson and Markus Strömbergsson as additional assistant referees. I had great confidence in everyone in the team, but also knew that UEFA didn't see it the same way.

Three weeks before the Euros, we had refereed the Europa League final in Basel between Sevilla and Liverpool. Sevilla won 3-1, and all English players and Liverpool supporters wanted three penalties during and after the match in different situations that I had judged differently.

Afterwards, I had received support for my decisions from both Collina and the formal observer Hugh Dallas, the Italian's right-hand man.

I had also disallowed a goal for Liverpool and later in the match allowed a controversial goal for Sevilla. Mathias had flagged for offside, but I shouted loudly "PLAY ON", because it was a Liverpool player who had played the ball, which nullified the offside. There too, I had received support from Dallas. Positive messages poured in after the match, and my former colleague Howard Webb, who was working for English TV, sent a text confirming that all our decisions had been correct, and that we deserved to celebrate properly. After the positive review with Hugh Dallas, he asked me to stay for a one-on-one chat. I had just refereed the biggest final of my life, made four major match-deciding decisions, correctly issued eight cautions, and was both happy and elated. I thought he would instil courage in me for the upcoming European Championship, talk about the Champions League final that I had been dribbled out of, or give me fuel to aim for another final in 2017.

Instead, Dallas expressed that UEFA's referee leadership was concerned about Mathias Klasenius's performances in recent matches, that his ratings in recent months had been below the expected level. Dallas suggested that I might start looking at a new assistant referee for my team in the future.

I was almost shocked by the criticism of Mathias. My feeling was that the criticism was a signal from above, that it was my colleague's centimetre-missed offside against Juventus in March that had given him an undeservedly bad reputation. That there was an agenda to get rid of him.

I couldn't accept that. I honestly answered that I heard what Dallas was saying, but that Mathias was an integral part of my team, and that I had no plans to replace him.

When I got home from Basel, I still looked through Mathias's matches to see if there was any relevance to the criticism against him. Because it's easy as a friend and close colleague to be blinded, to perhaps not see weaknesses, less good performances, or a negative trend.

But there was no substance to the criticism. During 2015, Mathias had fourteen straight matches with maximum ratings, before he missed a centimetre offside in Munich. After that, maximum rating in the quarter-final in Portugal, and then a fail in the final in Basel (although his error didn't affect the result).

After refereeing a series of international tournaments in recent years, we had learned how to prepare in the best way, how to think mentally, physically, and how to avoid boredom when you're closely, closely together with your team for four, five intense weeks.

Our goal for the season had been to reach the Champions League final, and the Euros had always been a bit subordinate. Hopefully, we could recharge in the team and get far into the knockout stages. Maybe even a final could be within reach, considering that Sweden would hardly go that far in the tournament.

We created routines even at Euro 2016. The most important was to always start the days with a joint walk around the lake that was right next to our hotel, wake up the body, talk through what had happened, look ahead and plan the day. Another was to train well, to always make sure not to follow UEFA's far too easy programme and occasionally dare to train extra hard in secret when no one was watching.

It was also important to relax and feel good. Therefore, we often gathered in a room, locked ourselves in, drank a cold beer and watched football. Since someone in the UEFA team felt sorry for us referees who were constantly scrutinised by Collina, we sometimes got to fill our backpacks from the fridge whose contents were actually intended for UEFA staff and the Referees Committee, and sneak up to the room with a few sponsored beer bottles.

Our first match was early in the tournament, at the Parc des Princes in Paris. A tough match between Croatia and Turkey, which I controlled with an iron fist. After just three minutes, it kicked off properly. The Turkish midfielder Ozan Tufan came in late for a challenge, and followed through - not unintentionally - against the Croatian superstar Luka Modrić.

It was early in the match, and I preferably didn't want to caution. I used all the energy, mimicry, body language, and leadership I could muster to find the balance between making the Turks understand that it wasn't okay, while at the same time making the Croatians feel that I would protect Modrić and the others for the rest of the match.

When I look at the situation with a bit of perspective, I understand that I am at the peak of my career during the Euros in France. I have a clear and convincing body language, my eyes are intense and determined, my signals are relaxed but at the same time confident, and my big decisions are always right.

The match was played as early as 3 pm, and we were back at the hotel just before 7 pm. I called home, talked to the children and my wife, and breathed out. My colleagues came by and we had a beer in the room before we went down for a joint dinner.

At the same station where hamburgers and sausages had been served three days earlier, Hugh Dallas snuck up behind me and sarcastically wondered if that was the best I could do.

Then he congratulated me on a fantastic match. He didn't mention Mathias with a word.

The day after the Euro opener, I had a wonderful feeling in my body.

We were showered with praise by everyone we met. In addition to all the praise I received from referee colleagues and UEFA, it warmed me that the esteemed French sports newspaper L'Équipe, after the first round, named me the best referee of the round.

In the evening, we were going to watch Sweden's first match in the Euros against Ireland, and the day after that, we would have our first completely free day after eight hectic days. Sweden played poorly, but it wasn't all negative. Even though I of course cheered for the blue and yellow, I didn't want the team to go too far, because this was my team's tournament.

Every time I visited the arenas during the Euros, I got goosebumps when I heard the music that built up the last fifteen minutes before kick-off. What you could only faintly perceive in the dressing room and in the players' tunnel was so powerful from up in the stands. As a spectator, I didn't need to be in the bubble of concentration, but could enjoy, hear, see, and listen to how a DJ built up a crescendo before kick-off.

The last thing played at full volume before kick-off, the official Euro 2016 song, was for once fantastically good and catchy. The theme song for the tournament was called "This One's for You" and was performed by French David Guetta and Zara Larsson. The two were supposed to sing the song live at the final, and in my dreams, I looked forward to Zara Larsson not being the only Swede at the Stade de France on July 10th.

Seven days later, we blow the whistle for another match in the last round of the group stage.

In Toulouse, we referee Russia against Wales - a perfect match to end the group stage with. Partly because I think it's nice to leave Paris and our hotel for a few days, and partly because the match is at the right level. We're refereeing two not-too-high-profile teams or big nations that shouldn't have anything to do with the last matches of the tournament. Because that's where we're aiming, anything less than a quarter- or semi-final would be a failure, we feel after our opening match. In the middle of the first half of the match in Toulouse, I also solve the problem that we couldn't handle in Basel a month earlier - but this time it's Daniel who hears my words that it can't be offside.

Daniel confirms that he hears me and therefore keeps his flag down while praising me for having perceived the situation and clearly communicated it. We cheer loudly in the team, without it showing on us with a facial expression. But we talk all the more between us.

The fourth official, the warm and generous Daniele Orsato from Italy, is full of praise in the communication equipment.

No one can criticise us after the match. We're praised in the media, and for the second time, L'Équipe picks me as the best referee of the round. Even the Russians, who now had to take an early holiday, thanked us afterwards, and I and the team can really rejoice in our dream start to the tournament after the match.

Our Dutch observer on site, however, says that he will unfortunately be forced to give me a failing grade. I understand exactly what he's referring to, and he's right in the meaning of the rule. It's really a trivial thing that makes me get my first failing grade after fifty-two straight matches.

With ten minutes left and the score 3-0 to Wales, the Russian substitute Pavel Mamaev pulls on Aaron Ramsey's shirt, just outside the benches. I see it clearly, know that it should be a yellow card, Mamaev's second, thus an expulsion. But I have such control, such confidence, and own the match so I ignore it. Everyone knows that the Russians are going home in ten minutes, a suspension doesn't matter because the competition is over for their part.

Wales doesn't react, and neither does anyone watching the match. But the observer, who actually agrees with me in principle, thinks I'm taking an unnecessary risk. At the same time, he says that the failing grade won't matter for my continuation in the tournament.

After the concluded group stage, we secretly received good news from one of the more senior members of UEFA's Referees Committee. We would skip the round of 16, but were set for a new match later in the tournament. It was only us, the Italian Rizzoli, and the Englishman Clattenburg who had UEFA's full confidence at the moment. A day or so later, UEFA staff talked to us and prepared me for the fact that it could be a long wait for me and the team until the next match. But it wasn't a problem because we knew that our fitness coach Gunnar, as always at championships, would soon come down and contribute with energy, mental coaching, and treatments for a few days.

It was fortunate, because it took sixteen days until the next match. I had time to be the fourth official on two occasions, and we had time to watch all the matches played in Paris and follow three of the quarter-finals in front of the TV before then.

With the decreasing number of matches left to referee in the tournament, referees were sent home as time went on. Some were told they were going home during personal meetings with the Referees Committee, others during the big meetings that all referees attended - others just got a text message from the airline that it was time to travel home.

The experienced Cüneyt Çakır, who two months earlier had sensationally refereed both semi-finals in the Champions League, was sent home more or less directly after his match between Italy and Spain. We never even got to say goodbye to the Turk and his team before they were back in Istanbul. My Norwegian colleague Svein Oddvar Moen, who made his championship debut in France, had a bit of bad luck in his two matches, Wales-Slovakia and Poland-Ukraine. When he then had his personal evaluation meeting with the Referees Committee, with Collina at the helm, no one said anything about his future or that he would be sent home. Svein went up to his room after the meeting and an hour later his phone pinged. It was a message that it was time to check in for his flight home to Oslo.

The conflict-averse Collina and his governing body couldn't even bother to tell Moen and his team that they thought they hadn't performed well enough and therefore would be sent home from the championship.

The days went by, we were left as one of the few teams and it was constantly whispered from informed sources that we would be allowed to stay until the end and fight for a final. We were told that four referees were now in contention for the last matches. It was me, Rizzoli, Clattenburg, and also the Hungarian Kassai who had done a fantastically good quarter-final in the match between Italy and Germany.

We constantly speculated during our morning walks, and came to the conclusion that if Wales went to the final, it would remove the Englishman Mark Clattenburg as an option. Moreover, everyone already knew that Rizzoli would never get to referee the Euro final, despite having had a fantastically good tournament. With a Euro final, Rizzoli would namely outdo Collina as the most meritorious referee of all time, and everyone who had worked with Collina understood how important it was for him to be considered the world's best referee of all time. Collina, namely, as an active referee, officiated four major finals: Olympics, World Cup, Champions League, and UEFA Cup. The only thing he lacked to complete his CV was a Euro final.

There he made two attempts. In 2000, he did his first European Championship. He reached the quarter-final, but because Italy went to the semi-final, he wasn't allowed to referee further in the tournament and was sent home to his great disappointment. In 2004, he did his second and last European Championship. Forty-four years old, it was his last chance to become historic - the first and only referee to reach all five major finals that a European referee can reach.

It started perfectly when Italy was eliminated already in the group stage, while Collina had done two really good matches. But when the referees for the tournament's three last matches were to be presented, Collina had to settle for the semi-final Greece-Czech Republic - the final would go to the German referee Markus Merk. At the appointment, Collina, according to a referee who was there then, had stormed out of the room in disappointment at not getting to referee the final.

Normally, it used to be an advantage as a referee to share nationality with the bosses within UEFA. Therefore, one might think that Rizzoli had an advantage before the selection for the Euro 2016 final. But that wasn't the case at all. In 2016, Nicola Rizzoli was forty-five and doing his last major championship. As an active referee, the sympathetic Italian had refereed three major finals: in the World Cup, Champions League, and Europa League. The only thing he lacked to complete his CV was a Euro final, and if he got that match, his four finals would outweigh Collina's four major finals - because a Euro in football is much more prestigious than an Olympics. Therefore, the theory, which Rizzoli's own team was also convinced of, was that Collina wouldn't give the final to his countryman but instead let the Italian referee the semi-final France-Germany.

If that theory was correct, there were three referees left - me, Mark Clattenburg, and Viktor Kassai - to referee two matches: the other semi-final, Portugal-Wales, and the final itself. It was a given that Clattenburg, as an Englishman, couldn't referee Wales' semi-final, and neither the final if Wales reached it. There were days of speculation, discussions, analyses, and gossip between colleagues. But we referees, as usual, didn't get to know anything. We interpreted all signs, tried to fish for information from the Referees Committee members, but nothing helped. We continued to train, killed time by coming up with fun things to do, and slowly started to long for home. One day I got a letter to our hotel room from my youngest daughter: "At football camp we saw a picture of you then I told some that you were my dad and I was proud. Miss, love you kiss." I cried by myself in the hotel room and longed for home. I wanted to do my last match as soon as possible and then fly straight home to what mattered most. It suddenly mattered a little less whether it was a semi-final or final, I wanted to go home after a month on the road.

Finally, UEFA called for a meeting on Monday, July 4th at 9:30 AM.

There, they would inform about who would referee the two semi-finals, and also which two referees wouldn't have matches in the semi-finals and thus be in contention for the final on Sunday. When I went to sleep the day before the meeting, the negative thoughts I had carried with me in recent months prevailed. I was convinced that I would never reach a final. On the morning before the meeting, Bosse Karlsson called, I answered immediately and my Swedish boss told me as expected that there would be no final for me this time either. But I had been assigned the semi-final between Portugal and Wales. It was secret until the meeting, but Bosse thought I deserved to know right away. I appreciated Bosse's call. And for the first time, I was neither disappointed, angry, sad, nor frustrated about a message about a missed final or an assignment that I didn't get. I could only state that it turned out as I felt it would. My colleagues and I took our morning walk and tried to focus on making a great match in Lyon on Wednesday and then going home and having a holiday with our families.

Portugal won their semi-final with a clear 2-0 and were ready for the final on the warm evening in Lyon. And I was satisfied. After concluding the Euros with yet another brilliant performance in the semi-final, we celebrated afterwards. When everyone had showered and changed, one of the three governing members of UEFA's Referees Committee, the Frenchman Marc Batta, who had also been an observer, asked me to stay behind for a minute. "Jonas," he said and looked me in the eyes. "The final on Sunday in Paris could just as well have been yours. I'm sorry for your sake, but glad that you performed so well in the semi-final tonight. You'll get a final next time, just continue like this." I had heard the same words from other people before, but since they had proved to be empty promises, I didn't take Batta's words seriously.

I was burnt, had already heard the fine words, the promising prospects for the future, which now meant nothing.

We squeeze into the bus that will take us back to the hotel. We've fortunately managed to get the driver to smuggle out some beers from the main sponsor, so when we sit down in the car, we can open a cold beer each and together enjoy that we now finally have a holiday. For real.

Me, Mathias, Daniel, Stefan, and Markus were all from different parts of Sweden. There was a four-year difference between the youngest and the oldest - we voted differently, had different views on a lot of important issues but were despite that all very good friends with a common passion: we loved to referee football. Otherwise, there were actually very few things that really united us, and music taste was just one example. Still, we always sang one song together after our matches - it had become a mantra in the team, in the same way that we always played Guns N' Roses' "Sweet Child o' Mine" before every match. In the bus on the way through the Lyon night, we sing loudly together Kenta's classic "Just Today I Am Strong". It has nothing to do with sympathies for the club Hammarby, which is associated with the song. Instead, it has to do with the fact that we've longed for that feeling you only get after you've refereed a difficult match with extremely high pressure and stress - and together can breathe out and enjoy for a short moment.

All of us in the team know that at the highest level where we find ourselves, there's an extremely high risk of failure. A single small mistake or controversial decision in a semi-final of a European Championship could have killed my refereeing career - regardless of what I had done before.

A refereeing career can collapse like a house of cards, just as quickly, just as unexpectedly and mercilessly, completely without warning, no matter how high and successfully you have built it up until that second it gives way.

We flew home to Stockholm the next day and in the late afternoon I got to kiss my family who picked me up at Arlanda.

Our daughters held up a big poster they had made with a referee with yellow and red cards.

"Welcome home, Dad, we've missed you so much we're bursting."

In the evening when the girls have gone to bed, I see in the background how France beats Germany and advances to the Euro final. The match is refereed by Nicola Rizzoli, of course. As both his team and I thought, he never got the chance to surpass Collina as the world's most meritorious referee of all time.

When I wake up the next day in Sigtuna, for the first time after thirty-three long days in France, I get a message from Mark Clattenburg:

"Cheers, mate. Thanks for making sure Portugal won their semi-final, it gave me the final on Sunday."

The Last Chance

As autumn 2016 approached, I felt uncertain about where I stood and where to aim next. After the promised Champions League final and a missed final in the Euros, I knew I couldn't rely on any potential promises from Collina or UEFA. I had two years left in my refereeing career.

The 2018 World Cup was still far off, but the tournament in Russia was a fantastic goal, an opportunity to crown my career. Shortly after the championship, I would turn forty-five, and my career would be over in any case. Life as a retired referee was drawing ever closer.

After an intense spring season and five long weeks in France during the Euros, I began to waver. I wanted more time with my family. In August, I wanted to prioritise spending a week with our youngest daughter at her football camp, be home when our oldest daughter had her birthday in the middle of an Allsvenskan round, and moreover, my wife and I wanted to take a longer weekend abroad somewhere. All quite reasonable things after missing so much of the summer away from family. Besides family, I also had a side project that was taking up more and more time and had a much longer horizon than the two years I had left as a referee.

In August, hockey profile Niklas Wikegård and I were set to open the gym in Sigtuna that we had been sketching out for several years. It had started as a loose thought back in 2012. At that time, we both trained at what was Sigtuna's only gym. A small, cramped, poorly maintained and generally unsavoury place where you absolutely didn't want to shower and where there was no space to hang around after your workout to chat and meet people.

In November 2015, Niklas had signed the lease for a suitable premises, and after that, work on the gym had intensified.

The ambitions were high. It was to be a meeting place with group training, the opportunity to have a coffee, staff who recognised you and had a personal approach, and not least, space so that you didn't have to be cramped. I had put hundreds of hours into the gym project, which we named WE after our surnames, and now as the inauguration approached at the end of August, there was more and more to do.

I emailed Bosse Karlsson, tired, sad and a bit dejected. I told him that I could consider terminating my employment, taking leave of absence or similar because I felt that I didn't want to be as available as my employers required. Bosse and I had a meeting, and we had a good chat. He understood my situation and helped me as much as he could in my role at home. I temporarily got a slightly calmer schedule in Sweden and didn't need to referee every round, so that I could recover from the international assignments and courses that took an enormous amount of time. With his own experience and insight into how everything was connected, Bosse was always good at listening, giving advice and simplifying my situation.

After the Euros, Mathias, Daniel and I had barely uttered a word about the future. None of us had had the energy or strength to lift our gaze, look ahead and set new goals for what we wanted with our refereeing. We in the team were to start the autumn with a half-day chat about our upcoming common goals in Jönköping, and then in the evening referee the home team J Södra against Östersund. It would be a calm match between two teams that weren't major crowd-pullers.

This spring, we had been involved in a nasty episode in our home series when we refereed IFK Göteborg against Malmö FF.

We had refereed the emotional meeting between Malmö and Göteborg on several occasions before. It was always packed with people and a good atmosphere, tough and intense matches with a lot of prestige at stake.

But what should have been a crowd-pleaser between two of Swedish football's finest and most successful clubs instead became a nightmare experience. In the final stage of the match, with just over ten minutes left to play, I perceive a sudden loud noise from the area where my colleague Mathias is. When I look out, I see a player sitting down on his haunches and holding his head. Someone has thrown a banger onto the pitch from the IFK supporters' stand.

When the players start leaving the pitch a second later, I see how the MFF player Tobias Sana runs down towards the section where the home supporters are, how he takes the corner flag and aggressively throws it up towards the stands. Several players and guards run there to stop him and then lead him away towards the player tunnel where the majority of the players are. We also withdraw from the pitch and lock ourselves in our room to investigate what has happened.

I look at Mathias who was just a metre away from the area where the banger landed. He is absolutely not feeling well, I can see that. He says there's a ringing in his ears, but I see that it's something else. He's absent, unfocused, doesn't answer my questions and starts crying when the shock subsides.

I hug him, calm and comfort him and ask the inevitable question of whether he can manage to go back onto the pitch. Mathias is not comfortable going out again. And even we others in the team feel the same way. If we're not safe, we can't resume the match after what has happened. It's a work environment issue.

I leave Mathias and the other colleagues in the referee room and go into an adjacent room. There I discuss possible scenarios together with the match delegate, representatives from the police and both teams. Everyone in the room is in complete agreement that we should abandon the match. Everyone understands us and accepts the decision: players, managers, representatives of the clubs, journalists and supporters. A steady stream of people comes to our changing room and shows their support, empathy and understanding for our decision. IFK Göteborg's sports director Mats Gren is one of them. He comes in, hugs Mathias and says in a cautious voice that he has full understanding for our decision and will accept it one hundred percent.

For us, a long evening followed writing reports, and after about a week came the Swedish Football Association's verdict: Malmö FF was awarded the victory with 3-0.

From our employer, the Swedish Football Association, we didn't get much support. At best a perfunctory call, but then it was I, Mathias and Daniel who were our own psychologists, therapists and processed the event and our feelings about what had happened.

We put the incident behind us and did our best to look ahead and had almost not a thought about the sad April evening in Gothenburg when we learned that the home team had appealed the verdict that they had previously said they would accept. All the fine and understanding words from Mats Gren turned out to be false and deceitful. According to the appeal he signed, the match should have been played to completion. According to Gren and the club, mistakes had been made by several involved, and therefore not only Gothenburg should be punished for the match being abandoned.

After three hundred matches in Allsvenskan and countless situations where one can think and feel differently, I had read numerous appeals and written exchanges, but I hadn't read a single one that was so full of lies as the one Gren had written. A person from IFK Göteborg's management team even called me the day after the appeal and apologised and told me that there were many within the club who didn't agree with the decision to appeal. The Disciplinary Committee rejected IFK Göteborg's appeal. We had been proven right again, the verdict stood. MFF won 3-0, and the person who had thrown the banger was later sentenced for causing bodily harm and received two months in prison.

Even though the verdict stood, I was personally angry and disappointed with Mats Gren, for his obvious lies, his false hug and fine words to Mathias in the changing room. I felt that I wasn't sure if I could handle it in a professional way when I met him in the future. Therefore, I made the decision that I didn't want to referee IFK Göteborg as long as Mats Gren was sports director at the club.

The traumatic event at Gamla Ullevi, and the sad aftermath, had left a sour aftertaste, but there and then, spring 2016, we were in the middle of a Champions League playoff and didn't let the episode affect us but kept our eyes on our goal.

I, Mathias and Daniel made a restart in Allsvenskan in August 2016. After a few weeks off, we were to referee Jönköping Södra against Östersund. We met early in the day, had lunch, talked about our future as referees, as a team, and what new goals we could set.

It was perhaps naive, but we talked about the Champions League final in Cardiff in May 2017 as our future goal. But since we hadn't got the final in Milan barely three months earlier after so many matches with good ratings, the chance was probably minimal that we would get any Champions League final at all. We therefore glanced further ahead, and already now talked about the World Cup in Russia in June 2018. There, at least, Collina wasn't the one in charge, and even though we all felt discomfort about working with FIFA chief Massimo Busacca on the way to Russia, we hoped that there at least we would get a chance to be judged more honestly. And if the World Cup in Russia was the goal, there was also a Champions League final in Kiev to aim for in May 2018.

After our discussions, it was time for our first match on the way to our new goal.

It was an absolutely fantastic evening at the idyllic Stadsparksvallen, warm winds, humid air, an almost still Lake Vättern just below and a grass pitch that smelled like the grass pitches smelled when I started refereeing football in division 5 almost thirty years earlier. A calm match with pleasant players, it felt like the perfect start to the autumn and a fine future - right up until the eighty-ninth minute of the match. That's when all hell broke loose. Daniel shouts loudly and stressfully that there's someone on the pitch. I turn around and catch sight of a masked man who from behind is about to attack Östersund's goalkeeper Aly Keita with punches and pushes.

I blow the whistle and in the tumult that arises, security guards seize the masked man. Keita is injured and neither can nor wants to continue playing the match after having received, among other things, a blow to the head.

The masked man has also made a bomb threat against the arena. Everyone present is shaken, shocked, dejected and questioning.

How could it happen here? On an idyllic football evening with two teams that just wanted to play football, where there is no hint of hatred and threats. There are no answers, other than that I know I'm forced to abandon my second Allsvenskan match in three months.

On the way home from Jönköping, I wondered if it was really worth it. So much time, so much crap in between. Tonight it didn't affect me and the team, but how long would we be able to handle being in these situations? I had refereed a number of matches with problems, with supporters who had crossed the line, with people who had taken liberties and thrown things in and created a work environment that was anything but positive for us referees. And it had become increasingly tougher during the years I had refereed at the highest level. Patience had become shorter, words ever stronger, objects thrown in more dangerous, attacks on referees and players considerably more aggressive and loud. It wasn't just a problem for football and the Allsvenskan stands. It largely reflected how society had developed over almost twenty years.

I slept poorly when I finally got home, but didn't have time to rest or recover on Saturday. I got up early, having barely slept an hour. It was a week until WE would open with pomp and circumstance, and I had so much to do with big and small things that needed to be fixed before the inauguration.

I know that I have an extreme capacity. I can work as much as needed, barely need to eat and sleep, have a good memory, can keep many balls in the air. On Sunday we would have a soft opening for the members who had already signed up. It became a packed day with work from early morning and when I had come home, eaten dinner and was about to put the plates in the dishwasher, everything went black before my eyes for a short second. When I looked at myself in the mirror, my face was pale despite the late summer having offered quite a lot of sun. I was tired, had slept too little during the past weeks and felt that I would need to take it a bit easy next week to recharge my batteries. But that was absolutely not an option. A thousand things remained to be done before the real inauguration of WE in six days. But before that, in just two days, I would referee a match worth a hundred million, a decisive qualifying match for the Champions League between Monaco and Villarreal.

I packed my bag and looked forward to travelling away for a few days to sunny Monte Carlo with my usual optimistic mindset. While my colleagues in the team read a book on the flight, I worked. After a good lunch on match day when my colleagues slept for an hour, I worked. I, who always used to sleep for one to two hours in the afternoon as preparation, this time only managed to sleep for fifteen minutes. All other time was spent preparing for the weekend's inauguration of WE.

Despite my less thorough preparation, the match went well, I thought, and so did the rest of the team. The players showed respect for me and my decisions, and even though Villarreal didn't progress and thought they should have had a penalty - but instead got a penalty against them - the protests were mild and respectful. Our Portuguese delegate said after the match that it was noticeable that they had seen me at the Euros, that I had a lot for free and solved the match in a fantastically good way.

Therefore, the Greek observer's review came as a hard slap in the face out of nowhere. He did say that I had done a good match, but that two big decisions had been wrong. Firstly, a missed handball in the first half, secondly when I had blown for a penalty for Monaco for handball where the ball actually hit the player's back. Two mistakes, both match-deciding, according to the observer.

Afterwards and on the way home to Sigtuna, I wasn't particularly worried.

Even though I had been dropped from the big finals at the last minute on several occasions, I knew that I was on Collina's and UEFA's inside list. They would surely correct one of the mistakes in my favour, I thought.

Back home from the match in Monaco, I didn't brood over the match and my incorrect decisions. I was fully occupied with the inauguration of WE. It was a success. We sold more memberships than we had dreamed of and received incredibly nice praise for the facility. Niklas Wikegård and I had managed to create something special, and it was an enormous kick. I had almost suppressed the match in Monaco when the rating came a few days later. The number was a hard blow to the stomach: 7.4. I had made two match-deciding mistakes, and UEFA's leadership had confirmed my clear errors. It was the worst rating of my career - not even my catastrophic match in 2009 between Glasgow and Sevilla had given that rating. My rock-bottom rating also meant that I would be suspended, which happened when you got a rating lower than 7.6. My stomach tightened. For the first time in seven years, I wasn't a regular when the thirty-two referees were to be selected for the first two matchdays of the Champions League. It stung and hurt my performance-addicted heart. I was ashamed of having to tell people that I would referee Europa League instead.

A week or so later, Pierluigi Collina called. On FaceTime. I was at home, sitting by the computer and my heart immediately started beating a little faster.

I adjusted my hair and answered with a voice that tried to be both positive and confident. Collina confirmed that I would miss the Champions League start. It was UEFA's rules that governed. At the same time, I knew that he could personally influence all ratings. If he didn't want to suspend a referee, he had all the power to ensure that the rating was raised so that the referee could continue. Collina was otherwise in a good mood, asked how I viewed the situations, I tried to argue that the first situation wasn't at all such a clear and obvious mistake as the observer and UEFA thought. He didn't agree with me at all, but the conversation was positive and Collina often laughed. Before we hung up, I plucked up courage and asked the only question that really mattered. That I asked it surprised me, as I knew I couldn't trust him. I asked straight out if it was worth it for me to keep the dream of refereeing the final in Cardiff in May 2017.

He replied that I was one of the best referees and absolutely had a chance to referee the final next year. It was the expected answer and I knew it didn't mean anything at all. Instead of refereeing in the Champions League, we got Fenerbahçe-Feyenoord in the Europa League. It was a big match in itself, on paper a better match than several of those played in the Champions League. The tempo was high, the situations tough and the crowd loud. But it still felt extremely strange and wrong that I wasn't refereeing Champions League.

The week after came an email from Collina where he questioned Mathias Klasenius' performances lately. That he had made mistakes that were not acceptable at this level. It hurt that Collina and UEFA questioned Mathias. He had been with me abroad since 2006, we had done nearly one hundred and twenty matches together internationally and he had been a contributing factor to why I was where I was today. He had always been loyal, stepped up, worked hard and over time performed fantastically well. I didn't buy that any single match with isolated situations that had drawn attention would be enough for UEFA to question Mathias. Did it have to do with the offside against Juventus? Was that still on the agenda in the meeting rooms in UEFA's long and not entirely bright corridors? I briefly replied to Collina that I thanked him for his feedback, and that I would take it further with Mathias in my own way. I chose to be completely open with Mathias. On the flight down to Belgrade the same week, I showed him Collina's email. I think Mathias appreciated my honesty and understood the importance of not getting involved in any controversial situations in the upcoming international match between Serbia and Austria, but also during the rest of the autumn.

In Belgrade, we refereed when the home team won 3-2, and both Mathias and I received maximum ratings (8.4) in the report after returning home. The rating that had been a given during the previous four seasons now felt like a great victory, especially for Mathias.

To perform so well under such great pressure was impressive.

After being suspended for the first two rounds, our real season debut in the Champions League came in October. We had been given the match between Tottenham and Bayer Leverkusen to be played at Wembley itself. Finally a big match, at a fantastic arena with lots of people in the stands. The desire for revenge burned in me. Now I would show everyone how good I and the team really were.

The preparation, however, would be completely different from what I had imagined. Wednesday morning, October 26, my older sister Jenny called shortly after half past eight in the morning. Jenny is two years older than me and we have had a very good connection throughout life, even though we are very different in many ways. While I have always taken up a lot of space since birth and shouted loudly when I lost, Jenny is my complete opposite. She is moderation personified and has always had fantastic patience with me. But we also have common sides. We are both Norrbottningar in every aspect imaginable: calm, secure, don't get upset unnecessarily and don't talk about feelings if we don't have to. When she now calls, I can immediately hear from her voice that something is wrong. I freeze, stiffen and hear her say: "It's not good with Dad. He was taken to Sunderby Hospital by ambulance last night, with a severe heart attack, he's in the emergency room now." Thoughts are spinning and I feel my heartbeats increase rapidly, while she explains that he seems to be okay under the circumstances, but that he will undergo an operation. Dad had had a bit of pain across his chest for a few days, felt a pain similar to heartburn and had rather clumsily tried to get an appointment at the local health centre. During the night it had become acute, he had broken out in a cold sweat, fainted and it had ended with mum having to drive him to the hospital. There he had suffered cardiac arrest, and they had been forced to restart his heart with a defibrillator.

After listening to what had happened, I decide that I want to fly to Luleå to meet Dad and Mum, and my sister, and get an idea on site of what had happened, how he really is and what happens now.

When I land at Kallax airport and turn on my phone, I have an uneasy feeling in my body. I know that Dad is getting the best help he can get, but also that the first 24 hours after a heart attack are always critical.

I go out from the terminal and see my mum sitting waiting in the car. I go over, she comes out and we hug each other. My mum Ann-Britt is calmness itself, never gets stressed, doesn't worry unnecessarily and most often states that "these things happen" when something serious has occurred. And that's exactly what she says when she picks me up, on this sunny Wednesday in October that I had actually planned in a completely different way. And when I ask how she herself is doing after a night without sleep, after her husband of almost fifty years had suffered a heart attack and she herself had driven him to the emergency room and with her own eyes less than twelve hours ago seen the medical staff save his life, she answers a bit laconically in Northern Swedish style: "Well, I'm fine. A bit tired, but it's no problem." We drive the twenty minutes to the hospital where Mum had worked her whole life. On the way we talk about what happened, how Dad is doing and that despite everything he's had insane luck to be alive. I scold her a little gently, that they must take warning signs more seriously, not be dutiful and stay at home until it's too late.

We arrive at Sunderby Hospital, park the car and go in. I have been fortunate and almost never needed to visit the hospital for my own injuries or ailments - and almost everyone close to me has also managed well. It strikes me when I walk through the doors that it feels heavy, strange, serious and a bit depressing to go in there. I travel back in time. My grandfather, my role model, he who was my hero, he who could do everything and knew everyone. In the summer of 1985, he suffered a stroke. After a few weeks, which felt like an eternity, I finally got to visit Grandpa in the medical ward in Kalix. I remember how I went into the room, saw a person who looked like my grandfather sitting up in bed. It was Grandpa, I understood that, but still not. His natural charisma, radiance and self-confidence were gone. His body and language were changed. When he saw me, he started to cry, uncontrollably. I remember being shocked.

My grandfather was the strongest in the world. He could do everything, knew everything, knew everyone and was always happy and strong. Now he was crying in front of my eleven-year-old eyes and it made me desperate and confused. Now thirty-one years later, I'm terrified that I will experience something similar with my own father.

I nervously enter the room where Dad is lying. He is indeed a bit pale, has some tubes and machines connected to his body, but he is completely clear in his head, seems cheerful and tells in his own words what he's been through.

He is to be operated on in a day or two, but isn't afraid. He has no fear of death, despite having been close to dying just a few hours earlier. He sees clearly what has happened, is just happy and grateful to be here, thinks that the healthcare is fantastic and that the staff here are so kind and friendly. I take the opportunity to scold him a little caringly: "Next time you have heartburn for a few days, maybe you should go to the hospital a bit earlier." We talk football, as always. Our smallest common denominator. About IFK Luleå, about Allsvenskan, about Champions League, about my next match which is planned for tomorrow, AIK against Häcken. I say that I'm unsure if I should referee it, that it depends on how he is doing and how long I stay here in Luleå. He looks shocked and surprised and says: "But for goodness sake, I'm okay, I'm getting great care. Mum and Jenny are here, of course you should referee tomorrow and next week in London." I'm glad he's doing well, and that my mum also seems to have taken the past couple of days in the right way. Dad is to be operated on once more within a day or two, then he can come home and with the right medicine, exercise and adaptation, he will be able to live a normal life going forward. At least that's what the doctors say.

I decide to travel home to Sigtuna the same evening. When I go to bed late at night, it's been a long day I have behind me. I have been on an emotional roller coaster over the past eighteen hours, but the ride is over and my father and mother seem to be doing well. Despite everything.

After that day, I became increasingly grateful that I and my loved ones were healthy, I no longer took health completely for granted. And from that day on, I always answered when my sister called - even if I was in the middle of meetings and presentations.

The match in London the following week went as well as I had hoped and dreamed. Not a single mistake, not a situation discussed afterwards - I thought we were back where we belonged, at the top of Europe. In November 2016, I equalled my perhaps not most flattering personal record when in the World Cup qualifier between Greece and Bosnia, I handed out as many cards in ninety minutes as I had in Munich in March of the same year. But in Piraeus, just outside Athens, I also had a serious sending-off of a player and as an end point, I reported the Bosnian national team coach Mehmed Baždarević after he followed us in the player tunnel after the match and shouted loudly about how catastrophically bad I was as a referee. Was it my fault that the players acted so indifferently and aggressively? Did it have to do with my leadership, my decisions and my way of acting? It had started already during the warm-up when the supporters threw fireworks at each other and made rushes - and continued during the match with constant problems in the stands, objects thrown in, players who were aggressive and didn't want to play football at all. According to the Slovak referee observer, who gave me the more than maximum rating of 8.6, it only had to do with the players. I was more critical myself. Had I perhaps missed a decision? Not been tough and clear enough? Did the Greeks have a negative image of me after the yellow card on Karagounis in Euro 2012?

Did the Bosnians have bad memories of me from the match in Romania in 2011 when they lost 3-0? I felt that I had lost energy, that I didn't feel the same flow as before, that I somehow lacked joy, confidence and motivation. Was that the puzzle piece that made me no longer able to convince players and leaders about my decisions? The autumn season that had started in the worst way in Monaco and then had stuttered with a suspension, a questioned team and a less good feeling, would in December conclude with a match in the Champions League. We didn't know until a day before which match we would get, and when UEFA revealed the match, Olympique Lyonnais against Sevilla, my feelings were mixed.

    I loved refereeing in Lyon. Not only had I become ready for the Euros right there in November 2011, I had also refereed a Euro semi-final in the city as recently as June. But this match was played in one of the toughest groups and was a direct decisive match for who would go through. The positive interpretation of that was that UEFA still had confidence in me. Really, I should have loved getting this match, that it was exactly my type of match, a sign of support from my bosses and a given step towards the big final I dreamed of. But in December 2016, something had happened to me. With perspective and the broken promises, I had begun to doubt that UEFA believed in me, and thus I had also begun to doubt myself, my competence and ability to succeed. It became a tough and nervous match, but I had full control of it, the players accepted my decisions and the twenty-two free kicks were evenly distributed between the teams. The match ended 0-0 and Sevilla went through. If Lyon had won 1-0, the home team would have gone through, and both Lyon's players and leaders were disappointed afterwards. But not a single person in either team said a negative word to us. On the contrary.

We were met with great respect from everyone.

The feeling in the dressing room was good, we generally got positive feedback about our situations from friends and colleagues who had seen the match on TV. There might have been a penalty to discuss, but those who had followed the TV broadcast gave us support for our decision not to blow.

After ten minutes in the dressing room, our observer came in, an Estonian who had happily told before the match that he travelled around Europe and took all the assignments he could get, that he took pride in never saying no to matches when UEFA asked. We knew in the team that he was appreciated by UEFA for just that, and maybe not for his competence.

The Estonian was satisfied, said that we had done a good match. There had been some difficult situations, he said, but we would talk more about that after dinner.

There was another knock on the door, and we opened. It was Olympique Lyonnais' charismatic owner and president since 1987, Jean-Michel Aulas. It rarely happened that the president of the clubs came into the referee room, the clubs usually sent in a representative of lower dignity to thank for the match and often hand over a gift from the home club. Most often we referees got a match shirt, some souvenir or present from the city or region we visited.

The president was very pleased with our performance, despite the team just missing out on the Champions League playoffs. When Aulas left the dressing room, I felt that we had succeeded. Even if we maybe, theoretically, could have missed a penalty, the overall performance was extremely good. That the observer had been in the dressing room and heard the losing and eliminated president's praising words should help us on the way, I thought as we left the dressing room and went to dinner.

In autumn 2016, there was a blog called Third Team. It was an open blog where people interested in refereeing could analyse performances of referees, speculate on who would referee certain matches, discuss rules, interpretations and even set ratings for referees and their performances.

I thought it was a fun initiative, even though I personally read it very rarely, in the same way that I chose not to read about myself in newspapers or on social media. I was convinced that I became a better referee by not taking in what other people thought about me - especially when they might not have all the knowledge, knew what rules applied or what interpretations and instructions we had received.

Instead, I chose to listen to my colleagues, my bosses and above all my worst critic: myself. However, I knew that several other referees followed the site slavishly, read every day and gladly took in criticism - whether it was positive or negative. Even observers read the site, as did Collina himself. During a presentation from the Italian's computer, I had seen that he even had the site as a bookmark.

During dinner we sat spread out around the table and talked to each other, while the observer mostly looked at his mobile phone.

After a while, he looked up and said to me that Third Team thought I had missed three penalties and two sendings-off. I tried to play it off as quickly as I could by saying that Third Team didn't always have a grasp on either rules or interpretations.

The dinner went on, but I had a lump in my stomach. I became more and more angry the more I thought about the observer seeming to care more about what had been written on a blog than his own assessment of the performance. It bothered me for the rest of the dinner so much that the food didn't taste at all.

The review then became a farce. There were apparently five key situations to discuss in the match, but when we left the review, neither I nor my colleagues knew what the observer really thought. Except that we collectively thought we knew that he supported us in all key situations.

We travelled home and I didn't know if I had done right or wrong.

I lived with a lump in my stomach that took energy and strength, and when the rating after just over a week landed in my inbox, I opened it quickly and froze: 7.4.

Again due to two clear and match-deciding mistakes. I was suspended again.

The dream of a final was dead. For real.

A week passed, then Pierluigi Collina called for the second time this autumn. It was Monday, December 19, five days until Christmas Eve, and I knew that it wouldn't be a pleasant conversation.

What was good about the conversation was that we agreed on the overall picture.

We also agreed that we would talk more at the course in Málaga in five weeks, with a little perspective. What was bad about our chat was that I still had got 7.4 in rating and thus was suspended for a match again.

This time I was so afraid of the truth, of an honest answer, that I didn't dare to ask about what I wondered most: if I still had a chance to referee the final in Cardiff despite everything.

I celebrated Christmas 2016 with a bad feeling, an uncertainty that I had almost never felt during my time as a referee at the highest level.

The new year began with a referee friend sending me an article. It was about the only official poll where the world's referees were ranked. The article lifted me a little out of the gloomy thoughts I had had about my refereeing life.

The article stated that I had been named the fourth best referee in the world. Ahead of me on the list I only had Mark Clattenburg, Nicola Rizzoli and Viktor Kassai. And since one had quit and another would quit shortly, I could in a way see myself as the world's second best referee. Although the poll was done by the International Federation of Football History and Statistics (IFFHS), which didn't contain any voters from either UEFA's or FIFA's referee committee, it was of course honourable to be at the top.

Jag förstår vikten av att översätta hela kapitlet korrekt från början till slut. Jag fortsätter nu där jag slutade:

Despite this, I felt neither joy, energy nor confidence when I travelled to the annual course in Málaga at the end of January. I knew that I was again suspended in the Champions League, that the dream of a final in the European cups was distant. But even the road to the World Cup in Russia 2018 was both long, difficult and pointed steeply upwards. Our World Cup qualifier matches during the autumn had given maximum ratings and good reports. That spoke in our favour, but what also happened at the end of January did not. A week before the Málaga camp, FIFA had appointed a new president of the referee committee after the suspended Spaniard Ángel María Villar Llona. Surprisingly, the choice fell on Pierluigi Collina. The world's most powerful refereeing personality had become even more powerful. The Italian now sat on more chief chairs than anyone else: FIFA's, UEFA's and the Ukrainian referee committee's. At first, many had been surprised by the appointment, but when I and other referees at the course in Málaga analysed the matter, the connection between FIFA's new president, Gianni Infantino, and Pierluigi Collina became very obvious. Both had Italian passports, came from the same confederation where they had worked together for a longer time with the now corruption-suspended Michel Platini as boss. Infantino was the highest official, i.e. general secretary, in UEFA in 2010 when Collina began his employment as the highest referee chief within the organisation. Moreover, there was a personal friendship between the men outside the football area.

Collina might have been the right man for the job as president of FIFA's referee committee - judging by merits and background. But that he would sit on so many chairs simultaneously, have so much responsibility in so many roles, meant that the power within the refereeing world was further centralised.

I was like many others shocked, but also a bit disappointed. I knew where I stood with Collina - for me he was a political liar, a moody and capricious person who protected those who helped him on the journey towards total power, who got rid of people when it no longer suited and who created an environment around him where no one ever dared to challenge him and his opinions or say what they really thought. Deep down, I already understood at Collina's appointment that the journey towards the World Cup in Russia would become even more difficult, that I now had a supreme chief that I knew I absolutely couldn't trust. But I didn't just think negative thoughts. To be able to cope with the effort, I forced myself to lift my gaze, think about how well I had refereed for several years with Collina as chief of UEFA - and that it could also mean an advantage for me in the hunt for my second World Cup.

It went so-so. The days at the camp in Málaga in southern Spain were depressing. I did pass the running test better than ever, weighed less than ever and had a fat percentage that was lower than before, but I got no praise for any of it, no encouragement or any confirmation from the chief who had suspended me on two occasions during the autumn. If you become a referee, you're certainly not in need of praise, a pat on the shoulder and kind words. But you at least need to have a boss who gives you his unreserved support, who builds your security and self-confidence for upcoming assignments. During the days in Málaga, I realised that we didn't have any match at all in February. In the Champions League we were suspended and we didn't have any match in the Europa League playoffs either, where you always used to get a match when you were suspended from the biggest tournament. Positively, I could, theoretically, be back for a quarter-final in the Champions League, and that I hadn't refereed more than four teams in two matches during this year's competition and that I therefore in theory could referee all teams, except Paris Saint-Germain. What was also good was that I and my team didn't appear on a single clip during the entire course. It was almost a bit remarkable, since I supposedly had made four major match-deciding mistakes during the season and these were usually shown over and over again and the referees were hung out to dry. Once I was even mentioned in a positive context by Collina. A large mass confrontation with twenty-two players in the match between Greece and Bosnia was described, with four yellow cards and one red card as a result. Collina likened me and the team to a Swedish peacekeeping team where only the blue UN helmets were missing. But that was also the only positive thing that happened in Málaga.

What bothered me most during the days at the course was that I, after having talked with a bunch of colleagues and heard how it had gone for them and other referees, realised that more referees during the autumn had had the rating 7.4, but they had not been suspended. That certain referees who I knew had made two clear match-deciding mistakes had not received the rating 7.4 but landed on 7.8 or 7.9 and thus got to continue refereeing in the Champions League. It was clear that there was a difference between referees and referees. Much depending on who they were, if UEFA wanted them to succeed and, above all, which countries they came from. That conclusion I could easily draw. I had suspected it before, but since the majority of judgments, assessments and ratings in recent years had been in my favour, I hadn't really reflected on it. Or seen the downside of it. It was previously only in the final stages of tournaments that I had been dribbled out and understood that it wasn't always the best referee who refereed the best matches, that there was another agenda. But now I found myself where many other referees had been over the years.

With the feeling that I wasn't being judged in the same way as everyone else.

After the next playoff round of the Europa League and Champions League had been drawn, I was in FAME several times a day to see if we had got any match. And one day I saw that three dates were shaded in April. That meant we were back in the Champions League.

We would referee in a quarter-final, either Atlético Madrid-Leicester or Bayern Munich-Real Madrid.

It was a small vindication to get a quarter-final. Part of me wanted to referee the biggest match (in Munich) to show myself, another wanted to referee inconspicuously and on paper as easily as possible (in Madrid) to have a greater chance of then reaching the final seven weeks later. The thoughts of miraculously reaching a final would soon be ruled out, however.

On March 20, I got a text message from the referee coach for Allsvenskan, Peter Fröjdfeldt, where he honestly and warmly congratulated me on my selection for the U20 World Cup in South Korea in May. At first I didn't understand anything.

No one had told me anything.

Many referees would have been overjoyed to have been selected for a U20 World Cup. But I mostly became angry and irritated. Partly because no one had told me that I was selected, that I sort of found out about it through the grapevine, but above all because the selection for the championship meant that one of the season's goals and dreams was crushed: the tournament in South Korea was played at the same time as the Champions League final. For my part, there would also be no participation in the Confederations Cup in Russia, the tournament that used to guarantee a place in the World Cup the following year. My irritation didn't subside, but I was forced to accept the facts. The day after Fröjdfeldt's text message came the formal invitation. It would be the U20 World Cup in South Korea for five weeks in May and June. I dreaded telling my family.

When I got the news, I had almost three weeks of constant travelling ahead of me. First I had a friendly international between the Netherlands and Italy in Amsterdam. It would be played on my birthday, which my daughters had become sad about me missing. Then straight home to travel the next evening to the Allsvenskan premiere between Halmstad BK and Östersund FK. Home the same evening with the last flight from Copenhagen and then the next day on to a week's FIFA course in Florence. After seven days there, it would again be a day at home and then straight off to the quarter-final that I, after all, was very much looking forward to.

The FIFA course in Florence was an important step further on the way to the World Cup in Russia 2018. With a newly appointed president from the region, it was no coincidence that the course was arranged in Florence, at the Italian federation's own facility, Coverciano.

The week was more chaotic than usual. The new system for video assistant referees, VAR, was to be tested. Several different technical solutions were in place and referees would test the system both on the pitch and in front of the screens. No one really knew what was to be done, what the purpose was, how we would be evaluated, what the referees should do. We referees at the course mostly looked at each other and shook both shoulders and heads. Yet we were constantly berated by Busacca for not doing what we should during the three-hour long training sessions. Collina walked around muttering, he wanted to break off the training. He saw that it wasn't working, that it was chaos - but Busacca chose to continue anyway, and was irritated at everything and everyone. At the system, at the technicians, at his instructors, at the referees. Above all at those who didn't come from Europe. At one point he completely lost his temper and shouted "If you do this again, I will kill you" to one of the Asian referees. Probably he had made an incorrect decision or not understood the instructions, which happened to most people. If you did it right, it was more luck than anything else. I can be ashamed that I didn't speak up and point out how inappropriate it was to attack a person in that way. Even though the words were certainly not meant seriously, it was unacceptable language and a threat against one of my colleagues. It sounded terribly bad, and there were many of us who heard it - but none of us cowards said anything. The practical training sessions during the week were as usual far too long, always over two hours. They generally contained very low intensity - only to then explode with four, five extreme exertions of one minute each. I could see that on my pulse curve afterwards. During one of the runs, I felt a twinge in my thigh. To not have to run another round and show that I was injured, I blew for a penalty, even though it probably wasn't one. Better that they concluded that I had given an incorrect penalty than that I became seriously injured, I thought. I didn't dare show that I was in pain afterwards, but secretly booked time with our physiotherapists later that same evening. It was a minor rupture, nothing major. But I shouldn't do any maximum runs for a few days, the therapist advised. But I had to ignore that, I couldn't rest, there was a running test the next day. To not run or, even worse, to miss it would be like saying no to next week's quarter-final. So I gritted my teeth, took painkillers and hoped that my body would hold up, despite everything. And it did, even though I was in pain. I managed the two forty-meter sprints, but also the longer interval run without problems.

The best receipt after the week was that during the practical training it was clear that FIFA had divided the twenty European referees into an A and a B team. The referees in the first lineup were those who were currently planned to referee the World Cup in Russia in fourteen months.

On that side were the German Brych, the Turk Çakır, the Russian Karasev, the Hungarian Kassai, the Dutchman Kuipers, the Spaniard Mateu Lahoz, the Serb Mažić, the Italian Rocchi, the Slovenian Skomina - and me. I was on my way to Russia. Despite everything. I had twice before refereed Atlético Madrid at the Vicente Calderón. Both times it had gone extremely well, I had travelled home with the highest rating and knew that the home team had a good feeling and good memories of me and my performances. Now it was time for a third match - quarter-final in the Champions League against the English success team Leicester.

As always, I looked for positive signs around my matches, all to build up my self-confidence and a good feeling before the trip to Madrid. I therefore thought about my previous matches with Atlético, about how much I enjoyed the city, how pleasant, good and professional our host Manuel from the football federation always was, how good it was to referee just the first match between the teams and not the second, decisive meeting, what good weather we would get in the Spanish capital and how much I was looking forward to some long-awaited Easter holiday with the family in the mountains, directly after the match.

And not least: we would get an observer that I had met before, who had given me maximum rating last time, who I perceived had a positive image of me and who I had also helped with the first important step into the European observer career when I had given him good testimonials after a Europa League match in 2008.

The man who would be the observer in the quarter-final was Luciano Luci, Italian according to his passport - but by profession deputy referee chief in Ukraine, where he reported to the highest responsible Pierluigi Collina. Collina and Luci therefore talked to each other several times a week, and I knew that a good match by me in Madrid would quickly, guaranteed already the same evening, be communicated further to the refereeing world's most powerful person. The bonds of friendship and loyalty between Luci and Collina were strong, important and also reciprocal. Without Luci on the ground in Ukraine, Collina would never have been able to take or keep his assignment and earn the reported forty million kronor that he received in compensation during the eight years he was responsible. And in the same way, Luci would never have been able to get or keep his lucrative assignment in Ukraine without Collina having a contract there. I hoped that Luci remembered that I had helped him on the way nine years ago, that I might have a small, small advantage if it came to grey area situations where there could be two truths - depending on who was looking at them.

The atmosphere at the arena was as always special. At several other Spanish arenas it could be a bit quiet, hesitant, almost cautious - but at the Vicente Calderón you always had to struggle a bit extra to be heard. It's not a particularly difficult match to referee with only three cautions, good flow and generally good mood between the players. Sure, the away team is disappointed with a penalty they get against them, and at the same time they think they should have had a penalty with them - but the reactions are still fully normal for being a quarter-final in the Champions League. I'm satisfied with the overall picture, the control and my leadership of the match, but during the review Luci fixes his eyes on me and says: "You clearly miss two penalties tonight." I feel like I'm about to faint. Did he really say two penalties? One I can possibly understand, if he really wants to look for errors. But two? Have we really seen the same match? What is he after? Is the thought that I should be written down so much that I don't get more matches? Luciano Luci brings up two situations where he claims that I have failed. First a penalty situation in the twenty-seventh minute when Antoine Griezmann in the home team drives the ball at high speed after a counter-attack. From the left side of the penalty area, he forces his way towards goal and is fouled by an opponent. That I should blow, everyone agrees on. But is it inside or outside? My decision must be made in a flash and I perceive that the first contact is outside the penalty area, but that the defender follows through and then there is more contact and that it is therefore inside the penalty area. I blow for a penalty. The second situation is even stranger. No one, and then I mean no one, except Luciano Luci wants a penalty after what happens in the thirty-fourth minute. Not the crowd, not the TV commentators, not any of the Atlético players who see the situation, not the hot-tempered coach Diego Simeone - and above all not number 8 in the home team, Saúl Ñíguez Esclápez, who is the player that Luci claims is fouled. And then I know from experience that players from Spain always want penalties for everything that happens in the penalty area against their own team. The observer who before the match had been pleasant, open, friendly and liked to discuss different situations is suddenly as if transformed. He is curt, brief and unpleasant. After the quarter-final between Atlético Madrid and Leicester on a fantastic spring evening in April, two nails were hammered into my career's referee coffin. One of them concerned this situation. Was Antoine Griezmann really outside the penalty area when Marc Albrighton couldn't keep up and fouled the Frenchman? Or did the tackle continue into the penalty area? Opinions were divided. I knew that I had read the game correctly, run along and had a good position to make my decision. I didn't hesitate when I blew for a penalty. But the Italian observer was uninterested in discussing and stated: clearly outside.

After fifteen years of international refereeing, I'm used to observers often first asking what you yourself think, if there's anything you want to discuss, any situation you want to talk about and gives the referee himself the chance to make an analysis. After that, the observer gives his thoughts and views, and discusses with the referee in an open and honest way. Tonight Luci doesn't give the impression of being willing to discuss anything.

I make an attempt anyway. I don't go into direct polemic with what Luci has decided is wrong, but I try carefully to adjust his image around the first situation, pause the picture when you see the second and third contact inside the penalty area.

I never say that he is wrong, but try to nuance it.

Luci says nothing, barely looks at the screen when I try to argue and seems more or less not to be listening. He has already decided long ago: it's not a penalty.

Regarding the second situation, which no one on site or even the bloodthirsty media corps in Spain, England or Sweden has picked up on, I'm more straightforward and explain that it absolutely can't be a penalty.

Luci seems uninterested, doesn't really listen to my comments or want to try to understand what I mean. Finally he says that he doesn't care about my explanations. I have made two big mistakes in the penalty area during the match and he will write that in his report.

"We'll see what UEFA says, if they think something different than I do," he concludes. UEFA in this case means Collina, and I have a definite impression that the two friends have already been in contact with each other before Luci presents his assessment to me. Luci would never dare to go against Collina's opinion, or dare to decide on a decision that Collina would then change. In any case, the report was approved by Collina faster than any other time during my refereeing career. Usually it took at least two days, but often much longer, for UEFA to review the match, verify key situations and approve the report and thus make it available to the referee. But the ten pages from Atlético Madrid-Leicester were approved already the afternoon after, despite there being several difficult-to-judge situations that should have been analysed by several people.

If my two tight situations in Madrid had been judged in my favour, the rating would have been the brilliant 8.6. Now it was instead 7.4 and pitch black.

It wasn't just me who felt bad in the time after the debacle in Madrid. Even the others in my team had the same uneasy feeling as I did. Something was chafing. Something wasn't as it used to be. I had previously taken two important wrong decisions during some match, that wasn't it. It was the way they had been judged as incorrect, so categorically, without a hint of possibility for me to even try to tell or argue why I had made my decisions. Those in charge at UEFA didn't have the slightest interest in looking at the situations in detail. None of us had experienced anything like it. I had no match to look forward to and thus no opportunity to take revenge. I pondered quite a bit. What should I do? I felt irritation and anger that I, in my opinion, had been wrongly treated in Madrid - so I decided to bring it up with Collina directly. It might have been typically Swedish and could possibly be perceived as naive to bring up a problem and a personal feeling with the refereeing world's most powerful person, but what did I have to lose? Through a referee colleague, I found out that Collina would come to South Korea during the upcoming tournament. It could be a suitable opportunity to bring up the matter with him. But during my almost five weeks in South Korea, Collina's arrival was postponed several times: he was first to come before the Europa League final, then after it, then shortly before the Champions League final, then directly after it, to later just show up at the final - and by then I had already gone home. After the tournament in South Korea, however, I felt less need to bring up the matter with Collina. We had done three top matches and received an enormous amount of praise from FIFA, had not ended up in focus and had avoided making any major mistakes. I had also shown that I understood how to referee with the new system with video assistant referees, VAR. On site in Seoul, we were intensively trained in VAR which was tested during the tournament. It was new for virtually everyone and we were instructed that the video referees should only intervene on what were clear and obvious errors by the referee - errors that the referee in a normal match, without VAR, would get a failing grade. I became a bit curious about what my colleagues at FIFA thought about my two situations in Madrid - those that Luci, Collina and UEFA clearly and obviously thought had been incorrect and thus given me a suspension. After support from several colleagues, I plucked up courage and showed them to Busacca as well, without revealing the background or my thought behind getting his feedback. To my delight, he also agreed that neither of the situations constituted any serious mistake on my part.

The last evening in South Korea, Daniel and I by chance met Massimo Busacca in a corridor. He wasn't a person you easily made small talk with. All social contacts used to be short, formal and a bit stiff.

We stop, opposite each other in the corridor. Daniel and I are silent and let Busacca take the word. "Thanks for everything. Fly carefully, see you in a year," he says. We thank him, shake hands and exchange some pleasantries. Daniel and I walk away silently, wait for the elevator and when the doors close I say to my colleague: "He said we'll see each other in a year. Does that mean we're set for the World Cup in Russia?" From the summer of 2017, I and the team counted down to two events. Partly towards the end of November when the referees for the World Cup would be selected, partly towards June 14, 2018 when the championship in Russia began. I saw a light at the end of the tunnel in front of me, a stop on the journey, a referee retirement at forty-five after my thirty-one years as active. I knew that I would hang up my whistle, that my career was soon over, that my focus would shift in another direction after the World Cup next summer. We made the restart already in South Korea in May, and the autumn started well - significantly better than the year before. The annual playoff match to the Champions League we refereed in Be'er Sheva in the Israeli Negev Desert. There I had a very difficult situation with a player who maybe, maybe was held back and if he was fouled then the next difficult and decisive question was: was it inside or outside the penalty area? I was of course burned after what had happened in Madrid during the spring. Based on that, I should have learned, I should have judged it outside and if there was also the slightest doubt that it was even unfair then my brain should have been programmed not to blow at all.

In hindsight, I can think that I maybe should have learned from my mistake. Once you've burned yourself, you should shy away from the same fire again.

But it doesn't work on me.

The situation went extremely fast, I followed my feeling and immediately put the whistle to my mouth and blew. Penalty.

The relief after the match when our Northern Irish observer hugged me and praised me for the decision was among the strongest I had experienced. To give a penalty to the home team was not at all the most important decision I had made in my career, it was neither the most difficult, nor the most decisive - but for my future, for my hope and my dream to be able to conclude with a second World Cup it was a key decision.

The next stop for the team became the political powder keg between North Macedonia and Albania. It was one of the tougher matches that I had refereed in my entire career, but all difficult and big decisions were correct according to our Dutch observer. But when the report came after a week, he had changed his mind.

I became incredibly disappointed. An observer who live from the stands thought I had done right, who when we after the match together looked at the images still thought it was right, who then a week after returning home had changed his mind after again looking at the same images. Or it was so that someone higher up in a position of power maybe wanted to influence my rating, contacted the observer and asked him to change his interpretation and his rating. It wasn't new and had happened on several occasions before. What happened in North Macedonia at least only gave "just" 7.9 - thus a failing grade that most referees had a few per season. It wasn't 7.4 and I wasn't suspended.

After that we refereed CSKA Moscow-Manchester United in the Russian capital's early winter cold. Even the away team's coach

José Mourinho was in a brilliant mood, and all irritation and anger over what happened during the Super Cup final a few years earlier seemed to be blown away. And he thanked me cheerfully after the match. What it depended on I understood immediately. Certainly I had been good, but above all his team had won 4-1, no one had been injured and this time I hadn't sent off any of his players.

The autumn went by and suddenly there was only one match left before the referees for the World Cup would be selected. I knew that match was extremely important.

It was with that rating, with that impression, that FIFA's referee committee on November 17 would sit down, analyse the referees, our performances and then select the nine or ten referees who would represent UEFA at the summer's World Cup.

My family had since the summer said that they wanted to travel away during the autumn break. I of course wanted to go along, but it wasn't possible. The autumn break was a Champions League week, and then I could have a match. My three girls chose to book a trip to Italy, to the eternal city, to Rome, to be tourists for a few days in a bit sunnier environment than Sigtuna could offer at the end of October. When I looked in FAME about a week before the autumn break, I saw that we had a match on Tuesday. I curiously checked which matches would be played that evening and was struck by the fact that a match would be played in Rome: AS Roma against Chelsea. That a family got to see a match for UEFA or FIFA was almost never possible, the finals excluded when you got tickets, and that the selection also became official in good time. So I cheered when I found out a few days before kick-off that our match was precisely the one in Rome. I loved Rome, the arena was magical and the atmosphere used to be magnificent, but above all my family would be able to sit in the stands. In secret, of course. That they were there was pure coincidence and not planned, and I didn't tell anyone at UEFA. I bought the tickets online, in my wife's name, and paid for everything myself. No one would be able to question my neutrality. A week or so earlier I had emailed Pierluigi Collina to ask him a bit about planning for the coming months. I did that occasionally. Not to know if I had a match or which match it was, but rather to know when they would select matches, so that I could best put together the schedule with everything else I was involved in.

This time I had asked Collina when they would select the twelve playoff matches for the 2018 World Cup that would be played November 9-13. If I had no assignment, my plan was to book some meetings, accept a lecture or maybe visit my parents in Luleå over a weekend.

Collina's answer was delayed a few days. It did that very often now, if you even got an answer. Either he had so much to do with being the highest responsible for FIFA and UEFA, or it was me who wasn't as prioritised anymore.

To have zero cautions doesn't say everything about a referee performance, but quite a lot. A good referee can control matches without waving cards time and time again. A competent referee lets the game flow when it can, blows the whistle when needed and can control it by just using the whistle and blowing free kicks.

This evening in Rome becomes one of the two occasions when I don't need to use the cards. The match in Rome is one of my best matches in my career. I'm in top form, feel good, am quick in the head, read the game exactly as you should, constantly look into the future and am in the right place at the right time, am both clear, angry, kind, personal and professional in my communication with the players. Everyone accepts me and I don't make an incorrect decision in the entire match.

My team works perfectly, we cooperate perfectly and solve all situations that arise. Twenty-two players thank us afterwards, no one has anything bad to say about our performance.

At dinner after the match, the otherwise quite strict German observer joins in the chorus of praise and gives us maximum rating and only positive comments.

The path towards the World Cup lies raked.

Friday, November 17 became a day I will never forget, but unfortunately for completely different reasons than I had thought.

I had long since written in "World Cup referees selected" in my calendar, and secretly counted down the days until I could celebrate my second World Cup.

Instead I sat alone in the kitchen at home in Sigtuna the day after. Without having celebrated, and without having a single text message to answer. And in my head my voice spoke to me over and over again. Said that it couldn't be true.

I'm tired but can't sleep. I'm hungry but can't eat. I'm sad but I can't cry. I don't know how long I sit there, but the light starts to peek in when my wife suddenly stands beside me. I haven't heard her come into the room. She lovingly puts her hand on my shoulder and gently asks if I've heard anything more. I have, already late last night. But I haven't dared to admit it, not even to my wife. What did I think? That I would wake up from a nightmare? That everything was just a misunderstanding? That the list of referees that the media had published was incorrect? I know the truth, the ice-cold news that will soon be out for everyone to read. I'm dropped from the World Cup, I've been fired, I'm not at the top anymore, my career is over, I'm finished.

I who have performance-addicted my whole life have failed to reach my final goal. The crescendo in my career is blown off, my planning for the coming eight months is blown away. I think that I as a person am a fiasco, that I have failed monumentally, that I have finally become a bubble that has burst, a lie that has been caught out.

I feel a shame before other people in my surroundings that I have failed with what would be the last in my long and successful refereeing career.

I who have always been good at separating criticism against me as a person and in my professional role as a referee suddenly have incredibly difficult to see a dropping as anything other than a definitive end for me as a person, that I'm not worth anything at all, that nothing I have done or will do will ever affect that. When my wife repeats her question for the third time, I wake up. "No," I answer, "but I know it's over. It says so in international media." Then I can't take it anymore. I break down. My wife holds me and tries to comfort me as best she can. Our five-year-old daughter who has just come into the kitchen stares horrified at me. She's not used to seeing dad cry, and hardly dares to come forward. I try to explain that I'm sad, that nothing dangerous has happened, that everyone is fine, that everything is just as usual, that dad is just sad because I won't get to referee the World Cup this summer. Our daughter cries, I cry and my wife tries to comfort us. I try to say that it doesn't matter, I lie and say that this is actually the best thing that could happen: "Because now I'll be home in the summer and not away in Russia for seven, eight weeks." The happy news about the summer plans comforts our daughter a little bit, and after a few minutes she has forgotten about my missed World Cup place. But I haven't.

I eat a little breakfast. The chews take a long time to swallow, and after a little while our oldest daughter comes in and she immediately feels that something isn't as it should be, and I have to explain to her too. I don't know how long I sit there, but finally only my wife and I are left at the kitchen table. The daughters have gone to their rooms.

Four years earlier I had celebrated my World Cup place as a winner with champagne - now I sit here as a loser, red-eyed and trying to understand what has happened.

I still haven't heard anything officially from FIFA, but the lists I've seen look like they come from them. That's all I know. It becomes my mantra during Saturday, while the first journalists start to contact me. I don't take any calls at all. Not from friends, colleagues or least of all journalists. Instead I get several texts from journalists who want to reach me. But I avoid answering them too.

Still want to believe that someone from FIFA will call me. Maybe Busacca, maybe Collina. Someone who calls and explains that it's a misunderstanding, that they had forgotten to put my name on the list.

Several times before in my life when I've had a lot to do, a problem has been in my head or a lump in my stomach, I've solved it by taking a long run in fresh air. It may sound banal, but forty-five minutes usually clears the head, makes my thoughts clearer, I become calm and get energy.

But it's difficult to get out and run just this Saturday for several reasons. Firstly, the weather is miserable. Sleet, windy and slippery on the ground, but above all, on Tuesday, a few days earlier, I had twisted my ankle during a training session and my right ankle is blue and swollen. It actually hurts far too much to even walk on it, let alone run. But I change clothes and finally get out anyway.

It's slippery, really crappy weather and I'm in enormous pain in my foot. Every step hurts, my pulse pounds and my right foot feels as if I've put on a ski boot by mistake and I try to run faster and faster despite the pain making me grimace.

People I meet don't recognise me. I've pulled down my hat properly, have my gaze constantly directed downwards towards the ground because I don't want to meet anyone at all.

I see afterwards that I ran 10.3 km, that I had extremely high pulse for almost half the time. It's one of the most strenuous training sessions I've done in recent months, but I don't feel any tiredness and after twenty-five minutes I also have no pain in my foot. Halfway through my run I stop in the forest, shake my head and start crying. I sit down on my haunches, have difficulty breathing properly - I don't know if it's because the training has been so intense or because of my disappointment. Probably a combination.

I feel a little better after my hour in the rain. But not my foot.

When I stop, the pain comes back, with increased pain. I limp in at home, slowly take off my clothes and see that I have more missed calls. Even more journalists. But I still can't bear to answer. I realise that I have to inform my parents and my sister about the news that will soon become official. They shouldn't have to read it in a headline on Aftonbladet. My mum and dad are on a longer cruise abroad, and my fingers tremble when I formulate my message to them. I let the phone be on around the clock for two reasons. First, for someone from FIFA to call me, send a message or in some other way maybe explain that it's a misunderstanding, that I am indeed selected for the World Cup. After a few days, when the news becomes official everywhere, I instead hope that someone from FIFA will just call me and tell me why I wasn't selected, why just I and my team got fired. How could I go from being ranked fourth in the world in January 2017 to not being among the thirty-five referees who had been selected? How could I go from having refereed the Europa League final 2016, semi-final in Euro 2016, quarter-final in U20 World Cup 2017, to now being completely isolated, frozen out and dropped?

I sat alone in the kitchen at home in Sigtuna and felt that all the energy had left my body. I was empty, felt dejected, and couldn't find any joy in anything at all. My wife and children tried to cheer me up, but I wasn't receptive. I was in shock. I had put all my focus, all my energy, all my time into becoming as good a referee as I possibly could. I had sacrificed so much, missed so many important moments with my family, always prioritised refereeing over everything else. And now it was all over. Just like that.

The days that followed were a blur. I avoided all contact with the outside world, didn't answer my phone, didn't check my emails. I just wanted to be left alone with my thoughts. But eventually, I knew I had to face reality. I had to start thinking about what to do next. My refereeing career was over, but my life wasn't. I still had many years ahead of me, and I needed to figure out what to do with them.

I started by reaching out to some trusted friends and colleagues. Their support meant a lot to me during this difficult time. They reminded me of all I had achieved in my career, of the respect I had earned from players, coaches, and fellow referees. They helped me see that while this was a huge disappointment, it didn't define me as a person or negate all I had accomplished.

Slowly, I began to emerge from my funk. I started to think about the future, about what opportunities might lie ahead. I had gained so much experience, learned so much about leadership, decision-making under pressure, and handling difficult situations. Surely these skills could be valuable in other areas of life.

As the days turned into weeks, I found myself reflecting on my career, on the highs and lows, the triumphs and disappointments. I realized that while the World Cup had been my ultimate goal, it wasn't the only thing that mattered. I had had an incredible journey, officiated at the highest levels of the game, and made lifelong friends along the way.

I also thought about the younger referees coming up through the ranks. Maybe I could use my experience to help mentor them, to share what I had learned and help them avoid some of the pitfalls I had encountered.

As I write these final words, I'm still coming to terms with the end of my refereeing career. It's not the ending I had hoped for or worked towards, but it's the one I've been given. And while the disappointment is still there, I'm beginning to see it as the closing of one chapter and the opening of another.

To all the players, coaches, and fellow officials I've worked with over the years, thank you. To my family, who supported me through it all, words cannot express my gratitude. And to the beautiful game itself, thank you for the incredible journey. It's been an honour to serve you.

The final whistle has blown on my refereeing career, but the match of life continues. And I'm ready for whatever comes next.

The Way Out

The days following the news that Mathias, Daniel and I had not been selected for the World Cup were dark indeed. I had been sacked, forced to leave the job I'd held for four years—despite being better on paper now, more experienced, weighing less and with greater stamina. After about a day, FIFA published the list of selected referees on their website, and the news became officially real. We received confirmation that I had been dropped and would no longer referee what should have been the final major tournament of my career.

I felt hunted and stressed. As always, I tried to be polite and respond to the journalists who contacted me, but my answer was flat, meaningless, yet entirely honest. I couldn't manage phone calls; it was just text messages to those who reached out. I politely replied that I knew no more than they did. For no one had contacted me. Neither President Collina nor Head of Refereeing Busacca. I knew that in January 2017, nine months before the selection, I had been named the world's fourth-best referee in the only official poll where the world's referees were ranked. Ahead of me were Mark Clattenburg, Nicola Rizzoli and Viktor Kassai—but since two of these had retired since then, I could consider myself number two in the world. To me, it was utterly absurd that in November of the same year, I wouldn't even be among the world's thirty-five best referees, for that many had been selected this time. It was ten more referees than at the Brazil World Cup, and yet I didn't make the cut.

Moreover, the year before I had been promised the Champions League final, refereed the Europa League final and received a semi-final at the Euros—and on the way there, I had officiated a long string of matches without a single major mistake.

Certainly, in the past sixteen months, I had officiated two or three matches with less than stellar ratings, with results outside the target. But we weren't talking about any major scandals, no decisions that had caused the media to write reams about my mistakes. Several of my colleagues had found themselves in similar situations, where at least I thought their mistakes had been bigger, more obvious and received more media attention.

My last five competitive matches, after a successful Under-20 World Cup in South Korea, had, with one exception, received good ratings: 8.5 - 8.4 - 8.4 - 8.4. That was sufficient to reach the World Cup, I thought. But despite that, I had been removed from the 2018 World Cup. The sucker punch that came out of nowhere was a fact. Was there a problem with my attitude? Had I said something to someone that affected FIFA's view of me? I hoped to receive a call from Collina or someone else who could explain to me what had happened. I was convinced that such a call would come. But regardless of whether I received a call, even if I got a good explanation, a sound and honest basis for the decision, there was a feeling that it had been planned for a long time that I wouldn't go to Russia.

For if FIFA had wanted me to succeed and they thought along the way that I hadn't delivered sufficiently, surely they could have said something to me, I thought. Perhaps called and told me that I needed to improve. Simply given me the opportunity to pull my socks up. The only time Collina had communicated with me since the course in Málaga in January 2017 was when he belatedly responded before my last match, Roma vs Chelsea, ahead of the World Cup selection. He then wrote that he was looking forward to a brilliant performance from our side. Something we had delivered with a maximum rating for everyone in the team in a perfect match. After the match, I heard nothing from Collina. There was no praise afterwards, no words of encouragement. It was there my real sense of unease began; it was as if he had hoped it would go badly for us in that very match, so that our performance could be an argument for us not being selected for the World Cup. I looked time and time again through the list of the ten European referees who had been selected, made my calculations, analyses and ponderings about how it could have gone as it apparently had. I could honestly and directly say that three of them were better referees than me—more experienced, with among other things a Champions League final each on their list of merits. But then none of the other seven referees could match me when it came to merits, number of matches, experience of major finals or representation in big tournaments—all such things that usually are decisive in the selection of referees for a World Cup. A referee like the Slovenian

Damir Skomina had, for example, merits that could possibly be considered close to mine. Two quarter-finals from Euro 2012 and Euro 2016—compared to my semi-final in France 2016. At the 2014 World Cup, I had reached a round of 16 match—while Skomina hadn't even been selected for the tournament. So as far as experience within FIFA was concerned, I was undoubtedly ahead of him. However, there was something about Slovenia that grated for anyone with a decent grasp of football and politics. The reason was spelled Aleksander Čeferin, the Slovenian lawyer, born in 1967, who had made a meteoric career in football. As late as 2011, he became involved in the national football association—and five years later, Čeferin was president of UEFA after the new election that was held when Michel Platini was suspended for receiving unauthorised payments from FIFA.

Slovenia is not a major footballing nation. Since the introduction of FIFA's world ranking of national teams, the country has averaged around fifty-sixth place—and as a country, Slovenia has reached two World Cups. Yet the country was extremely well represented in refereeing matters, especially after Čeferin became president of UEFA. Damir Skomina was an incredibly competent referee, but his greatest successes undoubtedly came after Čeferin became president in the autumn of 2016. In the spring of 2017, Skomina refereed the Europa League final at Friends Arena between Manchester United and Ajax—a year later he got the Champions League final between Tottenham and Liverpool. Regardless of how you compared my CV with Skomina's, I understood the football politics in Skomina being selected ahead of most other European referees, including me, given his nationality and the connection to UEFA's president. But it still hurt like hell. Further down the list of European World Cup referees, it hurt to continue reading. All had far less merit than I did, and it seemed obvious that they had been selected more because of where they came from than anything else. The host nation Russia had got Sergei Karasev in, France Clément Turpin, Italy Gianluca Rocchi and Spain Antonio Miguel Mateu Lahoz. I really did wish Antonio a place at the World Cup. He was a master on the pitch, a fantastic personality and the kindest and most ordinary person I had met among all the referees. But I knew that he too lacked any form of major tournament experience—that I was completely superior to him in terms of experience. But the fact that he came from Spain decided in his favour. It didn't matter that in the decisive qualifying match between Italy and Sweden, before the eyes of Vlado Šajn as an observer, he may have missed three or four penalties, he was still selected for the World Cup. I, who was a performance junkie, who always wanted to be the best and who didn't want to experience not belonging to the top, considered quitting on the spot. The day after the official announcement, the phone rang constantly. One person who really wanted to reach me was the Allsvenskan referee coach, Peter Fröjdfeldt. He called three times, but I couldn't bring myself to answer. Then a text message came. He wondered how I viewed the future and how he should plan and think ahead of 2018.

That I, the day after the nightmare, after the sucker punch, should be forced to consider my future in Allsvenskan was not only a question posed with very poor timing—it was also provocative. I became angry that I was being pressured to make a decision about my future when I was floored with disappointment.

Apart from Mathias and Daniel, I talked a lot with Bosse Karlsson, my Swedish boss, my mentor, the one who "discovered" me in 1996 and who had been by my side the whole time. He was encouraging and supportive, but at the same time blunt and stated that I had been treated like shit and that he was as surprised as I was. The week after, Bosse went away on a UEFA course for observers. I asked him to keep his eyes and ears open to find out what was being said. Was there an explanation? What did people in general think about me being dropped as a World Cup referee? At least fifteen observers had approached him and were puzzled that I wasn't included, Bosse told me after the course.

Whether Bosse was being honest or whether he said it to comfort me, I don't know. But it felt good that I wasn't completely alone in my surprise.

I had planned nine intensive months of hard work that would culminate with the World Cup in Russia and then retire as a referee.

Now the playing field was completely different. In the long term and in the short term. Next up, I had written in my calendar a FIFA course in the United Arab Emirates for ten days—but when I had been dropped from the World Cup, I was no longer welcome at the camp that would prepare the World Cup referees.

The emptiness was enormous and the lump in my stomach constant. My wife noticed my restlessness and how badly I was feeling. One day she said that she thought I needed to travel away, change environment and think about something else for a while.

I understood that she was right, and I loved her for seeing what I myself couldn't perceive. I had difficulty getting away, but finally she forced me to sit down at the computer and book a trip.

Preferably far away, at least a week. Almost randomly, it became a trip to the USA. First to Boston, then New York for a few days and then home—the same day I had planned to come home from Dubai and the cancelled course.

I landed in Boston on the evening of Thanksgiving itself. The normally vibrant city was almost deserted, and only I and the down-and-out wandered along the streets—everyone else was at home with their families, socialising in the warmth. I ate dinner alone at a seedy Chinese restaurant in central Boston.

The day after, I met an old referee friend, Alan Kelly from Ireland, who had been living in Boston for a few years and was refereeing in MLS as a professional referee. We ate dinner and had a few beers, talked about old times, the World Cup selection and how I viewed the future, which I still had no answer to.

Then followed four days in New York without a real agenda. But it was as if the pieces of the puzzle were starting to fall into place. First, I met Mark Clattenburg, my former colleague who was now head of refereeing in Saudi Arabia. He was in the USA for some TV work. We ate dinner, had a few beers and talked quite a bit.

Then I hung out for two days with Howard Webb, my colleague from Euro 2012 and the 2014 World Cup who then quit and became head of all referees in the American professional soccer league, MLS. We ate dinner and I visited him at his workplace the day after.

Both Mark and Howard thought my dropping was surprising, that I should have been selected given my merits—but that as always with FIFA, it's politics, politics and more politics that govern, instead of competence. That it was of course a big disadvantage for me to come from a small country.

Certainly, it was the case that the larger countries were usually favoured in the political circus that existed within FIFA and UEFA. And that key persons such as chairmen, presidents, general secretaries and other individuals obviously influenced in the way they wanted—not infrequently in their own national direction. No one doubts that Lennart Johansson surely did a good job for Sweden and Swedish referees during his time as UEFA's highest chief. Even though Lennart, when you had met him and knew what he stood for, was not a man who used his position to give political favours to either individuals or countries.

But it is, for example, perhaps not an advanced guess that Anders Frisk's chances of refereeing the Euro 2000 final did not exactly decrease because Lennart was UEFA's president. On the contrary, it was perhaps Lennart's mere presence and position that actually gave Anders the final that he already deserved on sporting grounds.

When I came home, I thought more clearly. I still hoped that Collina would get in touch, but I also felt that I had a choice to make. I landed on the fact that I had three options: The first involved an angry and honest email to all those in charge, a resignation, an end with immediate effect. The second meant that

I would stop as an international referee, but that I would continue to referee the 2018 season in Allsvenskan. To make an end with dignity. The third was that I would swallow everything, that I would accept the setback, that I would clench my fist in my pocket. But that I would travel to the course in Malta at the beginning of February stronger, faster and lighter than ever before. It took time, I bounced options off myself, off my wife and then the sporting aspects with Mathias and Daniel. Both were the same age as me and had been on the journey for a long time, received the same sucker punches and heard the same empty promises, they understood my situation one hundred percent. But none of us wanted to give up, none wanted to see the battle lost—we wanted to try to get back somehow, reclaim some pride and just keep refereeing to have fun, even if we understood that our future was anything but bright.

In the end, I landed on the third option: swallow everything, clench my fist in my pocket and come back better than ever before.

The first step back towards a normalised refereeing life was to start refereeing again. And not at just any level—my first step back was to referee in the Champions League for the forty-sixth time in my career.

My first match after the negative World Cup decision I should actually have refereed in Munich—Bayern against Paris Saint-Germain. Just that in itself was extremely strange, since I had clearly said in previous years to UEFA that I didn't want to referee PSG due to my connection to the team's president.

I had never before in the Champions League since 2011 when I declined to referee Paris Saint-Germain, been selected to referee them. Not even by mistake by Collina. For the Italian was not a person who forgot or left anything to chance—he had control of everything, regarding everyone.

But now I was still selected to referee PSG. I found that out right after our match in Rome, that is, long before I knew that I wouldn't be selected to referee the World Cup in Russia. I had reacted immediately and via Bosse asked Collina a question to remind him of the inappropriateness of me refereeing PSG. Then I didn't hear a word. About a week after being dropped, when the year's last match in the Champions League was approaching, we were removed from Bayern Munich against Paris Saint-Germain, and instead got to travel to Porto to referee their match against Monaco. That it was due to my relationship with PSG, I understood, I had pointed out the inappropriateness to Collina myself, but why had he even selected me for the match? He who usually had control of everything and everyone? It seemed strange and highly unreasonable.

I let it go then, but in retrospect, I had thoughts about how it all came about. And if it had somehow affected the World Cup selection a few weeks later. I analysed and put together a puzzle.

My friend since my time in the TV rights business in the early 2000s, Nasser Al-Khelaifi, has since he stepped in as president of Paris Saint-Germain become a real power player in European football, gained an enormous network within the sports world and the prime example of this is that the Qatari is today a full member of UEFA's Executive Committee and also president of ECA, the largest clubs' joint organisation. But in mid-October

2017—two weeks before I was strangely enough selected to referee PSG—something happened that really put Nasser on the agenda, with dark, negative headlines. All with a clear connection to FIFA. He was being investigated for bribery. According to the articles in the media, the suspicions against Al-Khelaifi had been uncovered in connection with a larger investigation of corruption within FIFA. Two people appeared in the investigation. One was Nasser, the other the former FIFA official Jérôme Valcke who had already been banned from all football in 2016 for twelve years after, among other things, having entered into a pact to illegally release thousands of tickets to the World Cup matches in Brazil 2014, as well as having secured private economic advantages from FIFA in various ways. Now Swiss authorities suspected that Al-Khelaifi had bribed Valcke so that the Arab TV channel BeIn Sports would get the broadcasting rights to the 2018, 2022, 2026 and 2030 World Cups. So I had, two weeks after the published articles (which surely had been the subject of many, long and large discussions in the FIFA house in Zurich) honestly and openly reminded the refereeing world's most powerful man about my connection to the main person Nasser Al-Khelaifi—a person who at that time risked dragging FIFA's name even deeper into the mud than it already was. Could it be that my email had somehow opened Collina's eyes, UEFA's and FIFA's? That it had set in motion a process that not only stopped me from refereeing Bayern Munich against PSG—but also from the World Cup in Russia? Had my information and voluntary reminder of my connection to Nasser made FIFA afraid to select me for the World Cup?

For everyone who wanted to keep their job and their power, it was important to distance themselves from Al-Khelaifi as much as possible—as long as he was accused. Not selecting me for the World Cup would solve that problem for FIFA. No connection would then remain between Nasser, me and FIFA. Could that explain Collina's non-existent communication? The match in Porto was special. Partly because it was the first time I would get back in the saddle after being dropped from the World Cup, partly because of an email that Bosse Karlsson had sent to all of refereeing Sweden and which was the first thing I read when I turned on my phone as we landed in Porto.

In the autumn of 2017, the whole world, Sweden and even the refereeing community were shaken by the Me Too movement. In the email from Bosse, he described how he had been accused by a woman on Facebook of an incident that had occurred more than twenty years ago. It was about him allegedly telling a female referee that he wanted her while implying that he could positively influence her refereeing career.

The whole incident was said to have caused the female referee to quit. He stated that in many people's eyes he was already condemned, and that he therefore could not continue a role that was based on trust and that he resigned with immediate effect. In the media, Bosse replied that he had no memory of the incident itself. I had of course no idea what had happened between the two people so many years ago and didn't want to comment on anything at all when the press persistently called me to get my comments or opinions. Neither I nor anyone else, except Bosse and the woman involved, can comment on the details of what actually happened that evening or how it had been perceived. It never became a police matter, thus was never investigated but Bosse was still condemned by the public. That I support the Me Too movement is obvious, that I am against all forms of sexual harassment equally so. The only thing I can say in retrospect is that Bosse Karlsson in my presence, towards me and the people I met together with him had always behaved correctly. Nor had I seen or heard of such behaviour from his side.

Bosse had always been there for me since the first time we met in a corridor in Boden, even if we had our disputes and disagreements over the years. Therefore, I suffered with him, as he now found himself in the middle of a storm that forced him to leave his life's work—Swedish refereeing. He was largely the man behind me and my successes, behind all Swedish referees' successes during the 2000s, behind finals, championships and top performances. That little, little Sweden with so relatively few active referees had had referees in practically all major championships since he took over was largely his merit.

Not having Bosse left as boss in Sweden affected me. Suddenly it wasn't as fun anymore. Our shared journey had come to an abrupt end.

I and the team arrived in Porto with a slightly dejected feeling. We had been assigned the same observer as in Moscow just two months earlier who had most questionably failed Stefan Johannesson for a penalty decision. Usually, you barely met the same observer twice during a career, but now in the second match out of three in the Champions League we got to meet the same person. It contributed to us asking ourselves what we were really doing there. But when the match between Porto and Monaco had finally begun, we still did what we did best, refereeing football.

The day after the match, just before our plane was about to take off, Pierluigi Collina called. Two rings, then he hung up. It mattered little, because I couldn't answer anyway. I quickly sent a text that I was on the plane and that he could call me later tonight or tomorrow.

Collina neither replied nor called back.

I couldn't be bothered to chase him anymore, it hurt too much, it became too humiliating that I should try to get hold of him for him to explain the reason why I had been sacked. Somewhere in my sadness there was still a pride.

On Christmas Eve three weeks later, a text message finally came from the refereeing world's most powerful man. By then, thirty-six days had passed since Collina had been personally involved in choosing to leave me out of the World Cup.

He had not had the courage, energy, time or strength to tell me himself. Collina now wrote that he understood that I was disappointed about not being selected for the World Cup, but that upcoming matches would be a chance for me to show FIFA that they had made a mistake in not selecting me. And then he wished me a good 2018.

What hurt extra was that I found out that Collina, after the selections had become official, had taken the time to contact several of the other referees who hadn't been selected for the World

Cup. That he had encouraged them, motivated and explained why they hadn't been selected and at the same time given them a vision for the future regarding how he saw their development going forward. Sure, I was approaching the end of my refereeing career and maybe didn't have the longest refereeing career ahead of me, but I thought that I as a referee at the highest level for nearly ten years at least deserved a simple and brief explanation.

First and foremost, I wanted to referee the World Cup in Russia. Secondly, at least an explanation and a justification for why I hadn't been selected. I got neither. It hurt. I travelled to the course in Malta in top form. I had trained better than ever before, was strong, enduring and the scales showed lower than in a long time. Even the fat percentage that UEFA and Collina focused so much on was low—I clearly showed that I was ready for a new season and that I had taken the setback in the right way.

I was tense to meet Collina and see how he would react and what he would say. In the text message he sent on Christmas Eve, he wrote that we would have time to speak with each other at the course in Malta.

Therefore, I waited for him to take me aside and for the Italian to finally give answers to some of the questions that I had constantly had in my head since being dropped. But once in Malta, Collina didn't want to talk to me, I felt that clearly. It was as if he avoided me. He didn't meet my gaze, always tried to be somewhere else than just where I was. One day passed, two days, the third day was almost over and we still hadn't talked. I had been convinced that he would take the initiative, that he would take me aside for a chat—but he didn't. Instead, it was I who had to pluck up courage to get a meeting.

After a theoretical lesson, Collina sat slumped in front of the computer.

While the others left the room, I took a deep breath, went up to him and asked if he had a few minutes for me. The question was rhetorical. I sat down without waiting for an answer and now found myself opposite the person who had crushed my dream and who then hadn't had the courage to call me and tell me why. I was silent for a few seconds, let the people who lingered in the room slowly walk out so that it was almost only me and Collina left. Then I spoke up and asked him how my position as a referee really looked now. After first trying to joke away the question, a long and political answer came. On the one hand this, on the other hand that. I absolutely had a future as a referee at the top level, he claimed. Getting to referee the Champions League final in May was not impossible, even if I didn't belong to the ten World Cup referees. He praised me for my fitness test, for my weight, that I looked slim and for working so hard despite knowing that I was disappointed after missing out on the World Cup. That I would definitely be involved in Euro 2020 if I continued to invest, and that he was prepared to give me the dispensation that would be required to continue refereeing internationally after the age of forty-five. Finally, after all the political bullshit and nice and false future prospects, I asked the question of why I hadn't been selected for the World Cup. Collina seemed to be a bit surprised that I asked it. He hesitated for a few seconds before answering that it was partly because I had had some poor ratings during the season, partly because they needed to rejuvenate the referee corps. Then he added that sometimes there could also be reasons that one couldn't always point to clearly after a selection, that played a part without being decisive. I asked if it was something that had to do with me as a person. He looked at me with his ice-cold eyes and shook his head and denied that it would be anything like that.

I was silent. I knew there was nothing to gain by questioning or challenging what I had just heard. None of what Collina had said had surprised me. I knew from before that he was a liar that I couldn't trust. When I left the course the day after and flew home from Malta, I had made up my mind. This had been my last course for UEFA. I was done. Six more months, then I would quit. But I would keep my decision to myself for now. I started planning for a life without a football World Cup. After returning home from the course in February, I talked to my wife, said that I thought we should travel far, far away in the summer, preferably right during the World Cup and be away as long as the five weeks that the World Cup was played. We eventually booked a five-week holiday on the US West Coast, in New Zealand and around islands in the South Pacific—as far away from Russia as you could get. It was departure on the same day the World Cup began, and return just when the final was played. It was a necessity for me, it would hurt too much to be at home, talk about the World Cup with everyone you met and have to answer the question of how it felt not to be there. I continued to be serious during the spring, took care of my training carefully and delivered my training reports on time. Even though I knew that I didn't need to care about what I sent in—I would quit anyway. But I took pride in finishing at the top, in being as good as I could be right up to the end.

I refereed Basel against Manchester City in the Champions League round of 16 without any problems, again got a maximum rating from the warm, friendly and honest Italian observer I had met several times before.

I told the observer that I had been crushed by being dropped from the World Cup, but that what hurt the most was that no one had contacted me to tell me the reason. "Collina is like that, he can't handle it. That's not how you do it when you work with people, but at the same time I'm not surprised," the observer stated. I knew that Collina's words about me possibly refereeing the Champions League final in Kiev in May were empty and something that couldn't happen. That match was intended for one of the ten referees who were selected to referee in Russia in the summer. But out of pride, I wanted to be involved as far into the tournaments as possible. My round of 16 match in the Europa League was the most high-profile of all, and I was glad that I got to referee Arsenal against AC Milan at the Emirates in London. But of all my international matches, it was probably just that one that created the most disappointment and frustration afterwards—even though I did everything right, and would have done exactly the same thing if I had ended up in the same situation again. At the end of the first half, after Milan had made it 1-0, the home attacker Danny Welbeck fell (or dived) easily in a challenge with Milan player Ricardo Rodríguez. From where I stood, with the angle and position I had, I saw no foul. But in my earpiece, I heard after a little while Stefan Johannesson call for a penalty. Stefan stood five, six meters away with a perfect angle, I just over twenty meters away with a poorer overview and also a bunch of players between me and the situation. So when I heard what he said, I of course blew for a penalty. Even if I hadn't perceived what had happened, I trusted my colleagues as always. That's how I had done my entire career, during all matches, since my first assignment with linesmen in Luleå sometime in the 1980s, and the match at the Emirates was no exception. Skilled colleagues, good cooperation and total trust in my team had always been a hallmark for me, one of my greatest assets—perhaps the single factor that had made me one of the world's best referees.

Now it was precisely my total trust, my delegation of responsibility to a colleague that ended my international career. But that's how I had acted throughout my career, and afterwards I felt that I would have done exactly the same if I had been given a chance to do it over.

However, if VAR had been introduced, as it was introduced in the Champions League barely a year later, then our mistake would have been discovered and it would not have affected the outcome of the match. It was a bit sad, a bit wistful, to have to end in that way. Even though I myself received a maximum rating from our Czech observer—since it was clear to everyone that it had been Stefan who had made the decision about the penalty and thus was failed—I understood that it was my last international match for UEFA.

I sent a text message to Collina to give him brief information about what had happened in the match, and that he could contact me if he wanted to discuss it. Of course he didn't. I was ice cold.

The only good thing about not being a selected World Cup referee was that you got to referee friendly internationals with World Cup-ready nations.

I received several nice invitations, and got to celebrate my forty-fourth birthday in Berlin to referee the two best national teams in the world, according to the then world ranking: Germany and Brazil.

The match was special, it was the first time that the Seleção would meet Germany after the embarrassing and humiliating 1-7 defeat in the 2014 World Cup. It was therefore anything but a friendly international. Both national teams played with their absolute best starting elevens, and while Germany rolled around and made five substitutions, Brazil made only one. It showed how incredibly important the match was for the away team—honour would be restored, Germany would be defeated.

When I went out to warm up before the international and saw the crowd and all the world-class players, I suddenly became unsure if I really should quit now. A few minutes later, during a tempo increase, my right thigh muscle started to cramp, and a worry spread through my body. Was it a tear? I took an unhealthy amount of Voltaren, got treatment from our masseur and when I left the dressing room before the match, I had promised myself that if I managed ninety minutes without breaking the match, then I would quit before the World Cup.

It was as if my body wanted to remind me. That my right thigh wanted to tell me that I had actually already decided to quit, even though I now thought it was so much fun to be at a packed Olympic Stadium with world stars everywhere that I once again considered continuing with what I actually loved most of all.

I stood completely alone in the players' tunnel a few minutes before kick-off. Not a single person was nearby, and it was so isolated that I couldn't hear a sound from the seventy thousand spectators who were making noise out there in the stands.

I remember how calm I felt, how secure I suddenly was in my decision to quit, that I was finished with this. That I would forever miss what had been a big part of my life—but that everything has its time, and that the time had come for me to hang up my whistle. During April and May, I slowly landed in the decision I had made. I realised that my career was coming to an end, that I would soon have a life without refereeing football. It was a cocktail of emotions. I thought it felt exciting and like a relief, but at the same time it was sad and terribly scary not knowing what I would do in life going forward. In retrospect, I realise that I became more afraid and cowardly in the last month of my refereeing career. I worried about getting injured, about failing or about not ending my long and successful career in the same way as I had refereed previously. When I had decided to quit but was still active, I became more hesitant, more afraid and cared about what people would think of my performances. I thought more about what people would think of me when I had quit than ever before.

I was also more concerned about injuries than before, and therefore I declined, for example, to referee the 2018 cup final between Djurgården and Malmö FF. I had a bit of pain in my thigh the days before and chose to withdraw. A year earlier, I would never have said no to a cup final, instead I would have done all the rehab needed, taken all treatments and medicated to manage the match.

I was quite uninterested, said that I hadn't even been told that I wasn't selected, that I would go to Malta on a course and meet Collina and that we would talk again afterwards. When I came home from Valletta, I was even more disappointed and dejected and firmly determined that I would stop refereeing before the World Cup. But also equally clear that I had decided to be away on holiday during the weeks that the World Cup was played.

But Marcus didn't give up, he chased me, sent suggestions, we discussed my role and finally he had convinced me that I should take the assignment for SVT. I understood that it would be good for me to have something else to think about during the World Cup, other than dwelling on the deep disappointment that I felt and that I knew would bubble up throughout the championship. I went home to the family, discussed with my wife, said that I wanted to work for SVT during the World Cup and that we could postpone the long trip until after the championship. As usual, I was grateful that my wife understood me, and let me do what I had to do to cope with the summer. She also understood that it was a new start for me, a way away from the world as a referee—and into a new world that I needed to discover in order to move forward in the best way. Moreover, there was another highly intentional upside for me in travelling on holiday after the football World Cup had ended. If we left Sweden on July 16, the day after the final, we wouldn't be back in Sigtuna again until exactly a month later. Then I would automatically miss UEFA's summer course. If I were to get cold feet later and change my mind, it would then be a practical impossibility. I planned my two last matches in my career in detail. In the last Allsvenskan match between Sirius and Djurgården on a sunny Sunday at the end of May, I had my family in the stands. All three got to come into the dressing room and we took a nice picture together. After that, it was time to tell everyone in my surroundings about my decision. First to our two daughters. The youngest cried, but was at the same time happy that I would be home more in the future. The eldest understood better and was happy for my sake, that I myself was satisfied with my decision. Then to my parents. They were, as usual, understanding and said they weren't surprised. After that, it was time to tell my closest colleagues, Mathias and Daniel. They had probably already sensed that the decision was coming, especially when I texted both of them simultaneously and asked for ten minutes together on the phone.

It wasn't really dramatic. They understood my decision, they knew how I had felt after the treatment we had received in the last eight months. Since the international season started anew in August, there was also time for them to reflect on their own future, find new referees to work with—but it wasn't particularly dramatic as both were the same age as me and only had one and two years left respectively. Mathias chose to quit in September of the same year, Daniel continued to referee, but only at the national level.

Bosse Karlsson also deserved a call after all we had been through together. He was certainly no longer with the Swedish Football Association, but still sat on UEFA's Referees Committee. It became a short but emotional chat where I told him about my decision and how I planned to communicate it. He was understanding, kind and had realised that the conversation would come soon. He had no plans to ask me to continue or try to convince me to referee on. Bosse, if anyone, knew how many blows I had taken, how many times I had been promised assignments that I never got, how hard I had worked and what priorities I had made to reach where I had nevertheless reached. I told Bosse that I absolutely wouldn't write a line to Collina or the rest of the UEFA leadership about my decision. Bosse could do that. I waited for UEFA's classification for the coming season which came on Wednesday, May 30—so that no one would think that I had been demoted and therefore had quit. I had never in thirty-one years' time been demoted a category or division. Nor had I missed a fitness test during that entire time. Quitting with the flag flying high and with dignity was a matter of course for me.

I had for several days written a farewell letter to all my referee friends around Sweden, the mailing list was ready and after proofreading the email one last time, I sent it off with a trembling hand and ended thirty-one fantastic years of my life.

In the email, I told, among other things, that the international match in Reykjavik a few days later would be my last, and that I had now decided to hang up my whistle for good. I also thanked everyone for all the support through the years. I described my decision to quit as a combination of wanting to have more time for my family, that I was starting to feel the desire wane and that I wanted to devote myself to new challenges, but I was at the same time open about the fact that I no longer had any confidence in the leadership within the refereeing world at the international level.

When UEFA's referees reassembled in Switzerland during the first three days of August to prepare for the new season, I was seventeen thousand kilometres away, on the Cook Islands, in the middle of the South Pacific, on holiday with my family.

A new life, my new life, had begun.

That I had quit before the World Cup and that I had worked for SVT during the summer's championship in Russia turned out to be exactly the start to life that I, as a forty-four-year-old retired referee, needed. Working together with a good team, with the fantastic André Pops as host, getting to talk in front of the Swedish people, educating them about refereeing and getting the chance to show that I knew more than just free kicks, yellow cards and offside gave me a new platform.

Before I went into the TV studio, I was recognised by a few as "the referee who missed out on the World Cup" – when I stepped out a few weeks later, I was known by everyone who had seen the broadcasts more as "the referee". Not as the one who had quit, the one who got sacked and didn't make it to the World Cup. I was simply associated with being a referee.

I had no problem being critical of the referees, but as always, I was careful to separate criticism of the referees' performances from their persons. Everyone makes mistakes, and if you have a public profession, you always have to tolerate people having opinions. The referees and players who can't stand criticism should change jobs.

I had never had a problem with receiving criticism, as long as it was factual and based on facts and rules – not on personal opinion. I tried to stick to the same philosophy in the studio during the World Cup. I, who throughout my refereeing career had had criticism, shouts, threats and hate thrown at me, suddenly received praise, kind words and compliments. I felt appreciated.

I also truly understood that it had been right to stop refereeing when I saw the World Cup, talked to my colleagues in Russia and saw how some of them were treated by FIFA. Everything was the same, according to the referees I talked to. The scoldings from a pressured Busacca continued, the lack of communication and moodiness in Collina's temper likewise, but also the overshadowing politicisation of selections and which referees would get which matches. Referees were sent home without being told why and some referees felt humiliated by the way they were handled in terms of matching and communication.

I was glad that I had started a new life, a new career and that I wasn't in Russia during the six weeks that the World Cup was on. Above all, my feeling was reinforced by the fantastic, slightly surprising Swedish successes in Russia. Janne Andersson and his national team not only progressed from the group stage, but also to a quarter-final against England. The World Cup final went to Néstor Pitana, the enormously skilled Argentine referee who with an ox's energy led the match with an iron fist. It was his fifth match in the tournament, he was tired in body and head and also had a muscle injury after many matches and the usual crazy FIFA training sessions. Another referee told me that it was as if the leadership from the beginning had decided that Pitana would get the final. But if anyone deserved a final, it was Néstor Pitana. A warm, funny and crazy person who without barely knowing a word of English managed to communicate with both players, leaders and colleagues. Regardless of the reason for the selection, he was worth the final that he eventually got. After everything I had experienced during my years as a referee within FIFA and UEFA, I knew that I would never, in the foreseeable future, want to work for either of those organisations. There is too much rotten in the walls. Far too much political play, cronyism and friendship corruption that affects people and makes which passport you have and who you know play a bigger role than how you perform.

My honour, my pride, my moral compass was, and is, stronger and more important than a suit with FIFA's or UEFA's logo on it, flights in business class, free match tickets to the best matches in Europe and a few hundred euros per day in compensation for my work.

When I had announced that I would stop refereeing, I had received hundreds of emails, texts and messages from Swedish and foreign friends, colleagues, players, leaders and supporters. All messages were friendly, kind, encouraging, positive, grateful and everyone who wrote to me got a reply. I was overwhelmed by all the kind words. It was a shower of self-confidence, a dose of confirmation, a large portion of appreciation for the many years that I had put into the service of refereeing.

I received emails from most of the members of UEFA's Referees Committee, from refereeing officers Hugh Dallas and Marc Batta. But not from Pierluigi Collina. After ten years of cooperation and employment, I didn't seem to be worth anything to him. I didn't care at all—I had freed myself from his leadership, from his domineering techniques and felt the joy from football slowly coming back when I didn't need to have him as my boss.

Collina might have become angry over the criticism I had expressed against FIFA, against the political agenda that governed the refereeing and that the right people were not selected for the right assignments, that nationality and friendship with the right people played a role. In SVT's World Cup studio, I went out brutally honestly at the beginning of the championship and critically stated that thirty-five selected referees from around the world was far too many. It was at least ten referees too many, a bunch of them were not up to standard. My detractors thought that I was bitter, that I was just angry because I wasn't selected myself. They were partly right. I was angry, but absolutely not bitter. And later it turned out that I was right in my analysis. When the World Cup was over and sixty-four matches had been played, only twenty-eight of the thirty-five referees had refereed their own matches. Eight of the referees had been given FIFA's trust to referee only a single match—it suggested that there were really only twenty referees that FIFA trusted and that they thought held the right competence.

Of the European referees that I competed with and that I thought I had more experience and better merits than, there was almost none who didn't deliver. All were good, maybe even better than I would have been. The Frenchman Turpin maybe didn't deserve to be there already in 2018 in terms of competence, but got to build experience for the future and will become one of Europe's leading referees with time.

There was one exception, a referee who clearly didn't meet the standard.

The Russian Sergei Karasev, who obviously was only there because he belonged to the host nation. He got one match, a meaningless bottom match between Australia and Peru. That's what happens when football's political snout shows up in the fine arenas.

I didn't regret for a second that I had stopped refereeing, especially not on August 1 when I was on a fantastic holiday on an island in the South Pacific. But the idyll was disturbed by several messages that made me wonder if I might have quit too early.

The reason for all the messages from the ongoing UEFA course in Switzerland was that during the first day it had been announced that Collina would leave UEFA, that he was no longer either chief refereeing officer or chairman of UEFA's Referees Committee. He chose to quit for personal reasons, it was said. When a person leaves a post for personal reasons, you avoid follow-up questions. Often it has to do with health, with family or other personal reasons that not even the media want to, can or should dig further into. But the reference to personal reasons in connection with Collina quitting was laughable. For those who understood something about the situation and knew that the Italian would leave UEFA, while he would remain as president of FIFA's Referees Committee, they understood that this was just a nicely formulated circumlocution for him having been fired, and that no one could now dig further into the cause. For everyone who had followed the media, it was no secret that one of the members of UEFA's Executive Committee, the powerful president and owner of Juventus Andrea Agnelli, during the spring of 2018 had been completely mad at UEFA's referees in general and Collina and his leadership in particular.

Everything took off after Juventus got a cheap penalty against them in overtime and were knocked out of the Champions League by Real Madrid. The referee Michael Oliver was criticised, UEFA likewise—but most of all Collina was criticised. Agnelli thundered that Collina was so eager to show that UEFA was not corrupt and judged in favour of the Italian teams that he deliberately had appointed anti-Italian referees.

Thereafter it was talked about that Agnelli together with representatives for Roma and Milan had turned directly to their countryman Giorgio Marchetti, UEFA's competition chief, and demanded Collina's immediate resignation. After that, it ended up on President Čeferin's desk. That Čeferin and Agnelli were close, close friends probably played a role in the decision. The Slovenian president had for a few years been godfather to Agnelli's daughter, and surely you can't say no to an urgent wish from the person who gave you the trust to be a godfather? In any case, Collina was dismissed, and replaced, of course, by another Italian. Roberto Rosetti, who I had refereed the U17 Euros in Denmark 2002 with, stepped into the role as the one who would be responsible for the European referees going forward. And it made a difference right away.

"You should have waited a while longer, it's a completely different mood and atmosphere now," texted a former colleague from the course in Switzerland.

I was happy for my colleagues on the course, but also for the future of European refereeing. But personally, I was regardless of that finished with my career.

As a newly retired referee, I set an enormous pace on life in the autumn of 2018, on all levels. I refused to sit still, rest or feel how I really felt, how it felt not to be a referee anymore. I was probably deep down afraid of the answer, that the longing would be great and I might regret it.

So I did exactly everything with my foot on the gas pedal during the autumn of 2018. I lectured more than ever, everywhere I got the opportunity.

I spent more time than ever before on our WE facilities. I travelled to New York for the US Open in August with a bunch of friends.

The weekend after, I saw England play against Spain at Wembley. I saw U2 play in Madrid in September. I trained hard and ran the New York Marathon in November. I coached both daughters' football teams, was referee responsible in Sigtuna IF, arranged outdoor days and chose to always increase the pace in everything I did. I didn't want to stop, didn't dare to make a slowdown for fear of ending up in an everyday life that I was afraid of not enjoying.

I continued to train hard. In fact, I became in many ways more fit than when I was active as a referee. I didn't need to think about planning, training diary, being in top form for a match once a week or that my fat percentage couldn't increase to over twelve percent because then I would hear sighs and groans from a staring Collina. My dream after the career was not to pass the yo-yo test twice a year. It was instead to run the world's six largest marathons, but that ambition took a little hit after the onset of the pandemic. But it will happen, the question is just when.

I have moved on, and I feel really good today. There is really only one thing that still hurts, even with a few years' perspective.

When the Champions League is shown on TV, I change the channel. I can't watch a match, a sequence, hear the anthem or see the logo. It still hurts too much in me. At the core, I am still today the same person as when I started refereeing football as a curious thirteen-year-old boy with a hockey haircut in Luleå. I don't think I have changed very much, I wanted to move forward quickly and preferably be at the centre. I was prepared to work hard and I wanted to have fun while doing it. I am eternally grateful to football, where it took me, for the way the sport developed me. And equally grateful I am to all colleagues, bosses, instructors, observers and other people who supported me along the way and helped me reach the top. You know who you are.

It is said that a referee makes three hundred decisions during a match that is ninety minutes. But how many decisions don't you make during a normal day? During a year? Or during an entire life?

My second best decision in life was that I started refereeing football.

My best decision in life was to go out to the nightclub Berns on a Friday in February 2003. There I met my future wife. Without her, I would never have got my two wonderful daughters. Without them by my side and their constant support and understanding, I would never have reached where I did with my refereeing.

Overtime

My match as a referee ended on June 2, 2018 and today I can of course miss the big matches, the audience, the adrenaline, the challenge, the tiredness and constantly being exposed to new trials. In my dreams, I sometimes find myself on a football pitch to referee. Big matches with lots of people, and I hear that cold, echoing, hard sound when the studs on the shoes rhythmically hit the dumb cement floor while the players walk out to the match. I also sometimes dream that I'm at a tournament, far from Sweden. That I long for home, but still want to stay.

There was no comeback on the pitch for me. No foreign career, no seasons in any other league to round off the career. If I had wanted, I would surely have had alternatives, opportunities and occasions to live outside Sweden for a year or some years, but it was never of interest. Most of my colleagues who do it have money as their main reason. But for me, the money was never the driving force, not at the beginning or during the career, and not at the end either. Money, taxes and Swedish FIFA referees have been a current topic during the time I've worked on this book. Information mainly in Fotbollskanalen has claimed that several Swedish referees have avoided paying tax on income from foreign assignments and that the Swedish Tax Agency has initiated reviews and in a number of these, corrections have been made. I of course don't know what everyone has done, how they have handled it, what knowledge they have had about the rules and what reasons there have been for a number of my colleagues missing to pay the taxes. They have to answer for themselves when someone asks the question.

I do, however, know what I have done. I have reported everything, always taken help from experts and tried to do what I can to follow the regulations that exist. I have neither been corrected by the Swedish Tax Agency nor been forced to make a correction myself. It is my responsibility, and I can answer for that. But I also know that there has always been a culture of silence within the referee group around everything concerning compensation, salaries and taxes. It's not something you have talked about, discussed or asked your colleagues about.

When I write the book's overtime chapter, I have just driven through the Norrbotten where my career began. Road signs to Brännberg, Vittjärv, Jokkmokk, Ullatti, Malmberget and Masugnsbyn remind me of meetings, challenges and tough matches where I learned that the best referee is the one who isn't seen.

I'm also reminded that all encounters with people, matches I've refereed or situations I've handled during my long career have shaped me into the person I am today. I'm endlessly grateful for that. But it also strikes me, especially now during the work on this book, how at the highest level there is so incredibly much filth and dirt in the game behind the sport, the part of football that is rarely or never seen by those who watch the matches. I have been astonished by how people have become speed-blind, greedy, lost their moral compass and done everything to always put themselves and their closest friends in the best possible position without a thought for honesty, fairness or fair play—words that once made me start refereeing football. I am also convinced that most people are tired of the cheating that is actually visible in football: that players are constantly diving, exaggerating and deceiving to gain advantages. Football must decide that it wants to remove this. With tools like VAR, it is now possible—it's just a matter of FIFA and UEFA deciding. I believe that a contributing factor to women's football being on such a strong upswing all over the world is that we rarely, or never, see cheating or diving when the women play. It's gratifying to see that interest in women's football is increasing, that the stars are becoming more popular and recognised, TV viewers are increasing and that national teams and club teams at all levels are investing in women who play football.

In my time, the refereeing chiefs were clear that men should referee men and women referee women—it was never up for discussion to mix different genders in terms of referee teams or that women could referee men.

But the more female referees we have at the highest level, the better the climate will be. After Stéphanie Frappart, as the first woman, had refereed the Super Cup final between Chelsea and Liverpool in the summer of 2019, everyone agreed: how well the men behaved when it was a woman who refereed.

If it's that simple, we should have significantly more women refereeing at the highest level. Not only on the pitch must it change and be mixed up, but also in all of football's committees and boards that decide about the future, more women are needed. But not only more women are needed, but also more people who actually dare to stand for something, to be honest, to question, challenge and speak up when friendship corruption, loyalty and nepotism take precedence over competence. In retrospect, I am absolutely not bitter about anything. I'm not sad or angry either. I don't really care what it was that made my own career collapse like a house of cards: whether it was my old friendship with Nasser Al-Khelaifi, my refusal to remove Mathias from my team, some missed penalties, an angered and powerful big club, too many commitments off the pitch or just the fact that I became a victim of a generational shift. It matters less because I have a richer and better life today—I feel better than I did during my years as a referee at the highest level. I have perspective, can see what I've been through with different eyes and am grateful for what I have experienced—but at the same time I'm glad that I have now stopped refereeing and left the refereeing world. You probably remember Sweden's fantastic playoff matches against Italy in November 2017. We won 1-0 on aggregate and progressed to the World Cup in Russia. We scored and performed better—despite Italy always usually being in the World Cup, that Italy with all probability had eleven players who were better than ours, that it really should have been they who made it to Russia.

But in football, the little team can win against the big one. The team beats the individual. Football's wonderful unpredictability means that the unexpected can happen—and the only thing you know for certain is that the team that has scored the most goals when the match is over wins. Now imagine instead that Italy against Sweden in the World Cup qualifier would be decided by FIFA's Executive Committee. They get to decide the winner in a meeting room where no one has access and no one gets to know what has been said. Do you think that little Sweden would have gone to the World Cup then? My, and all other football referees', careers lay in the hands of powerful men with proven dubious motives and methods. And the cronyism, concentration of power and friendship corruption have hardly decreased since I quit. The best referee during Euro 2021 was Cüneyt Çakır from Turkey. He refereed two group stage matches and an absolutely fantastic round of 16 match between Spain and Croatia. Then there were no more matches at all. He was sent home without getting any of the last seven matches in the tournament. Everyone with insight understood why. The reason was a match in October 2019. Çakır refereed Slovenia against Austria in a decisive match to qualify for Euro 2021. UEFA's president, the Slovenian Aleksander Čeferin, sat in the stands and thought that Çakır missed an absolutely obvious penalty for handball. Slovenia were knocked out and the president was furious at the performance in an interview afterwards. "I was crazy, it was a clear handball. People were looking at me in the stands, like: 'Who the fuck are you if you don't have any influence?'", said Čeferin.

Çakır was immediately removed from his next match in the Champions League, and after that UEFA put him in the freezer. The Turk who had refereed a Euro semi-final, two World Cup semi-finals, a Champions League final and six semi-finals in the same tournament was after the match in Slovenia not allowed to referee further than to the round of 16 in the Champions League and during the Euros. Does anyone seriously believe that one of the world's best and most experienced referees really became such a much worse referee after the match in Slovenia, regardless of whether he missed a handball or not? Politics is today just as dominant within UEFA and FIFA as when I was active. The new system with VAR, however, carries with it a potential advantage for the referees who operate at an international level. A lot of gross and obvious errors, those that previously lowered the grade, suspended referees and in the worst case could ruin a career, can now be avoided.

For Swedish referees, however, VAR is an obstacle to making an international career. That the system is completely absent in Swedish football, that Allsvenskan clubs generally have been negative, will likely result in the Swedish referee teams becoming less relevant for international assignments. The teams that are selected for the big tournaments, the international cups and international matches today usually contain VAR referees. And because it is completely lacking in Swedish football, the chance and opportunity to be able to make the journey I made will be limited as long as Swedish football stands outside what has become the norm in Europe.

Despite all the downsides of the job, all the pressure and stress that comes with it, I recommend everyone to become a referee. It's the world's best job.

It will develop you, make you smarter, better in your civilian job, teach you to work under greater pressure, make wiser decisions, keep track of your emotions and maybe, maybe you'll get to be at a World Cup in the end. And who knows, maybe the leadership has become different when you finally reach there. And if you choose not to become a referee, then for heaven's sake make sure to act wisely and respectfully towards the men and women in black on and beside the pitch. Realise what a difficult and exposed job they have, how much time they put in and how little money they earn. If you also sometime see a young person refereeing, then go up afterwards and praise him or her. Then you contribute to us getting more and better referees in the future. For don't forget: without referees, it's not possible to play football.

Printed in Dunstable, United Kingdom